'Set against the backdrop of one of the most turbulent periods in Scottish history, this is the story of forbidden but enduring love, of the strength of the female spirit in a world dominated by men, and above all of an extraordinary woman far ahead of her time. It held me captive from the first page to the last. Utterly breathtaking'

TRACY BORMAN

'A really thrilling discovery – a sixteenth-century woman writing, and she's a professional clerk, and she's a poet, and she's writing love letters to another woman and she's Scots. This is a real extension of our knowledge of women of the period, engagingly told'

PHILIPPA GREGORY

'*With My Own Hand* is a necessary act of queer historical reclamation. In recovering Marie Maitland from the margins of manuscript culture, Ashley Douglas does more than reconstruct a life: she demonstrates that women's same-sex desire was part of the lived and articulated reality of the early modern world. At a time when the legitimacy of queer lives is again contested in public discourse, this return to a sixteenth-century woman who loved women feels not antiquarian but urgent. The power of the book lies in its archival seriousness, in its patient reading of documents, contexts and silences, and in its refusal to allow women's desire to be footnoted or euphemised out of history. This is not simply biography; it is the restoration of a lineage. Douglas reminds us that queer history survives not by accident, but because someone chooses to look for it. An important and timely contribution to the history of women who loved women'

CHRISTOPHER STEPHENS, author of *The Light of Day*

'Absolutely mesmerising, Douglas's meticulously detailed research reveals a fascinating story that's been lost for centuries'

Sara Sheridan, activist and author

'Engaging, evocative, enthralling: Ashley Douglas shines a light on a part of Scotland's history – and a fascinating Scotswoman – too often overlooked or not even written in'

Steven Veerapen, author of *The Wisest Fool: The Lavish Life of James VI and I*

'Though a work of non-fiction, this is a teasing and tantalising historical drama, beautifully written by Douglas'

Sass MacDonald

'Beautifully written and meticulously researched, *With My Own Hand* immerses the reader in Marie Maitland's sixteenth-century world from the very first page. By reconstructing Marie's exceptional life through in-depth and careful analysis of a range of legal and literary records housed in archives across Scotland and the UK, Douglas challenges dominant narratives that have rendered stories like Marie's invisible and forgotten for centuries. What emerges is an utterly fascinating account of a sixteenth-century woman who loved other women, and who bravely defied the limits placed upon her within the patriarchal world of early modern Scotland for much of her adult life. Thanks to Douglas' passion and ingenuity, Marie Maitland will no doubt be restored among the great historical figures who shaped early modern Scottish history'

Dr Rebecca Mason, expert in early modern Scottish women's legal history

'The joy of this book, for me, is its vivid evocation of a secret love story – a love story between women in the sixteenth century. It has all the drama and complexity of the best romances. Ashley Douglas has created a clear and accessible narrative that takes us right into the thoughts and feelings of Marie Maitland, allowing us to see and experience as she did, over a gap of hundreds of years. The academic rigour with which Ashley Douglas has researched her story clearly establishes a truth too often obscured by the ignorance and biases of earlier historians. Women have always loved other women, romantically and sexually. Queer love has been part of human history as long as humans have existed. But centuries of homophobic assumptions mean that truth is still disputed. Ashley Douglas uses original source material, without speculation, to demonstrate a love that cannot, now, be denied or argued out of existence. By the end we feel certain that this is only the tip of an iceberg of untold historical love stories that might be found if others looked with the same energy and meticulous care'

Rona Munro, playwright

'A remarkable exploration of a little-known, sixteenth-century manuscript which reveals the secret life of Marie Maitland who inserted, amongst the poems of her father, her own verses as erotic and sensual declarations of her illicit gay love. Using the manuscript as her map, Ashley Douglas leads us through the social and political upheavals of a Reformation Scotland to tell the story of a defiant and independent woman who insisted on having a voice'

Clare Hunter, author of *Threads of Life* and *Embroidering Her Truth*

With my own hand

Also by Ashley Douglas

The Lass and The Quine

ASHLEY DOUGLAS

With my own hand

The secret life of Marie Maitland, Scotland's sixteenth-century Sappho

HEADLINE PRESS

First published in 2026 by Headline Press
An imprint of Headline Publishing Group Limited

1

Cataloguing in Publication Data is available from the British Library.

Hardback ISBN 978 1 0354 3060 4
Trade Paperback ISBN 978 1 0354 4916 3

Designed and typeset by EM&EN
Printed and bound in Great Britain by Clays Ltd, Elcograf S.p.A.

MIX
Paper | Supporting responsible forestry
FSC® C104740
www.fsc.org

Headline's policy is to use papers that are natural, renewable and recyclable products and made from wood grown in well-managed forests and other controlled sources. The logging and manufacturing processes are expected to conform to the environmental regulations of the country of origin.

Headline Publishing Group Limited
An Hachette UK Company
Carmelite House
50 Victoria Embankment
London EC4Y 0DZ

The authorised representative in the EEA is Hachette Ireland,
8 Castlecourt Centre, Dublin 15, D15 XTP3, Ireland (email: info@hbgi.ie)

www.headline.co.uk
www.hachette.co.uk

Contents

'My hairt heir I present, In pledge perpetuall'

For Eilidh

someone will remember us
I say
even in another time
Sappho

to your self maid ane immortall name
Marie Maitland

Preface

To your self maid ane immortall name

In 1586, in Scotland, a remarkable woman named Marie Maitland put the finishing touches to a manuscript she had been labouring over for years.

A member of an influential family, the Maitlands of Lethington, Marie's sense of achievement must have been tinged with sadness as she dipped her quill into the ink, ready to apply the last strokes. Her illustrious father, Scottish statesman Sir Richard Maitland, whose poetry made up many of the manuscript's pages, had only recently died, and his funeral was still fresh in her heart.

At least she'd ensured him the peace of mind of knowing that his verse had been preserved for posterity, Marie might have comforted herself, as she inscribed her name onto the title page – not just once, but twice, in two different ornamental scripts. She was, after all, the manuscript's creator, and she wanted that to be known.

What's more, it was not only her father's poetry that she had diligently recorded within its pages.

Far from it.

Within the leaves of her manuscript, Marie had also concealed a whole host of poems written not just by herself but by the women around her. Astonishingly, among this female-authored verse is some of the earliest known lesbian love poetry in Europe since Sappho of Lesbos. The celebrated ancient Greek poet had lived in the seventh century BCE and immortalised her love for other women in her work, giving us the very words 'sapphic' and 'lesbian' that we still use to describe women who love women today.

If Marie emerges from sixteenth-century Scotland as an early successor to Sappho, the world's original lesbian, on the one hand, her life also predates that of Anne Lister, the world's first modern lesbian, on the other.

Anne's unparalleled diaries have, in recent years, secured her rightful place in history. It was in 1821, in an uncomprehending England, that Anne committed to paper her disarmingly bold declaration that 'I love, & only love, the fairer sex & thus beloved by them in turn, my heart revolts from any other love than theirs.'[1]

But it was more than two hundred years earlier, and in the yet more hostile climate of the aftermath of the morally suffocating Scottish Reformation of 1560, that Marie Maitland poured out her heart in verse: declaiming, inspired by her love for another woman, that 'thair is mair [more] constancy in our sex, than ever among men has been'.*

Like Anne, centuries later, Marie's bravery of spirit was not restricted to the page: it defined the way she interacted with the world around her, in public, as well as the contents of the poetry she wrote, in private.

As much a feminist as a sapphic icon, Marie broke free of the strictures that should have restrained her and lived a unique life for a woman of her time. For decades, she eschewed the standard path of marriage and childbearing, instead pursuing a rich education and wielding substantial social and financial agency, which she used to further her own interests, as well as those of the other women in her life.

---

* All translations into Modern English of the poetry of the *Maitland Quarto* manuscript in this book, full or partial, are the author's own. Please see the 'note on language, dates and documents' at the end of the book for further information and context.

We know from Marie's poetry that as a woman of both the European Renaissance and the Scottish Reformation, she found inspiration in the classics, as well as her Bible: in the devotion embodied by the biblical figures of Ruth and Naomi in the Old Testament, the epic love story of Achilles and Patroclus, heroes of the Trojan War, and, of course, the poetry of Sappho.

She would, I think, love the idea that people today might now find the same sort of inspiration and symbolism in her own story, through this, the first book ever written about her. Marie's poetry, and her story, have certainly had a profound impact on me.

*

'You wield me wholly at your will and ravish my affection,' declared Marie to her female lover in one of her poems, in a line on par with the most erotically charged of Sappho's lyrics – one which still pulsates with sensuality, more than four hundred years on.

Later in the same poem, the forty-ninth in her manuscript, Marie stated unequivocally her desire to marry this woman that she so loved. Their love, she claimed, was 'mair [more] holy and religious' than any other. One of the hallmarks of the newly reformed Scotland in which Marie lived was its Calvinist emphasis on the authority of the word of the Bible. In this poem, Marie – momentously – prays in aid of that very scriptural unassailability to validate her sapphic love; 'as the scripture sayis [says]', she wrote. If only they could 'with joyfull hairt [heart]' honour their love through the bond of marriage, Marie continued, they would no longer be the two 'unhappie women' that they were, forced apart by the accident of their shared gender, in their sixteenth-century world.

Eventually, Marie has to concede that, as two women, they can never really be wed to one another. However, even after that admission, she maintains that 'nocht but deid [nothing but death]' will ever truly 'divorce' them; that, in their hearts, it will always be as if they were bound by the vows of marriage.

On one level, Marie's staggering statement of love for another woman in this poem is impassioned and defiant. She even appeals to her bible in justification. Ultimately, though, Marie admits defeat to their reality. She sets out her fervent wish to be wed to the woman she loves, and why such love is righteous and holy, yet ends her poem with the acknowledgement that it can never happen; that, despite the depth of their mutual devotion, 'friendship' is the only real option available to them.

However heartbroken it left them, however unfair it felt, Marie and her lover had no choice but to concede that, in their world, *marriage* between two women was simply impossible.

*

In 2017, in Scotland, I had the singular joy of exchanging vows with the woman I love. Hearts full, tears streaming down at least my face (my now wife, Eilidh, managed to maintain better composure), we pledged to love each other, to the exclusion of all others, as long as we both shall live. We did so lawfully, in the eyes of the state, and in front of our friends and family – something that Marie could scarcely have conceived of.

Truth be told, we could hardly believe it in 2017. Equal marriage had been legal in Scotland for only three years when we married. At the time of writing, it has been legal for only around a decade; some still vocally oppose it. As a gay woman, I can't help but be conscious of the fact that my right to be married, to live my life with the same equality, dignity and safety as others, is never a given. And if things remain challenging in twenty-first-century

Scotland, how much worse the situation was for Marie and her lover in their time.

Marie's world was that of Mary, Queen of Scots and radical reformer John Knox, among the most famous, or infamous, figures in Scottish history. Her life coincided with the cultural revitalisation and embracing of the classics of the Renaissance, but she also lived through the transformational counterforce of the Reformation, when Scotland abandoned the old Church for one of the most extreme and austere forms of the new.

Marie thus fell in love with a woman, and penned her love poetry, in a punishingly Protestant Scotland, fizzing with all the zeal of the newly converted. It was a time and place where women were viewed as inferior to men in all ways, and where same-sex relations – 'sodomy' – whether between men or women, was one of the worst transgressions imaginable, societally condemned and formally penalised.

And yet, here was a woman with the strength of character and unshakeable sense of self to maintain her conviction that her love for another woman was just as valid as – even superior to – any other. Here was a woman who lived hundreds of years ago, but who walked the same haar-drenched streets of Edinburgh that I do today, in the shadows of the same ancient volcanic hulk of Arthur's Seat – and who, like me, loved another woman so much she wanted to formalise it in marriage.

Only one copy of the manuscript that Marie created exists in the entire world. The first time I held it in my hands, I opened it to the middle pages and placed my left hand where its forty-ninth poem begins. My wedding ring, symbolising my marriage to another woman, touched the words on the page, ink etched onto paper by a woman who, some four hundred years ago, would have given anything for the right I now had.

If only Marie could know how far we have come.

*

Women who love women (whatever they might or might not have called themselves) have always been here. Sappho, in the seventh century BCE, was one such example. Marie Maitland, in the sixteenth century, was another. Anne Lister, in the nineteenth century, another still. They will not have been alone: they are simply rare examples of women of the past who were both capable of leaving a record of themselves *and* chose to do so. For much of our history, each of those conditions has represented a massive hurdle.

In Marie's world of sixteenth-century Scotland, most women (and, indeed, men) could not read or write. Meanwhile, elite women with sufficient socio-economic privilege to enjoy literacy, as part of a fashionable Renaissance education, were expected to restrict their creative activities to the penning of demure, devotional poetry, to know their place as the intellectual subordinates of men, and as humble Christian servants.

They definitely weren't meant to exalt lesbian love in verse.

Through the moral clampdown that followed the Reformation, the people of Scotland found their private lives policed like never before, with zealous neighbours breathing down their necks and rabid Church authorities eager to weed out and punish any and all kinds of 'immoral', 'illicit' and 'deviant' behaviours – which, it was implied, had been allowed to flourish under the old Church.

Women, in their moral weakness, were viewed as particularly susceptible to the sins of the flesh, and 'sodomy' was abhorrent, conflated with witchcraft and the demonic. In these circumstances, the overwhelming majority of women who loved other women in Marie's time were either unable or unwilling to leave us any trace of their lives in writing.

Demonisation by Church and state leads, for the most part, to self-preserving self-censorship. Combined with widespread illiteracy, this means that much of the limited evidence for the existence of people who loved those of the same gender from this era takes the form of criminal and condemnatory records, written by others.

But these very same sobering realities make Marie's poetry, as a positive record of a woman's love for another, in that woman's own hand, from the Scotland of more than four hundred years ago, something of exceptional rarity and preciousness.

Against all the odds, Marie was both able and brave enough to write it in the first place; and, against all the odds, it has survived to this day.

*

These days, the manuscript that Marie created is known as the *Maitland Quarto*, based on its petite, quarter-sized ('quarto') pages and its connection to her historically important Maitland family, the men of which dominated in royal administration and politics.

Her father, Sir Richard, was a statesman, judge, poet, historian and Keeper of the Privy Seal (that is, he was responsible for the seal used to authorise important state documents) under Mary, Queen of Scots. Her eldest brother, William, served as Secretary of State to the same queen; another sibling, John, would be raised to the position of Chancellor at the court of her son, King James VI (later also James I of England).

We know that the manuscript was written by Marie, because she wanted it to be known. She left no end of unmissable signs among its pages, not least that she emblazoned her name on its title page – twice, for good measure – or that several of its poems explicitly refer to her as the manuscript's creator.

At its most fundamental, the manuscript is a collection of ninety-five poems in historical Scots, still the language of the Scottish kingdom in Marie's time. The script, meanwhile, varies between the Scottish 'secretary hand' of the era and the new 'Roman' or 'italic' form of handwriting of the time.

Secretary hand was generally the preserve of men, as it was a technical skill for professions (such as legal clerks) that only they could practise. Its fast-flowing, joined-up letters and contraction-heavy nature was about speed and efficiency of writing. Italic, meanwhile, was more aesthetic, associated with the humanist educational project of the Renaissance, and was commonly taught to women.*

A scribal showboater, Marie flits seamlessly between these two scripts throughout the manuscript. She records its poems in a combination of both, adorned with a range of calligraphic flourishes and decorative elements.

Finalised in 1586, the year that Sir Richard Maitland died, the manuscript opens with a poem extolling his achievements and closes with a series of poems lamenting his recent passing. In between, the bulk of the poems in the manuscript itself are by Marie's father: it is the most comprehensive and pristine compilation of his poetry that we have today.

---

* Though italic was also used by men who had received a Renaissance humanist education. Please see the 'note on language, dates and documents' at the end of the book for further information and context.

Marie also included a selection of poems attributed to other important men and court poets connected to the family, reflecting her father's status and legacy. These include one by King James VI himself, and several by his right-hand man, Marie's influential politician brother, John.

But only on the surface is this manuscript a literary commemoration of Marie's father, a celebration of Sir Richard and his male compatriots. Look just a little bit closer and this manuscript emerges – dazzlingly, unmistakably – as a precious primary record of the lives and loves of women, created by a woman.

For nestled among the pages of poetry attributed to the male great and good of sixteenth-century Scotland are around thirty technically 'anonymous' poems – many of which can safely be attributed to women.

There was little reason for men of the time not to attach their name to their work, or to limit its circulation; indeed, Marie diligently attributes much of the poetry that she recorded in her manuscript to the male pen that first produced it. What's more, the men whose verse is preserved in her manuscript also had wider reputations as poets, their work appearing in other sources.

By contrast, many of the 'anonymous' poems appear uniquely in this one, female-authored manuscript. And some are obviously by, or about, Marie.

Many are female or gender-neutral in voice and treat female themes from female perspectives: from sadness at an unwanted arranged marriage to appeals to classical goddesses. Three of the manuscript's poems chart the soul-shattering love story of Marie and another woman – and, even though it played out almost half a millennium ago, the emotional force of that story remains palpable to this day.

Women were not meant to write such bold poetry, never mind explicitly attribute it to themselves, with the aim of wide circulation. In this context, Marie deftly exploited the means at her disposal to record her own poetry and that of some of the women around her. Surreptitiously but effectively, she slipped their work in, unsigned, among the pages of a manuscript compilation dominated by the poetry of men.

Perhaps never has Virginia Woolf's observation that 'Anon, who wrote so many poems without signing them, was often a woman' rung quite so true than in the case of the 'anonymous' poems of Marie's manuscript. Today, they are the literary legacy of a small community of sixteenth-century female poets, friends and even lovers, with Marie at its heart.

*

The *Maitland Quarto* may have long been perceived, and celebrated, as a manuscript of the poetry of Marie's father and other men (the cover story has been almost too effective) – but it is, ultimately, her manuscript. And nowhere is her literary appropriation more clear than in its very first poem.

Unsigned, but written by Marie, it is headed: 'Ane [A] Sonet to the Authour in Commendatioun of his Buik [Book]'.

So far, so – seemingly – straightforward: an apt title for an opening verse addressed to her father, the main 'authour' of the poems that follow, and a commendation of what is thus 'his Buik'.

Or is it?

In the sonnet, Marie extols the achievements of their shared Maitland ancestors and gushes about how her father has done the family name proud. In its final lines, she writes that, even when he has departed this world for the next, his poetic legacy will keep his name alive. He has 'with the pen the poetis pairt weill playit', thereby 'enlairgi[ng]' his family's 'fame' and ensuring himself 'ane immortall name'.

[. . .] with the pen the poetis pairt weill playit	*with the pen the poet's part* *well played*
Whairby your lordship enlairgit has thair fame	*Whereby your lordship has* *enlarged their fame*
And to your self maid ane immortall name	*And to your self made an* *immortal name*

On the surface of it, a fine and fitting introduction to the collection of her father's poetry that she has created.

Except, in reality, this poem is not dedicated to her father at all.

Look carefully, and this poem is Marie *dedicating the manuscript to herself.* For those paying attention, 'maid ane immortall' is a near-perfect anagram of 'marie maitland'.

to your self maid ane immortall name
to your self marie maitland name

To draw attention to the anagrammatic line, in case readers missed it the first time, someone – perhaps Marie herself, perhaps a woman close to her, in on the manuscript's secrets – conspicuously copied out the words 'maid ane immortall name' again below.

And there are yet more clues that this poem (and, indeed, the whole manuscript) is really far more about Scotland's sixteenth-century Sappho than it is about Sir Richard.

In a manuscript where most of the poems appear with no title at all, later on in its pages, Marie recorded a poem that is clearly about her (poem 85) with the standout title 'To Your Self', directly connecting it to this momentous, revelatory line in this sonnet, poem 1. Likely written in Marie's honour by a woman who knew her, not only does poem 85 refer to Marie as the manuscript's creator – she is described as writing 'this buik' – it also directly compares her to Sappho.

Some of the signs that Marie left are obvious, and some are more coded. But they all have the same aim: of making sure that later readers would know that this 'buik', although technically dedicated to her father, is Marie's; and that the 'immortal name' she was concerned to make through it was not, ultimately, her father's but her own.

*

Such an impressive manuscript can only have been the culmination of an extraordinary life, lived by a singular woman.

So who, really, was this Marie Maitland, who lived in a newly reformed Scotland, and combined her Protestant faith with an unapologetically passionate sapphic love? What conditions endowed Marie with the bravery or recklessness, or both, that led her to record her illicit love, her desire even to marry another woman, concealed behind only a flimsy cloak of anonymity?

A highly educated woman, who could write fluently in multiple scripts at a time when most could not write at all, what circumstances led Marie to compile a manuscript collection of her father's poetry – and thus also to the opportunity of a lifetime to make her own immortal name?

In the pages that follow, we will trace Marie Maitland's remarkable life for the first time, told in the context of her living present

– her family and the turbulent decades and iconic figures of Scottish history that defined her.

More than four centuries on, some aspects of her story are irretrievably lost to us and must be left to educated guesswork – but so much can be gleaned from what remains. Marie left behind a mountain of clues in her own manuscript. There are details and secrets preserved within its pages, steeped in classical legend and biblical scripture. And the poetic record is supplemented by authoritative primary documents relating to Marie and those around her, recorded in places such as the Register of Deeds of the Court of Session and the monarch's Register of the Privy Seal.

Much is already known about the illustrious lives and careers of Marie's father and brothers. By contrast, many of the records relating not just to Marie but to the other women in her story, I have only recently unearthed from the archives, as part of my original research into Marie's life.

Building on all that we already know about the Maitland men, and combining formal records (many unseen for centuries) with poetic testimony throughout, we will get as close as we can to the woman who was Marie Maitland, Scotland's sixteenth-century Sappho.

Chapter One

Who does not know the Maitland blood?

Quha dois not knaw the Maitland bluid The best in all this land[1]	*Who does not know the Maitland blood The best in all this land*

Marie Maitland was born around the late 1540s, most likely at her family's stronghold of Lethington Castle. A stone's throw from the ancient royal burgh of Haddington, it was also perilously close to the border (about a day's ride) at a time when the still independent kingdoms of Scotland and England were frequently at war. Marie was the seventh and youngest child of Sir Richard Maitland of Lethington and Mariota Cranstoun.

Some years earlier, on 8 December 1542, another Marie had been born, one better known today as Mary, Queen of Scots. Mere days after her birth, on 14 December, Mary's father, King James V, died at Falkland Palace. So it was that the Crown of Scotland passed to a six-day-old baby girl. Our Marie entered the world during the first years of the minority of this infant Queen, when Scotland was under the rule of Governor Arran – James Hamilton, 2nd Earl of Arran – next in line to the throne.

The family that Marie was born into was firmly of the landed elite, as their castle home suggests. Although not among the highest and mightiest of the titled nobility (the men were not yet earls or lords), the Maitlands were a well-established Lowland family, with property, power and royal connections. The presence of men with the French-descended 'Mautelant' name is attested to in Scottish charters from the 1200s onwards. The original ancestral lands of the Maitlands were those of Thirlestane, in Lauderdale, a bit further south. In the mid-1300s, they also acquired the lands of Lethington, in East Lothian, by royal charter. From this point onwards, the family generally styled themselves 'of Lethington'.* By the time young Marie entered the world, generations of Maitlands had called Lethington Castle home. She would later write a poem praising its glory, as well as boasting of her Maitland blood as 'the best in all this land'.

A few decades before Marie's birth, in 1513, the fateful Battle of Flodden had taken place. A disaster for Scotland, many thousands died, including King James IV himself, in a devastating defeat at the hands of the English. Among the many men who perished alongside the king on the battlefield that day was Sir William Maitland of Lethington, Marie's paternal grandfather. His teenage son, Richard, would have processed the news of his father's death alongside the reality that, as his heir, he now carried responsibility for the family name and its furtherance.

The young man destined to become Marie's father pursued a path typical for educated Scotsmen at the time, attending the University of St Andrews – established as Scotland's first such centre of learning in 1413 – before making his way across the sea to Paris to pursue his studies further. When he returned to Scotland, learned and eager to serve his country, Richard embarked on what would be a long and illustrious career in service to Crown and state, with his name first appearing in the records in connection with the court of King James V (1513–42).

---

* Marie's brother William is best known for his role as 'Secretary Lethington' to Mary, Queen of Scots. Marie's brother John, however, styled himself as 'Maitland of Thirlestane'. Her father was known as 'Sir Richard Maitland of Lethington' or 'auld [old] Lethington'.

By contrast, and as is so often the case when it comes to women in history, we know next to nothing of the life of Marie's mother, Mariota Cranstoun, before she married. Even when she does enter the historical record, we learn little other than the names of her father (Sir Thomas Cranstoun of Corsbie), her husband (Sir Richard Maitland of Lethington) and the surviving children that she bore (William, Elizabeth, Helen, Isobel, John, Thomas and Marie). Similarly, we know far more about the Maitland brothers than we do about Marie and her sisters.

Marie's life story played out at a time when women were defined entirely in relation to the men they were connected to, by birth and then marriage. Prior to marriage, a woman's social value was rooted in her virginity and her dowry. After marriage, fertility was the quality most valued, along with deference to her husband. This was a world of strict patriarchy and limiting gender roles, where the general expectation of those born female was simply to transfer from the household of their father to that of a husband, and then be in a near-constant state of pregnancy in order to produce as many offspring as possible. Tragically, many infants did not survive their first years, and so the pressure to continuously reproduce was acute. For elite families in particular, having legitimate heirs to inherit their wealth and titles, and to be strategically married into other elite families for political and financial gain, was paramount, and the expectation upon women of status to marry well and produce heirs was even greater.

Marie's parents married in 1522, when Richard was twenty-six and Mariota likely around eighteen, the average age of first marriage for a woman of the social elite. By the time that Marie came along, they had been building a life together for several decades, and were already raising six children, three sons and three daughters.

It is most unlikely, though, that Marie's mother escaped the sad fate of so many women at this time – to also endure the sorrows of miscarriage, stillbirth and infant mortality; indeed, there are suggestions that she gave birth to at least four more children. A poem that Marie wrote in her adulthood, preserved in her manuscript, refers to her father having had 'seven sonnis [sons]'. And, in a letter written in his old age, Marie's father would himself reflect that 'I have been the father of mony [many] sonnes'. Although we know of only three Maitland boys by name today – William, John and Thomas – it seems that four more had been born to Marie's parents, but did not make it past their early years. This apparent loss is representative of the harsh reality of infant mortality, a heartbreakingly common occurrence at this time, the boys' fleeting lives attested to now only in brief nameless reference in a poem and a letter. There may well also have been more daughters but there is no trace of them in the record – not even in Marie's poem, which is focused on her father's male – that is, his most meaningful – offspring.

Of the cast of six that Marie joined, her eldest sibling was her brother William. Likely born some time between 1525 and 1528, not too long after their parents' marriage, it is natural to assume he was named after the grandfather who had fallen with James IV at Flodden. Following in his father's footsteps, William matriculated at the University of St Andrews in 1540, before continuing his studies in Paris. By the time that his baby sister, Marie, was born, he would have been in his twenties, and already out making his way in the world.

Although precise years of birth are similarly difficult to give for Marie's remaining siblings, especially her three sisters, we know that the two brothers who survived into adulthood were born much later than William. John's year of birth can be narrowed down to around 1543, while that of Thomas (likely named after his maternal grandfather, Sir Thomas) is generally given as around 1545. The Maitland nursery that newborn Marie joined would certainly have been noisy and busy, though Marie's mother, as a woman of the elite, would have had servants to help her care for her many children, including a wetnurse.

If Thomas and William were, as it seems, named in honour of male family members, Marie's naming suggests more royal roots. The men of her family were closely associated with the courts of both Queen Regent Marie de Guise and her more famous royal daughter. Although best known in anglicised form as 'Mary, Queen of Scots' today, the Queen styled herself in her own lifetime as 'Marie R' (the R representing Regina, the Latin word for Queen). She was also commonly referred to as 'Marie' by her contemporaries, in both Scots and French. As well as a statesman and lawyer, Richard, our Marie's father, was also a passionate poet and historian. One of his historical endeavours was to compile, in Scots, a 'Tabill or Cathalog of the names of the kingis of Scotland, France and England'. On multiple occasions within it, he records the name of the royal 'dochter to James the Fyft' as 'Marie'. He also penned a poem in her honour, predominantly in Scots, but the final line of which exclaims, in French: 'Vive Marie, trenoble Royne d'Escos!' Sir Richard's youngest daughter was born just a few years after 'Marie R' and, it seems plausible, named in honour of the young Queen and in reflection of the Maitland family's commitment to the Crown.*

Marriage between a man and a woman at this time was very rarely about romance or sexual attraction but an economic,

* Marie was also a popular Christian name, given its associations with the Virgin Mary.

religious and social requirement. A public rather than a private affair, it was more akin to finding a job than finding 'the one'. Nonetheless, genuine affection could sometimes coincide with conjugal necessity – whether from day one, in the uncommon case of a 'love match', or developing organically over the years – and Marie's parents appear to have been among the lucky few. Their decades-long devotion to one another would later be honoured in poetry and, tellingly, there was no whisper of any illegitimate Maitland offspring. At a time when many men were not, and bairns born out of wedlock abounded, Sir Richard seems to have been entirely faithful.

But if Marie was born into a fairly loving and stable family setting by sixteenth-century standards, the relative peace of her home environment was not matched by the world outside. On the contrary, Marie was born into a Scotland not just rocked by internal factional divisions and international warfare but in the throes of religious revolution. So turbulent and transformative was the chapter of history that formed the backdrop to the beginning of her life that its main characters and events still rank among the best known of Scotland's past. Marie's youth was the Scotland of John Knox and Mary, Queen of Scots, of the ruptures of the Reformation, and the dramatic and tragic reign of one of the world's most famous queens.

*

Behauld the warldis instability	*Behold the world's instability*
That never still intill ane stait	*That never remains still in*
does byde[2]	*one state*

Marie first drew breath in a Scotland where the reek of burning reformers – to the establishment, 'heretics' – was blowing across the land. She would have been baptised according to the elaborate rites of what was still the only Church of the land, but which was rapidly becoming the 'old' or 'Papist' Church, as the reformist movement, with its emphasis on pared-back rituals (reflective of its altogether more austere ideology) gained ground.

When Marie was born, St Andrews Cathedral still towered above the sea, seemingly impregnable, the tallest and grandest building in Scotland. By the time she entered her teens, its mighty walls had come crashing down, along with the once unassailable authority they had for centuries symbolised in stone.

The scene had been set decades before, in 1517, when Luther hammered his explosive theses into the door of Wittenberg Castle Church, setting passions ablaze across the Continent and beyond. In 1525, the Scottish Parliament had banned the import of 'heretical' books, anxious to suppress the spread of Luther's radical thought, which threatened to overturn the Christian belief systems and structures that had held sway for so long. And when banning books proved ineffective, Scotland's increasingly worried authorities turned to burning people. In 1528, Patrick Hamilton was condemned as a heretic and brutally burned to death in St Andrews, becoming the first martyr of the reformist cause.[*] Persecutory panic continued apace: in 1546, another martyr, George Wishart, met the same grisly fate as Patrick.[†]

Marie's household, under the leadership of her father, remained unmoved by the revolutionary ideas flowing in from Europe, and

* Today, the cobblestoned initials 'PH' mark the place of Patrick Hamilton's death outside St Salvator's Chapel; viewed as cursed, they are anxiously avoided by St Andrews University students to this day.

† The cobblestoned initials 'GW' mark the site of George Wishart's burning outside St Andrews Castle today.

by the burning of heretics, or sacrifice of martyrs, at home. Shortly before his execution, George Wishart had, in fact, while preaching in Haddington, overnighted at Lethington Castle, where he might have set eyes on, or heard the cries of, a newborn Marie, as she was tended by a nursemaid. However, any attempts to convert Sir Richard were resolutely unsuccessful. Even John Knox, the most influential Scottish reformer, responsible for the radicalisation of countless of his countrymen and women with his rallying tirades against Rome, had to admit defeat when it came to Marie's father, conceding that he was 'ever civil, albeit not persuaded in religion'.[3]

Like many Scots, Marie's father very much recognised the failings of the Church and supported the need for internal reform. Unlike the radicals, however, he did not support burning the whole thing to the ground, either literally or metaphorically. In this respect, the eldest Maitland son took on his father's views. William Maitland and John Knox were both big political players, and frequently clashed at court. William did little to disguise his disdain for the foaming-at-the-mouth preacher, once dismissing him as nothing but 'a drytting prophet' – or, in modern English, 'a bullshitting prophet'.* The old Church might have had problems to solve, but Knox's vision was not, for the Maitlands, the answer.†

While Marie was brought up by a father who valued restraint

* William Maitland as quoted in John Skelton, *Maitland of Lethington, and the Scotland of Mary Stuart; A History* (William Blackwood & Sons, 1887–8) volume 2, p. 412. 'Drytting' comes from the historical Scots verb 'dryte'. Of Old Norse origin, it means 'to void (as) excrement'.

† Poem 13 of the *Maitland Quarto* by Marie's father seems to have been written as a thinly disguised attack on John Knox, on the occasion of his taking a seventeen-year-old bride, at the age of fifty, in 1564. Entitled 'Amang foleis [follies] ane greit folie I find', it is a lampooning of old men who take far younger brides.

and moderation, Knox and his comrades continued to be driven by untempered extremism. Their response to Wishart's execution in 1546 was the ruthless retaliatory murder of Cardinal Beaton within the walls of St Andrews Castle, outside of which Wishart had met his end. Having snuck in disguised as stonemasons, the Protestant rebels dragged Beaton from his bedchamber and stabbed him to death, before hanging his body from the castle, exposed for all to see. Backed by England, the reformers occupied the castle, while pro-French Scots relied on the support of a French fleet to help liberate it.

Representatives of what was, increasingly, the 'old Church' tried their best to hold fast as the waves of reform gathered momentum. But the previously incontestable status of God's own representative on earth, the Pope, was suddenly up for debate, while once respected priests were now publicly denounced as morally dubious peddlers of fiction. Even the monarch's divinely appointed position in the hierarchy was starting to look less secure. The 1540s were a time of old truths and orders being blasted apart, and new ones readying themselves to take their place. Everyone, from the mightiest of monarchs to the lowliest of paupers on the street, could feel the ground shifting beneath their feet. It really wasn't the best time to be a king or queen in Europe; and, in Scotland, the music first stopped with a young King James V, at whose court Marie's father served early on in his career.

Much like Richard Maitland, King James V was unpersuaded by religious reformist extremes, although sympathetic to the need for Church reform. The Scottish King was also resistant to political pressure from Henry VIII of England to follow his lead in breaking with Rome; in 1534, the English Parliament had passed the Act of Supremacy, which rejected the authority of the Pope and established

Henry VIII as the supreme head of the Church of England. Instead, James V sought to stem the tide of subversive religious thought flowing into Scotland and took steps to improve the state of the Church, passing legislation against heresy and imploring the clergy to improve their moral conduct. We also hear how James V personally intervened to convince Katherine Hamilton, in a private conversation during her trial, to recant her heresy and avoid the same sorry fate as her brother, Patrick, the first martyr.*

But all James's efforts weren't enough. When he died unexpectedly, following defeat at the Battle of Solway Moss in 1542, the flames of reform blazed on. With the religious situation so febrile, the throne passing to his six-day-old baby daughter, who now became Mary, Queen of Scots, didn't exactly provide for royal stability. Scotland was soon plunged into warfare over which nation, England or France, was to claim Mary's tiny hand in marriage. This was particularly bad news for the southern regions, where the castle home of Marie's family was left vulnerable.

*

I have na will to sing or dans	*I have no will to sing or dance*
For feir of England and of France[4]	*For fear of England and of France*

Scotland had long been strongly connected to France through the 'Auld Alliance', while England had been the 'Auld Enemy' for centuries. But the shifting of the tectonic plates of religion had thrown everything up in the air.

King Henry VIII had led England to sever links with Rome,

* Katherine Hamilton was the subject of modern Scottish playwright Rona Munro's enrapturing 2024 play *James V: Katherine*, part of their acclaimed 'The James Plays' series.

while France remained committed to the old faith. This left Scotland's path uncertain: to remain rooted in the past and the familiar with France, or to embrace an old foe and take a leap of faith into a religiously reformed future? Scottish reformers looked south to England for support, while Scottish Catholics continued to gaze across the water to France. This fork in the road was embodied by a baby girl, Mary, Queen of Scots. Was she to be betrothed to Henry VIII's infant son, Edward, thus uniting the kingdoms of Scotland and England, or to Francis, the dauphin of France, cementing the Franco-Scottish alliance?

For Henry VIII, France was a looming Catholic threat, and Scotland, as a French ally on his northern border, a perpetual liability. He saw the perfect opportunity to solve the problem by wedding his son to the young Queen of Scots, bringing the country into line with England and Protestantism – and he was not inclined to take no for an answer. His response to Scotland's rejection of this proposal, and Mary's betrothal instead to the French dauphin, was to send in his army, leading to the Anglo-Scottish Wars, which raged from 1543 to 1550.*

In this conflict, in which religion and politics were inextricable, Marie's father aligned with the Franco-Scottish Crown establish-

* This is the conflict often referred to as the 'Rough Wooings'. This problematic term has weak origins in a contemporary source, but was popularised by later writers, including Sir Walter Scott (1771–1832), who referred to 'so rough a mode of wooing' in *Tales of a Grandfather* (1828). It has gone unchallenged for too long, and particularly when we know that rape and gendered violence, then as now, were inflicted upon women as 'weapons of warfare'; primary sources tell us that this was the case during this specific conflict. To further compound the distastefulness of the term, Mary, Queen of Scots herself would also later be raped, as an adult, by Bothwell. Following the lead of expert on the period Dr Amy Blakeway, these years of conflict are referred to simply as the 'Anglo-Scottish Wars of the 1540s' in this book.

ment and the Catholic status quo. Throughout his life, he erred on the side of the moderate and the known, and away from the disruptive and the fanatical. He abhorred unrest and upheaval, which was bad for the commonweal,* or welfare, of the nation. Unenthused by the intemperate zeal of the reformers at home, his conservative sensibilities were left equally cold by the blunt violence of English attempts to force a new political and religious order upon Scotland.

In September 1547, English forces crushed a Scottish army at the Battle of Pinkie, not far from Haddington and Lethington Castle. But this victory for England did not achieve the aim of forcing Scottish agreement to an Anglo-Scottish marriage alliance. Quite the opposite, it led to little Mary, Queen of Scots being whisked off to her maternal homeland of France for safety, and further strengthened the alliance between Scotland and France, already bolstered by France's pivotal intervention in the siege of St Andrews Castle (1546–7).

Mary, Queen of Scots might have been safe over in France for now, but the Maitlands, left behind in Scotland, were not. Hot on the heels of the devastating Scottish defeat at Pinkie, Haddington found itself at the epicentre of hostilities. And where earlier English incursions into south Scotland had tended to be more 'smash and grab' affairs, what now played out was a full-blown, sophisticated siege. Known as the 'lang [long] siege', or simply 'the siege of Haddington', it lasted from July 1548 until late 1549. Lethington Castle, located only about a mile from the burgh, was dangerously

* A Scottish term that is still used today, the 'commonweal' was the subject of many of Sir Richard's poems. See: Roger Mason, 'The idea of the commonweal in sixteenth-century Scotland', *Journal of the Northern Renaissance*, 15 (2025).

close to the fighting and violence of the English occupation. An account of the period written sometime later, by Sir Richard's grandson James Maitland – Marie's nephew and the son of brother William – narrates how, unlike most of his fellow local lairds, Richard Maitland refused to side with the English: 'most pairt of the Gentlemen of Lothian, Merse and Teviotdaill did assure [swear loyalty to the English], but my grandfather would not assure, albeit the English did possess Hadington'.[5]

On the side of the Franco-Scottish faction, the Maitlands' castle home of Lethington became the military base for part of Scotland's Highland forces, fighting alongside troops from elsewhere in Scotland and France to liberate the strategically important burgh. Records from the time describe Lethington, along with Haddington, being targeted by burning attacks by the English.

During this long siege, Marie is likely to have been just starting to form her first syllables, perhaps to take her first tentative toddler steps. With their home transformed into a military base, at the centre of a warzone, we can safely assume that the young Maitland children would have been evacuated away from the frontlines to relative safety. As a wealthy laird with frequent business in the capital, Marie's father would have had a residence or some sort of lodgings in Edinburgh, and the resources to evacuate his wife and young family there. Although the capital was still on a war-footing itself, the Maitlands would have been in less immediate danger there than at Lethington. Equally, Marie's father may have sought refuge for himself and his family with local landed friends, such as the Dundas family, based at Dundas Castle, just north of Edinburgh. Plague was rife in Scotland during the 1540s, particularly in the towns and cities; these risks will also have been a consideration in deciding where to go, and may have made such a country residence more likely. Wherever they sought refuge, it can't have been an easy time. The same account by Sir Richard's grandson describes how his grandfather, 'thairfore did live al that tyme with very great difficulties, having a wyffe, many children, and a great family'.

After eighteen months, in September 1549, the siege of Haddington finally came to an end. By the spring of 1550, all hostilities had ceased. A peace treaty, the 1550 Treaty of Boulogne, was signed, the English withdrew and the Franco-Scottish faction emerged victorious. Now that it was safe to do so, a relieved Sir Richard could return home to Lethington Castle with his family.

The world that Marie was born into, then, was tumultuous, to say the least. Death was close at hand, whether from the various afflictions that took so many babes when their lives had barely begun, the ever-present and indiscriminate threat of plague, or the religious–political warfare that ravaged the nation throughout most of the 1540s.

The dawn of the 1550s, however, heralded better times for the Maitlands of Lethington, safely ensconced in their castle home once more, and with political events developing in their favour.

*

In 1554, Governor Arran – who had, until this point, ruled Scotland on behalf of the infant Mary, Queen of Scots – was ousted from power. While the young Queen, now twelve years old, continued to be brought up in France, Scotland came under the rule of her mother, Queen Regent Marie de Guise. Marie's father, Richard, and eldest brother, William, both found strong favour at her court, reflecting their learned reputations and the good standing they had built up over the previous years.

Back in 1552, under Governor Arran, Marie's father had been one of the commissioners appointed to negotiate the dispute around the borderlands, which resulted in the successful conclusion of a treaty. Under Marie de Guise's regency, Sir Richard not only remained such a commissioner but was also made an Extraordinary Lord of Session; that is, he was appointed to sit and vote with the Lords Ordinary, or ordinary judges, of the Court of Session.* These were special and rare appointments – only three or four such Extraordinary Lords existed – made at the pleasure of the Crown.† While Marie's father was making his mark in the sphere of law and order, brother William was striking out in politics, entering the service of the new Queen Regent as her Assistant Secretary of State in 1554.

And there was soon to be cause for celebration closer to home, as Marie's father had also been busy applying his diplomatic and legal skills to securing a good union for his eldest daughter, Elizabeth. On 30 May 1555, when she is likely to have been around eighteen, it was agreed between Sir Richard Maitland of Lethington and William Douglas of Whittinghame elder that Elizabeth would wed the latter's son and heir, William Douglas of Whittinghame younger. This branch of the Douglases were, like the Maitlands, a prominent local landed family. As the desirable eldest son, Elizabeth's new husband stood to inherit the family estate at Whittinghame, a parish about seven miles from Lethington.

The soon-to-be husband and wife's feelings were not particularly important; each would have understood that they had

* The term 'Lord Ordinary' is still used to refer to a judge in the Outer House of the Court of Session in Scotland today.

† Extraordinary Lords were abolished in the 1700s.

to make a strategic marriage – and the surviving contract sets out carefully agreed details regarding the movement of property rights and wealth. It stipulates that William elder is to grant Elizabeth and her new husband the family estate of Langtoun, in joint ownership, as an immediate source of wealth, and as a place to stay until such time as William younger inherited the main estate of Whittinghame. William elder is also to provide the couple with, specifically, eight oxen, six cows, two horses and as much wheat, barley, peas and oats as could be sown at Langtoun, which was a valuable set of assets in kind. However, William elder also agrees in the contract to 'sustain and hold the said William younger and Elizabeth . . . in household with him as long as they please to remain'. That is, although being set up with their own estate at Langtoun – a valuable asset, whether or not they opted to actually reside there – Elizabeth and her spouse also had leave to reside at Whittinghame, probably the superior property, if they preferred, until such time as William younger inherited it.

A widow in Scotland at this time was automatically entitled to 'a widow's third' or 'terce': in essence, lifelong enjoyment, or 'liferent', of one third of the heritable estate (immovable property) possessed by her late husband. 'Liferent' means that the woman had the right to use and benefit from the relevant property during her lifetime, but not to sell or transfer it to anyone else. That is, she didn't actually *own* it but had simply a personal right to enjoy it as long as she lived. As an extra layer of insurance, this marriage contract also provided that, if Elizabeth survived her husband but found herself, for whatever reason, unable to claim her terce, or third, she was instead to be provided by the Whittinghames with an annual income of sixty Scots merks.* This would be a secure source of income, alongside her lifelong right to reside at and benefit from the estate of Langtoun, which she had already been granted upon her marriage.

The dowry ('tocher', in Scots) that Sir Richard had to shell out in exchange for these terms, setting up his eldest daughter for life, was 1,200 merks: 600 upon completion of the marriage, and the remaining half within three years thereafter. This part of the contract was followed by the disturbingly pragmatic caveat that, should Elizabeth die within a year and a day of the marriage without begetting heirs, then William Douglas elder would be obliged to repay Sir Richard the sum paid out before her decease and renounce the remaining unpaid amount; a sobering reminder of the extent to which marriage in this era was about property and progeny, not love; duty and necessity, not choice. It is also a reminder that people died early of all manner of diseases and, in the case of women, of childbirth. Nonetheless, Sir Richard had performed the first duty of a father to his daughter by marrying her into a powerful and wealthy family, on good terms.

A young Marie would no doubt have been delighted to join in with the grand feasting and festivities that would have attended the happy occasion – though her excitement at all the fuss may have been tinged with sadness at losing the company of her older sister. But Elizabeth was the first of the Maitland daughters to reach marriageable age, and her time had come to duly embark on the path of wife and mother that had awaited her since the day that

* Due to inflation and other factors, accurate modern equivalents for figures are tricky to provide. Please see the 'Note on language, dates and documents' at the end of the book for further information and context.

she was born. In any event, it wouldn't have been a farewell forever; Elizabeth was moving only a matter of miles away and would have maintained close links with her Maitland family. Women in Scotland did not, in fact, take their husband's surname at this time but retained their father's, and so she remained, literally, Elizabeth Maitland.*

Just a few years later, in 1558, there were yet more nuptial celebrations, of even greater significance. On 24 April, amid extravagant festivities at Notre Dame in Paris, Mary, Queen of Scots was wed to Dauphin François, eldest son and heir to King Henry II of France. In Edinburgh, the massive cannon of Mons Meg was fired from atop Castle Hill to mark the occasion. This was a coup for Marie de Guise and the Franco-Scottish faction in Scotland, cementing the bond between the two nations, and keeping England out. For Scots of other persuasions, however, it sparked heightened fears – both religious and political – that their country was becoming a mere outpost of Catholic France.

The marriage of the young Queen across the water was certainly enthusiastically celebrated in the Maitland household. Ever loyal to the Crown, and unimpressed by the fanaticism of the reformers, Marie's father wrote a poem celebrating the 'greit blyithnes and joy inestimabill [great happiness and inestimable joy]' of the news of the 'contract of mariage honorabill betwixt the Quenis maist nobill majestie and the gretest young prince in Christintie . . . the Dolphin, first sone of King Henrie'.[6] In it, he exhorted his fellow Scots to rejoice at this splendid union: to clad themselves in their finest dress, take part in tournaments, stage

* This did not begin to change until around the 1800s; keeping your own name, as a woman in Scotland, is thus far more traditional than taking that of your spouse.

banquets and let the wine flow. He also encouraged them to take to the streets to dance and sing, and to relish in the festivities that Marie de Guise ordered to take place in Scotland that summer, including grand processions and dramatic performances. Desirous of peace above all, and thus committed to the success of the Franco-Scottish union, he implored that Scotland and France 'defend ane other bayth by land and sea [defend each other both by land and sea]'. Anyone who would 'mak sedition' between them should, declared Marie's father, be punished: 'Scottis or Frenche, what man that ever he be, with all rigour put him to punition'.

Marie would surely have remembered, for the rest of her life, the fizzing excitement of Queen Mary's first marriage, as bonfires lit up the streets of Haddington and Edinburgh on the orders of the Crown, celebrating the wedding in Paris of the young royal she had yet to set eyes on but with whom she shared a name, and who would already have loomed large in her imagination.

And this celebratory spring of 1558 would have been a time of welcome frivolity for Marie and her remaining two unwed sisters, amid the serious business of preparing to become respectable young women, worthy of the Maitland name – which very much included gaining a solid education.

*

As a girl, Marie would not have had the privilege of attending the local grammar school (Haddington's was highly rated). She certainly didn't have the opportunity to attend university in St Andrews, before continuing her studies on the Continent, like all the men of her family. She would, however, have received an education, most likely in the form of private instruction in the household, delivered by a tutor, and perhaps supplemented by the direct guidance of her father.

Sir Richard was a man aligned with the humanist educational project of the Renaissance, with its growing acceptance of the idea that even women – or, at least, elite women – should receive a degree of education. In his own words, parents should 'bring up thy barnis [bairns/children]' in 'vertu [virtue], science [learning] and knawledge of God'.[7] This special emphasis on learning and education in the Maitland household, driven by Sir Richard, means that Marie and her siblings may well also have been taught by their own father, when he was at home. His humanist sensibilities would certainly have inclined him towards taking on some of the duties of educating his children, including his daughters, himself. Prior to the Reformation, it was also possible for young women to attend schools run by religious houses.

Whatever form, or forms, Marie's early education took, by the time she entered her teens, she would, like her sisters, have been educated in the classics and taught the fundamentals of reading and writing in her native Scots, as well as French, and likely also Latin – alongside domestic tasks, such as sewing.*

But although the Maitland girls were fortunate to have a father who believed in them receiving a decent education, and who would support them in making a good marriage, that, ultimately, was the extent of what they could hope for in life. Any other paths remained closed to them, due to the simple fact of their gender. By contrast, there were no limits on the education of the Maitland boys, or

---

* Marie's sister Isobel, who received the standard education for a Maitland daughter prior to a prompt marriage, had a library valued at £10 upon her death, including a collection of 'Frenche buikis [French books]', reflecting both her general learnedness and her specific abilities in French.

on what they could achieve: and they exploited the freedom of having been born male to the full, William leading the way. In 1558, the same year that Scotland was celebrating Mary's marriage to the Dauphin, William was elevated from Assistant Secretary to Secretary of State for Life at the court of Marie de Guise.

Marie was brought up in a household where the Queen Regent Marie de Guise and her daughter, Mary, Queen of Scots were spoken of with not only requisite deference but personal familiarity, rooted in her family's intimate connections to the royal court. The Maitlands were not the masses: they knew the colour of their monarch's eyes, not just the outline of their face as stamped into coins. They didn't just hope for a glimpse of royalty, as they progressed down a street thronged with crowds, but shared tables, food and wine with them in private. During these formative years, on the cusp of becoming a young adult, Marie would have begun to develop an understanding of her family's closeness to the Crown, and of the significance of the roles of her father and brother. Hers was no ordinary family, and she was no ordinary girl but a Maitland of Lethington, she would have come to realise with an increasing sense of self and pride – qualities that would define so much of her later life and writing.

*

At the beginning of 1558, the political climate seemed fairly stable – just as Marie's father liked it – albeit most unfavourable to those of a Protestant persuasion. Mary, Queen of Scots had married the heir to the French throne, and Marie de Guise was running the show in Scotland until her daughter was ready to take over herself. Not only did Scotland seem to be firmly aligned with Catholic France, the reformers had also lost the allyship of a Protestant-leaning England. In 1553, England had returned to Catholicism under Mary I (also known as Mary Tudor, or 'Bloody Mary', for her persecution of her Protestant subjects). It was in this context that Knox penned his furiously misogynist tract, *The First Blast of the Trumpet Against the Monstrous Regiment of Women*. In it, he condemned female rule as an unnatural abomination, very much inspired by his particular outrage at Mary Tudor and Marie de Guise, their gender as offensive as their 'corrupt' faith.

However, if things had been looking bad for the Scottish Protestants at the start of the year, a series of deaths was about to change everything in their favour, no doubt convincing them that God was on their side. In November 1558, Mary Tudor died and a Protestant Queen, Elizabeth I, acceded to the throne of England in her stead. This re-emergence of a potential ally to the south gave a huge boost to religious idealogues in Scotland, as well as to the band of rebels known as the 'Lords of the Congregation', who were driven as much by politics as by religion. For many, alignment with England and Protestantism presented itself as a means to preserve Scotland's political independence from increasing French encroachment. Among these lords was one William Douglas of Whittinghame, Marie's brother-in-law.

In May 1559, these lords began to wage a rebellion (now known as the 'Reformation Rebellion') against Marie de Guise. And they did not have to hold out long: barely a year later, in June 1560, the Queen Regent of Scotland also died. A power vacuum now opened up. With Mary, Queen of Scots, Scotland's rightful ruler, still across the water in France, the Protestant Lords seized the opportunity of the pause between scenes to usher in a religious and political revolution that would change the face of the nation forever.

In August 1560, religious fervour joined forces with political pragmatism to powerful effect as the Lords of the Congregation staged an effectively illegal Parliament – the Queen had not called it – at which the celebration of the Mass was outlawed and the authority of the Pope denied. The old Church had been abolished; Scotland was now Protestant. And this momentous Parliament, held without royal authority, was presided over by none other than Marie's brother William Maitland of Lethington.

The last that we heard of him, William had been dutifully serving as Secretary of State to the late French Catholic Queen Regent, Marie de Guise. However, in an example of the sort of shapeshifting that would define his entire political career and earn him infamy as the 'Scottish Machiavelli', William now appeared on the other side of the aisle. Like his father, William was uncharmed by the violent zealotry of Knox, and was far from a Protestant extremist. However, he also recognised the flaws of the old Church, and the increasing power of the reformers. Whether selfishly unprincipled or sensibly pragmatic, he seems to have arrived at the position that, if the Protestant faction was about to take over, he would rather be inside the tent, able to exert control over events and temper reformist extremes, than on the outside looking in.

Whatever the precise constellation of William's motivations, or of anyone else present at that fateful 'Reformation Parliament', the deed was done. Although technically not a legal session – it had entirely bypassed the requisite authority of the Queen – the practical reality was that Scotland was now a Protestant nation, and it had gone for the full-fat option, adopting a most extreme and austere brand of Calvinism. Scottish Protestantism replaced a cult of the sensual and the visual, of ceremony and celebration, saints and intercession, with a colourless and joyless cult of the word. Pilgrimage and relics, imagery and incense, feasting and Mass were out; self-castigation and study of scripture were in. And adherence to the new faith and the moralistic policing of people's private lives would soon be enforced with zeal by local kirk sessions up and down the country.

By his actions, William Maitland had explicitly aligned with the new regime. As for Marie's father, it was not in his nature to be a rebel, which, at this point, cleaving to the old Church would have demanded of him. In any event, he had long recognised the failings of that Church, and some elements of the new Church would probably have appealed to him, such as its emphasis on everyone being sufficiently educated to be able to read the Bible for themselves.

So, in the interests of pragmatism and self-preservation, the Maitland household, headed by Marie's father, quietly fell into line with Protestantism, as the new status quo. Richard Maitland constantly strove to remain above the fray of the fierce political and religious struggles of the era. Studious and sedate, the nuances of the personal faith of this scholarly patriarch never translated into impassioned extremism. In politics, too, moderation was his watchword, and he was ever a dutiful servant of royal authority itself, as opposed to the individual who happened to embody it at any given time. Deeply concerned with peace and good governance, he rejected bitter partisanship and eschewed the nasty business of politics, preferring to direct his energies towards history, poetry and the law. This is very much reflected in his poetry, which, although it often deals with highly charged subjects and events, always carefully avoids favouring one side over the other. It is frequently at pains to urge both sides to find common ground, for the sake of the commonweal of the nation.

Given the conservatism and conflict avoidance of her father, along with the ruthless pragmatism of her influential eldest brother – and the documented distaste of each for Knox – it seems unlikely that Marie would have been subject to any sort of extremist Calvinist tirades at home. She would, however, have absorbed an understanding of the nature of the dissatisfactions with the old Church, and of the magnitude of the changes afoot. For whatever the precise nature of their personal faith, the Maitlands, like everyone else, would have been confronted with the immediate practical consequences that flowed from the revolutionary declarations of the Reformation Parliament.

On the cusp of adolescence at that seminal moment in Scotland's history, Marie would have been attending Mass for as long as she could remember. Now, overnight, it was abolished; she would never attend Mass again. The inside of the church that she knew would also have changed dramatically, stripped of all imagery and decoration in the name of spiritual purity and the elevation of the word. The days of elaborate ritual and sensuality were over. There would be no more celebration of saints' days or intercessory prayers; if Marie had developed an affinity with any particular saint, to whom she prayed and whose feast day she celebrated with particular enthusiasm, she would have had to abandon this 'idolatrous' habit with immediate effect. And if Marie, growing up in the shadows of one of the grandest abbeys in Scotland, led by a prioress, had harboured any idea of becoming a nun – the only valid path for an elite woman aside from marriage – the possibility had just vanished.

As part of their campaigns against the old Church, the reformers had tarred nuns and monks with accusations of sexual immorality and 'sodomy'. Monasteries and nunneries were suspect same-sex enclaves, keeping men and women from their one rightful and intended path, they insinuated, which was to marry, procreate and raise their legitimately begotten bairns in fear of God. Women living together alone, with no men to defer to, were an abomination. What were they getting up to behind those walls, away from prying eyes? And what sort of woman was content to live hidden away from the world like that, without children to raise or a husband to serve? Likewise, men living only with other men, not fathering any children or heading any devout households, was surely not God's plan? Cloistered celibacy was no longer considered a good life choice; what had once been viewed as selfless religious devotion, deserving of respect and support, now inspired suspicion, at best. Time was up for the monasteries and nunneries that had been a feature of Scotland's landscape and culture for centuries. A new regime was in town, and they now went the same way as the Mass – abolished and, in many cases, destroyed.

Haddington Abbey was no exception. On the eve of the Reformation, it was one of the largest and wealthiest abbeys in all of Scotland. First founded as a Cistercian convent by Countess Ada of Northumbria, daughter-in-law of King David I, back in the 1100s, it had loomed over the burgh for centuries. It was within its walls, in 1548, that the Scottish Parliament had met to ratify the betrothal of the young Queen Mary to the French Dauphin, as the siege of Haddington raged outside. Now, it had been disbanded as a religious house, and swiftly demolished. Nothing remains of it today, but for Marie, born in its shadows, it would have been a dominant feature of her local landscape and early life. She would never have dreamt that, before she had outgrown her teens, it would be no more.

Such was the dramatic and destructive impact of the Reformation of 1560, which transformed the face of Scotland both physically and culturally. Marie spent her childhood in one world, but she matured into a woman and lived out her adult years in a different one entirely. And the new world order, as embodied by the figure of John Knox, was underpinned by intemperate, moralising zeal in general (people were sinful and needed to be punished and controlled), and misogyny in particular (women, being inherently weaker and more sinful than men, were in need of special control).

Nonetheless, people continued to live their lives, as best they could, while the upheavals of revolution raged around them. Barely a month after the Reformation of August 1560, both of Marie's remaining unwed sisters found themselves pledged to marry sons of local landed families. The negotiations for these unions had no doubt begun when Scotland was still loyal to the old Church; by the time that they were concluded, it had been abolished.

On 1 October 1560, at Lethington Castle, Marie's father signed his name to two marriage contracts. One was an agreement with Patrick Cockburn of Clerkington (a nearby parish in East Lothian) that Richard Maitland's daughter Helen would wed his son and heir, John Cockburn of Clerkington – once again, the sought-after eldest son, who stood to inherit. Similar to the terms that Richard had negotiated for his daughter Elizabeth five years earlier, the contract stipulates that Patrick had to house and provide for the couple and any children they might have during his lifetime; that is, until such point as John inherited the Clerkington estate upon his father's death. The terms of the contract also included for Helen either an entitlement to an income of 100 merks a year or, if her father-in-law preferred, he could instead grant the couple the estate of Newbigging, giving them an immediate residence of their own and landowning status.* The dowry due by Sir Richard in return for these terms was not far off the 1,200 merks he'd had to shell out for his first daughter's marriage in 1555: this time, 1,100 merks, 600 upon completion of the marriage and 100 merks annually thereafter, until the full sum was paid.

It was a busy and costly time for Sir Richard, as the father responsible for arranging and paying for all these marriages. For it was on the very same day that his third-born daughter, Isobel Maitland, was contracted to marry the eldest son of another local landed family: James Heriot of Trabroun younger, son and heir of James Heriot of Trabroun elder. The full contract of marriage has not survived in this case. However, from records that refer back to it, we know that it was also signed on 1 October 1560, and that the total value of the dowry was 1,250 merks.† The finer terms of Isobel's agreement to marry into the house of Heriot of Trabroun would no doubt have been as carefully negotiated as those of her two older sisters, her lifelong rights to a good residence and a good income diligently ensured by her father.

*

---

* The latter property option was, ultimately, the more valuable deal, with the 100 merks a year cash clause likely inserted as a back-up option. In similar vein, it could be that the 100 merks were to be paid until the estate was handed over.

† The Register of Deeds volume for the relevant year is badly damaged, with some pages missing entirely; a truncated sliver of paper signals to the researcher where the missing pages recording Isobel's contract once would have been. However, an entry in the Register of the Great Seal tells us that her marriage contract was also signed on 1 October 1560. Then, a series of acquittances – essentially, receipts – preserved in the Register of Deeds records payments made by Sir Richard to James Heriot senior, meaning that we can deduce that the total dowry payment came to 1,250 merks, with an initial portion paid upon the marriage (as standard) and the remaining balance duly paid in the years thereafter.

Before the year 1560 was out, all three of Marie's sisters had flown the nest. They had departed their father's household and taken up residence with a husband, in fulfilment of the fate they had been born to. Marie, around her early teens, was now the last remaining unmarried Maitland daughter still at home. Whether she'd once harboured hopes of becoming a nun – bitterly dashed with the abolition of nunneries following the Reformation – or whether she'd never anticipated any more than soon following in the footsteps of her sisters and being contracted in marriage to some son of a local laird, life had other plans for her. And they were just about to become clear.

Chapter Two

Because I cannot see

And thocht that I to serve be not sa habill	*And though that I to serve be not so able*
As I wes wont, because I may not sie	*As I once was, because I cannot see*
Yit, in my hairt, I salbe firme and stabill	*Yet in my heart I shall be firm and stable*
To thy hienes with all fidelitie[1]	*To thy highness with all fidelity*

The year 1561 marked a momentous turning point for both Mary, Queen of Scots and her likely namesake Marie Maitland.

Mary's young husband had become King of France, as Francis II, in 1559. But his health had always been frail, and he ruled for barely a year before succumbing to a fatal illness in December 1560. The accession of a new French King – his brother, Charles IX – left little space for the young widow, Mary, in France. Across the water, meanwhile, her mother's death earlier that same year had left Scotland without a ruler. The time had come for Mary to return.

In August 1561 – by which time Scotland had been without an adult monarch for nearly two decades, and without a legitimate government for over a year, since the death of Marie de Guise – a teenage Mary, Queen of Scots set foot in the country of her birth once again, stepping ashore at Leith.

It was the death of a king, and her own birthright as Queen, that sent Mary back to Scotland, changing the direction of her life, as well as the fate of nations. The event that transformed Marie's life, by contrast, was not the sort that shaped the course of history or that was written about in foreign chronicles. In truth, it was probably of little consequence beyond the immediate environs of her family, but that did not make it any less transformational for her father, and for her. Around the very same time that Mary, Queen of Scots was preparing to return to Scotland, Marie's father, whose eyesight had long been deteriorating, went blind. This was the moment that changed everything: the chance occurrence that redetermined Marie's life path in a way that would otherwise have been unthinkable. To continue to write, and to be able to serve the young Queen, her father would need to pass on his pen.

*

Marie's father confirmed his state of blindness in August 1561, in his own words, in a poem that he addressed to Mary, Queen of Scots upon her return to Scotland. Its opening stanzas – among the first that he must have composed in his mind and dictated – combine gushing flattery with sage advice to the 'maist nobill Quene of bluid [blood] under the air', who, with all his 'hairt and micht [heart and might]', he welcomes 'hame to thy native people and countrie'. However, he then laments that, although he served as a 'trew servand [true servant]' to her mother, Marie de Guise, nowadays he 'may not sie [cannot see]' and is thus 'not sa habill [not so able]' to serve her royal daughter as he would like to be.

However, despite his reservations, not only did Marie's father continue to write poetry in his blindness (the majority of his poetry, including this verse, in fact, postdates his loss of sight) – but his long career of service also continued and flourished.

First, on 12 November 1561, Sir Richard was appointed as a Lord Ordinary; that is, made a full judge of the Court of Session, having participated since 1554 as an Extraordinary Lord.[2] Contemporary records make reference to this elevation taking place despite the 'notoriety' of his 'infirmity'.[3] It was the next year, in 1562, that he was first nominated to the Privy Council and made Keeper of the Privy Seal under Mary, Queen of Scots.[4] He also began to compose his 'practicks', a valuable collection of summaries of decisions of the Court of Session, which would cover up until the year 1577.*

This impressive array of professional promotions and contributions, in the period immediately following his turning blind, reflects the extent to which Marie's father's learnedness was valued by those around him, a point laboured both in his own time and in the literature that has been written about him since. For example, one later edition of his poetry declares that his appointment as a full judge, despite his 'suffering under so fatal an infirmity', constitutes an 'uncommon proof of the respect in which his learning was held, and the confidence which was reposed in his attainments for this honourable and important office'. It proves, it goes on, 'how far we are justified in forming so high an estimate regarding him'.[5] Another source states that he 'bore the affliction with characteristic calmness and cheerfulness' and that 'fortunately, it did not incapacitate him'.[6] Yet another source gushes that, despite 'this venerable judge' having had the 'misfortune to be deprived of his eyesight . . . his vigorous and cultivated mind supported him under this calamity'.[7] One essay on Scottish legal history even goes as far as to suggest that 'perhaps his very disability led the old man to pay all the more attention to the argument and to have all the more time of an evening to dictate the rubric'.[8]

This high praise is no doubt all deserved, but Sir Richard needed the support of more than just his mind to discharge

---

* 'Practicks' means cases or precedents; essentially, they are early law reports and remain today a significant source of Scottish legal history.

his many duties, in his blindness. The identity of the person, or persons, to whom the blind Sir Richard was dictating the rubric (his summaries of legal decisions) of an evening – or his poetry or letters or anything else – is left unanswered, but the fact that he must always have been dictating to *someone*, whose shadowy presence is implied while the spotlight shines on Sir Richard, is taken as read. But who were these mystery people? As well as the support of court clerks and his well-educated male servants, Sir Richard could also turn, when he was at home, to his dutiful youngest daughter, Marie.

By the time Marie's father lost his sight, at the age of sixty-five, three of his four daughters had already been married off; they were no longer living in the family home but firmly set up in the households of their respective husbands, the chapter of their lives as wives and mothers well underway. His three sons, Marie's brothers, meanwhile, were out making their way in the world on their own terms, as was their male right.

John and Thomas, closest to Marie in age, would have been off pursuing their studies at the University of St Andrews. The much older William, meanwhile, remained a key player on the national political stage. Despite his abandonment of the late Queen Regent and switch to Protestantism, he was appointed Secretary of State by her daughter, the newly returned and Catholic Mary, Queen of Scots. William's reputation preceded him; even his most bitter enemies had to concede his undoubted personal charm, along with his sharp political skills. Queen Elizabeth I of England famously praised Marie's eldest brother as 'the flower of the wits of Scotland', and he nurtured a rich rapport with both the English monarch and her own formidable chief advisor, William Cecil.

Although religiously tolerant, as a steadfast Catholic herself, Mary was acutely aware that she inspired fear among Protestants in both Scotland and England. In this context, she understood the advantages of appointing a prominent but moderate Protestant, with good relations with the English court, as her closest advisor. William would feature at the centre of the events that would come to define Mary's Scottish reign, ensuring his fame, or infamy, in the annals of history as her 'Secretary Lethington'. As his nineteenth-century biographer Skelton put it: 'Maitland, as the Prime Minister of the Queen, was the most conspicuous figure at the Scottish Court. In all Scotland, indeed, no man, Knox only excepted, was more widely known . . . he had attained a great political position.'[9]

Thus by 1561, only Marie remained in the family home. A scholarly man who well understood the value of learning, Marie's father had ensured that all of his children, including his daughters, had received a good education. Little could he have known that, in one of them, he was training a future scribe. But now, in his time of need, it was one of those daughters who could assist him – and Marie was only too willing to do so.

Initially, Marie would have had only italic script at her disposal, learned alongside her sisters as part of her early education. However, sometime in the early 1560s, as her commitment to supporting her father became apparent, coupled with her sharp mind and aptitude for learning, it appears that Sir Richard instructed that Marie also be trained in secretary hand, likely by one of his high-status male servants. We know some of these men by name, such as Andro (Andrew) Cleland or David Auldinstoun, as they appear as witnesses to Maitland family documents, as well as being referenced in other records.

Marie would also have supplemented this instruction with self-directed learning and practice in her own time – the traces of which appear to be preserved among the pages of a manuscript (a miscellany of historical and legal writings) known to have been in the possession of her father at this time. Tantalisingly, at various points we see examples of someone diligently practising secretary hand letter forms and words in the margins, using the previous hand as a guide – quite possibly a young Marie, in the process of learning, and on her way to being able to take on secretary hand duties herself.

In any event, as the new decade dawned, so it was that Marie, in her teens, took her first steps into the role of secretary, or amanuensis, to her blind father, committing his valuable thoughts to paper when he could no longer do so himself yet still had so much to contribute. We might imagine the elderly laird sat beside the fire in his favourite spot at Lethington Castle, or in his lodgings near the court at the heart of Edinburgh, dictating his learned thoughts on the most pressing legal matters of the day, or conveying his concerns about the state of society in lofty poetic form, his devoted youngest daughter sat at the table beside him, quill in hand, dutifully noting it all down on his behalf – and absorbing much learning along the way. For where her blind father benefitted from crucial in-house support, enabling him to pursue both his professional and personal interests, Marie's accidentally created scribal support role afforded her a unique degree of personal freedom and opportunity for growth, as a young woman. Liberated from the immediate expectations of marriage and motherhood, her education instead flourished far beyond that of her sisters and other women of her status.

In the process of providing invaluable support to her father, Marie was also nurturing her own intellect, finessing her own calligraphic skills and honing her own literary talents. When she wasn't busy transcribing his works, she would have taken advantage of his expansive library, reading everything she could get her hands on. She would also have begun to pen her own verse; faltering, at first, but becoming more accomplished over time. And, as the months and years went by, Marie would have been able to express herself on the page in secretary as well as italic hand.

*

Marie was benefitting from an enhanced education, but the flipside of her role as her father's secretary was that she was missing out on the social and financial security of marriage – a situation that became only more acute the older she became. The average age of marriage for elite women like Marie and her sisters was eighteen, and such women could certainly expect to be wed by their early twenties. When Marie first began to assist her father, she was likely still only in her mid-teens, and thus not quite ready for marriage yet in any case. For the first few years, therefore, her secretarial support role was straightforward enough. Marie was still comfortably living as a child under her parents' roof, her financial security and place of residence provided unproblematically by her father. There was not yet any pressing conflict with society's expectations of her, or any concern about how she would ensure her future wellbeing.

Once Marie reached, and then exceeded, properly marriageable age, however, the situation became quite different. As the years went on, her unmarried status would have been increasingly conspicuous, and a cause for comment and concern. Her already aged father could not live forever and, by this point, society expected that responsibility for her wellbeing would have passed over to a husband.

However, in spring 1569, instead of another marriage contract, Marie's father concluded a very different type of agreement on behalf of his youngest daughter – one in which Marie was assigned not a husband, but an income. This document marks the first time that Marie appears clearly in the historical record by name, and would have been drawn up when she was in her late teens or early twenties; that is, very much of the age by which she should, in the normal manner of things, have departed the house of her father for that of a husband.

Dated 5 May of that year, the contract sets out how Sir Richard Maitland of Lethington obligated a local landowner named William Sinclair to pay his daughter Marie the sum of 110 Scots merks a year, in two equal payments of 55 merks. When he had negotiated the marriage of her sister Helen in 1560, Marie's father had ensured that she had the right to an annual income of at least 100 merks; around 100 merks a year was thus clearly deemed an appropriate amount of disposable income for a woman of Marie's social status, their bed and board otherwise covered. But where Helen's bed and board was taken care of through marriage, Marie's was still the responsibility of her father. Indeed, as well as being described in this 1569 record as 'dochter lautfull [lawful daughter]' to the 'honorable man schir richert maitland', Marie is also described as 'ane noble damsell'. Each descriptor is a clear flagging of her unmarried status: a young woman, or damsel, still defined in relation to her father.

The money being directed towards Marie is described as 'annualrent'. A historical term referring to the interest due on a loan, it can essentially be read as 'annual interest', with such payments tending to represent about 10 per cent of the loan sum. This first income of Marie's is thus likely to have had its source in a loan of around 1,000 merks made by her father to Sinclair, with her father here arranging for the interest due on it to be paid to Marie, instead of him. And the contract stipulates that Marie is to receive her payment in the 'usuall money of scotland'; that is, not in kind (in barley or oats or anything else) but in hard cash.

Instead of preparing for marriage, Marie had spent the past years, as she matured into a young woman, dutifully learning the skills to support her father. With the establishment of this income in 1569, it was formalised that she would, for the time being, be continuing in that role. The Maitlands were highly adept at using the law to protect their interests, and everything here was done by the book.

The original contract between Marie's father and William Sinclair had been signed on 5 May; soon after, on 16 May, its terms were recorded and approved by the authority of the Great Seal, as a further formality. Through the official confirmation of the state, Marie's entitlement to her income was made very secure and very public – as, indeed, was her lack of availability for marriage. If any local landed family or eligible young bachelor at court had had their eye on the hand of Sir Richard's youngest daughter – who came from a good family with impressive royal connections, and who would also come with a good dowry – this was not the turn of events they will have been hoping for. But Marie had no pressing need to obtain the practical benefits of a marriage, in the form of a residence and an income, both of which she had, for the time being, through her father. More than occupied with her role supporting him, she was not in a position to leave her family home to become someone's wife, bear and rear children and run her own household. The message was clear: the 'noble damsell' referred to in the contract was, for now, remaining one.

*

For Marie, then, the 1560s were defined by a conspicuous lack of marriage, eschewed in favour of serving her father and nurturing her own self-development. For Mary, Queen of Scots, by contrast, the same decade was defined by two disastrous marriages, with events spiralling increasingly out of her control. A Catholic Queen returning to a rampantly misogynist, freshly Protestant Scotland, the scene was set for conflict. And not just at home: Mary's additional claim to the throne of England meant that she also instilled fear, or inspiration, in royal rulers, religious radicals and political players far beyond Scotland's borders. Even then, nobody could have predicted quite how badly Mary's Scottish reign would transpire. And, because the fate of Marie's family was inextricably bound up with that of Mary, Queen of Scots, the disaster of her reign, and the ensuing civil war, would lead to disaster for them, too.

In 1565, Mary, Queen of Scots wed Henry Stuart, Lord Darnley. A dashing young nobleman, he had, like her, a strong claim to the thrones of both Scotland and England. He had grown up in England and is said to have spent his first night on arriving across the border into Scotland at Lethington Castle – in which case, a curious Marie would, no doubt, have been most interested to make the acquaintance of the soon-to-be second husband of the Queen.

By all accounts, Mary and Darnley were, at first, genuinely infatuated with one other. However, they fell out of love as quickly as they'd fallen into it, their initially heady romance descending into complete relationship breakdown. In 1566, Mary's close friend and private secretary, the Italian David Rizzio, was brutally stabbed to death in front of her at Holyrood Palace, in the gory execution of a political plot approved by Darnley – an episode emblematic of both the turbulence of Mary's Scottish reign and the volatility of the world Marie lived in, especially as her eldest brother was never far from the drama.

William Maitland, or Secretary Lethington, was among the powerful men at court disgruntled by Rizzio's increasing influence over the Queen and involved in the scheming to get rid of him. Where William was driven purely by political self-interest, however, Darnley was driven by both political dissatisfaction and toxic sexual passion. Rumours of an affair between Rizzio and the Queen swirled around the court – and there are also hints that Darnley may have been as upset at the idea of being spurned by Rizzio as he was by allegedly being cheated on by his royal wife. English ambassador Thomas Randolph perhaps implied a carnal relationship between the two men with his reference to Rizzio as Darnley's 'only governor', alongside suggestive reports of the two sharing a bed.* Darnley was also infamous for his frequent presence at brothels, and promiscuous debauchery with both women and men, more generally. There is disparaging contemporary reference to his addiction to 'base and unmanly pleasures'

* The act of bedsharing was, of course, common in this era, and cannot be taken as evidence on its own. However, read alongside other factors, references to it in this case appear suggestive. Acclaimed Tudor historian John Guy, for example, firmly maintains that the two men were lovers.

and he was gossiped about as troublingly effeminate: he was 'more like a woman than a man, for he was very lusty, beardless, and lady-faced', stated Sir James Melville of Halhill, a diplomat and courtier at Mary's court.[10]

In early 1567, less than a year after Rizzio's bloody end, Darnley was also murdered, aged just twenty-one, when the house in which he was staying, just off Edinburgh's high street, was blown up using gunpowder (although his strangulated body was found in the garden outside). Darnley had many enemies, but suspicion fell predominantly on the Earl of Bothwell, an influential nobleman who had long harboured open ambitions of marrying the Queen and assuming power himself – her married status, and her consent, regardless. The fact that Bothwell was also already married was similarly but an inconvenient detail in the face of his bigger plans.

Unfortunately for Mary, Queen of Scots, she also had many enemies – and, seeing an opportunity to destroy her, they now attacked. In the wake of Darnley's murder, a propaganda campaign of pamphlets and placards proliferated across Edinburgh, accusing her of being in love with Bothwell and having plotted with him to murder Darnley in a crime of passion. All of this sent shockwaves across England and the Continent. Other rulers were terrified by the trend that might be set by the assassination of a King, and horrified by the rumours of Mary, Queen of Scots as an adulteress and murderess.

At pains to defend her reputation against these damaging accusations, it is truly difficult to think of a worse, more ostensibly incriminating course of action for Mary at this point than marrying Bothwell. And yet, mere months after Darnley's murder, Mary found herself wed to none other than the chief suspect of the crime, with whom she was accused of being in love. The political suicide and self-incrimination of this marriage is the first and most obvious clue that Mary can hardly have meaningfully consented to it. However, any remaining doubt is stilled by the contemporaneous record, which makes clear that Mary was abducted then raped by Bothwell, leaving her with little realistic choice but to wed him.

In April 1567, on their way back to Edinburgh from Stirling, Mary and her companions – including Marie's brother William and the courtier James Melville – were ambushed and kidnapped by Bothwell and his men. They were taken to Dunbar Castle, where Mary was violated by Bothwell while held captive. In his memoirs, Melville states bluntly that Mary was raped, and thus left with no meaningful options: 'whither sche wald hir self or not . . . the quen culd not bot mary him, seing he had ravissit hir and lyen with hir against hir will [whether she wanted to herself or not . . . the Queen could not but marry him, seeing as he had ravished her and lain with her against her will]'.[11]

Mary also confirmed in her own words that she had been raped, in terms as explicitly as she was able to while preserving her integrity, writing that she and her supporters 'fand his doingis rude [found his doings rude]', whereby the word 'rude' at this time had connotations that went far beyond merely the impolite, also encompassing violence and barbarity. In the days following her rape, Melville relates – again, from first-hand recollection; he was there – how he heard the Queen, 'wha was sa disdanfully handlit [who was so disdainfully handled]', ask for 'a knyf to stik [stab] hirself, or elis, said sche, "I sall drown myself"'.[12] Despite wanting to die, however, Mary remained alive; and she then also had to endure the further nightmare of marrying Bothwell. Rape had long been wielded as a 'weapon' of warfare; with a woman on the throne, it also presented itself as a 'weapon' of politics. Bothwell had calculated that forcing himself onto the Queen was the way to force her into marrying him, and he was right.*

This was the sort of society in which Marie Maitland existed, as a young woman. And these were among the seismic events of the Scottish 1560s that she lived through, and which will have dominated discussions in her family and social circles. As a Maitland of Lethington, Marie was not, like the masses, dependent only on what she heard on the streets, or read on placards, but would have learned about events far more directly, not least from her brother William, when he returned home to Lethington Castle (an avenue named 'Politician's Walk' still marks where the famed Secretary once strode up and down).

It is unlikely that Marie would have heard anything favourable about Bothwell from her brother. Not only were the two long-standing enemies but William had been captured along with Mary and held at Dunbar, and so would have known exactly what happened there. As a sister of Secretary Lethington, we can safely assume that Marie was more persuaded by the version of events whereby the Queen had been forced into marriage by Bothwell, as opposed to the propaganda efforts, aimed at the masses, that painted Mary as Bothwell's accomplice in a crime of passion. And Marie, no longer a child, would have been horrified by the reality that no amount of power or social status, not even being Queen, could truly keep a woman safe in this man's world.

There was great, and varied, discontent at the Mary–Bothwell marriage. In June 1567, a band of Scottish Lords took up arms

---

* Modern Scottish playwright Rona Munro brought this shameful episode of Scotland's history powerfully to light through their play *Mary*, first staged in 2022.

against Mary and Bothwell at the Battle of Carberry Hill, near Edinburgh, which the 'Confederate Lords' won. Bothwell managed to escape. He fled the country, and Mary would never see him again. Mary, meanwhile, surrendered. On paper, she was still Queen; in reality, she was now a subdued captive. And she wouldn't even remain Queen on paper for much longer. After a brief imprisonment in Edinburgh, she was whisked north to her second prison of Lochleven Castle. It was here that hostile Protestant nobles forced her to sign papers abdicating the Scottish throne in favour of her one-year-old son, James, the only child from her marriage with Darnley. With Mary deposed, he was crowned King James VI of Scotland, with the Earl of Moray appointed as Regent for the infant ruler.

Disempowered and imprisoned, Mary, as if she hadn't suffered enough, discovered her rape had resulted in her conceiving twins, which she endured the trauma of miscarrying at Lochleven. She famously managed to escape from her island prison and raise an army, but she was defeated at the Battle of Langside. At this fateful fork in the road, Mary opted to flee south to England, trusting that she would find refuge and sympathy with her fellow female ruler and cousin, Queen Elizabeth I. Instead, from 1568, she found herself imprisoned once more – a state in which she would remain until her death.

While Mary languished in England, civil war broke out back in Scotland – with serious consequences for Marie and her family. On one side was the Queen's Party, supporters of the exiled and imprisoned Mary, Queen of Scots. On the other was the so-called 'King's Party' – really, the enemies of Mary, rallied around the infant King James. Marie's brother William had distanced himself from Mary, and been implicated in her deposition. However, as slippery as ever, rather than join the ranks of the King's Party, he now entirely recanted and became a leading light of the Queen's Party, where he was loyally joined by his younger brothers. Both John and Thomas very much followed their older brother into the turbulent world of politics, rather than adhering to their father's example and sticking to the quieter life of literature and the law. And John's decision, in particular, to jump headfirst into politics would have severe consequences for Marie in later life.

Truly, the paths pursued by the sons could scarcely have departed more drastically from the sober example set by their scholarly patriarch father. If Marie's father was a sort of historical civil servant, dutifully serving the government of the day, while avoiding becoming personally embroiled in the messy business of party politics, then her brothers were early modern politicians, up to their necks in politics proper, and unafraid to get their hands dirty.

In representative fashion, where all three of Marie's brothers were active in the Queen's Party, their father took no side at all in the Marian civil war. To his horror, however, this did not prevent him from being cruelly punished, by a series of King's Party Regents, for the actions of his boys. There were perilously tough times ahead for Sir Richard and his household – which very much still included his unmarried youngest daughter, Marie.

Chapter Three

In this troublesome tyme

The chaos caused by the deposition of Mary, Queen of Scots led to stormy years for Scotland, with a revolving door of ill-fated regents attempting to govern while civil war raged.

The Earl of Moray, Mary's half-brother, first led the King's Party from 1568 until 1570, when he was shot dead by one of Mary's followers as he progressed through Linlithgow on his way from Stirling to Edinburgh. The Earl of Lennox – Darnley's father and little James's grandfather – took over next but fared little better. In another very early example of assassination by firearm, he was murdered in a shooting attack by Mary's supporters after barely a year as regent.

Next to sup from the poisoned chalice (perhaps literally) of the Scottish regency was the Earl of Mar. His time in charge was similarly short-lived, beginning in 1571 and ending in 1572. His demise might have been due to natural causes or it might have had more sinister origins, if rumours about his poisoning at the hands of the Earl of Morton were true. Given the murky and murderous nature of this era of Scottish politics, the latter feels plausible; not least as it was the selfsame Earl who next stepped into the role of Regent, where he would remain until James came of age, in 1578.

Unfortunately for Marie and her father, one constant among the various King's Party Regents was Sir Richard's unjust persecution at their hands. In the spring of 1570, his lands of Blythe in Lauderdale were attacked, as collateral for the political choices of his sons. His sheep, cattle and horses were stolen, his properties despoiled and his lands ravaged. Marie's father lamented this in a poem, which relies heavily on word play with the Scots word 'blyithe', meaning 'happy'. At the poem's opening, he implores himself, a 'blind man', to 'be blyithe', even though he has been 'wrangit' and his lands of 'Blyithe' attacked.

Blind man, be blyithe	*Blind man, be blythe [happy]*
Thocht that thow be wrangit	*Though you have been wronged*
Thocht Blyithe be herriet	*Though Blythe be plundered*
Tak nae melancholie[1]	*Be not melancholy*

Marie's father and his household would at least have been safely ensconced at their main residence of Lethington while this plundering of Blythe took place to the south. But things were soon to get much worse.

The forfeiting of lands and property was a standard form of punishment for the social elite at this time. Soon after, in the middle of the civil war, the ruling King's Party not only denounced the Maitland brothers as traitors and stripped them of their assets but also spitefully confiscated Lethington Castle from their father, who had done nothing to merit such punishment. For likely the second time in her life, Marie was thus forced into exile from her castle home as a casualty of war – and, this time, the trials of exile would have to be endured for much longer.

Amid the upheaval of regime change and civil war, the plundering of land and confiscations of property, one thing the newly Calvinist state still found time for was the punishment of 'sodomy'.*

* In England, Henry VIII's 'Buggery Act' of 1533 stipulated that the 'detestable and abominable Vice of Buggery' be punishable by death. The first execution under its terms took place in 1540. We don't know exactly when the death penalty for 'sodomy' was introduced in Scotland, but it had clearly become established as a capital offence by the mid-to-late 1500s, with the first recorded execution in 1570.

On 1 September 1570, John Swan and John Litster were found guilty of the 'crime' and sentenced to be strangled and burned at the stake at Edinburgh's Castle Hill; the grave consequences of the earliest known surviving conviction for 'sodomy' in Scotland. A decade after the Reformation – which had already rid the country of 'suspect' monks and nuns, living in their same-sex enclaves – and no doubt aimed at setting a deterrent example to the general populace, this scandalous case cannot have escaped Marie's attention, especially given her father's close involvement with the legal system. If Marie was in Edinburgh on the day of the men's execution, she may have found herself caught up in the crowds thronging up towards the Castle to watch the spectacle; she may even have gone to watch herself. By contrast, although Darnley's engagement in sexual acts with men had been an open secret, he was never hauled before a court, let alone sentenced to death for 'sodomy'. His behaviour may have scandalised the court, and been gossiped about in appalled tones up and down the country, but serious consequences there were none. Neither of the two men executed at Castle Hill, by contrast, were powerful; they both worked for the same master, as simple smiths and servants.

Not long after, there would also be a death closer to home for the Maitlands. In 1572, while abroad in Italy, Thomas, the third Maitland son, died of quartan fever. Born around 1545, he can't have been much older than Marie, the youngest sibling. In his short life, he made his mark in politics, and left behind a rich poetic legacy, predominantly in Latin (as opposed to the Scots verse of his father and sister Marie).

News of the severe blow of Thomas's death reached Marie and her family at an already tough time. His own neutrality apart, Marie's father was still very much paying the price for the Queen's

Party allegiance of his sons, finding himself under merciless persecution by the King's Party and their English allies. With Lethington confiscated from them, the Maitlands are, once again, likely to have taken refuge at Marie's father's lodgings in Edinburgh or to have availed themselves of the hospitality of friends outside the capital, such as their close friends at Dundas Castle. They were at Dundas at least some of the time, as records testify to the presence of 'auld Lethingtoun and his wyfe' there in April 1572. What's more, in a poem written around the same time, Marie's father seems to suggest that Edinburgh was not presently a safe place to dwell, due to the civil war: 'The toun, quharin [wherein] to dwell was best,' he wrote, is now 'with men of war richt sair opprest . . . in this troublesome tyme'.[2]

The civil war would, at least, soon be over, but the Maitland boys had backed the wrong political horse, and Marie's father's troubles would continue for quite some time more.

*

By the beginning of 1573, after years of fighting and shifting fortunes, victory was within touching distance for Regent Morton and the King's Party. Only Edinburgh Castle was still meaningfully held by the Marians and, in February, it surrendered, marking the end of the civil war and confirming the deposition of Mary, Queen of Scots. The fall of Mary also marked the end of the career and life of Marie's brother William, who had been part of the forces holding the Castle until the last.

When William had first embarked upon his political career years earlier, his father had penned a poem to guide him along his way. Later recorded in Marie's manuscript with the title 'The Laird of Lethingtounis Counsale to his Sone, Beand [Being] in the Court', he began by imploring William to 'imprent . . . this, my counsale, into thy mind'. In the stanzas that followed, he urged his son to 'be not blawin with windis of all airtis [directions]', but rather to be 'wyise and tenty [wise and cautious] in . . . governing'. Steer clear of 'other mennis faillis [failures]', guided his father, and be wary 'whomto thy counsale thow reveill', as 'sum may seme trew, and yit dissemblit be [some may seem honest, but be pretenders]'.

As in so many of his poems, Sir Richard's concern for the state of the nation also shines through. 'Let na thing the commoun weill elyde [let no thing quash the commonweal]', he instructed William: 'invent na thing that may the realme devyide; ay [always] nourisch peace, flie troubill and debait', and 'at all tyme maintein justice and richt'. Pertinently, he also cautioned his eldest son to be wary of how swiftly a man's fortunes can change:

Thocht thou in court be with the hiest placit	*Although you are placed in court with the highest,*
In honour, office, or in dignitie,	*In honour, office or in dignity,*
Think that sumtyme thow may be fra it chasit	*Be mindful that you may sometime be chased from it*
As sum has been befoir and yit may be	*As some have been before and may yet be*
Neidfull it is thairfor to gang warlie	*Therefore it is necessary to proceed warily*

His father's best efforts notwithstanding, all the wisest advice in the world could not protect William from his fate. He had played with political fire his entire career and, this time, he had been well and truly burned. After the fall of Edinburgh Castle, William was thrown into prison in Leith, where he swiftly died. He had been unwell for some time, and his death may well have been due to natural causes; however, the particular timing provoked suggestions that he had poisoned himself in order to avoid the fate of execution.

With William's death in 1573, Sir Richard lost his eldest son and heir. With his youngest son, Thomas, having died the year before, he had only one son left. And that son, Marie's only remaining brother, John, was imprisoned.

*

Your grief is greit, I graunt, in sa greit age[3]	*Your grief is great, I grant,* *in such old age*

Marie's father's grief at losing two sons in quick succession must have been overwhelming. It was around this time that Marie wrote a poem to comfort him. Although left unattributed when she later recorded it in her manuscript, the author of this poem could only have been Sir Richard's loyal daughter, by his side throughout his troubles. The poet displays not only intimate knowledge of, and great pride in, Maitland family history, along with a solid understanding of the family's present-day perils, but also a keen personal concern for Sir Richard's emotional wellbeing. Marie also deploys in this poem specific phrasing and themes that she would return to in a later poem, which would also be recorded in her manuscript. In both poems, for Marie, her father is so 'wittie [intelligent]' and 'wyis [wise, erudite]', and their Maitland ancestors 'manfull [brave and resolute]' men.*

---

* The later poem, which echoes themes and phrases in the consolatory ballad, is poem 1. Although it appears as the first poem in the *Maitland Quarto* manuscript today, Marie wrote, and added it into her manuscript, much later.

In her manuscript, Marie gave this earlier poem the title 'Ane consolatore ballad [A consolotary ballad]'. In it, she acknowledged her elderly father's great grief while urging him not to despair but to trust in God's plan and display stoicism in the face of adversity. Reflecting both her own faith, and her erudite intimacy with the scriptures, Marie invoked figures from the Old Testament, such as Job, who had their faith tested through having to endure great suffering. She also appealed to their shared family history, noting how their Maitland ancestors 'bitter blastis ay buir with breistis bauld . . . and stormis withstuid with stomak stout and stoic [always endured bitter blasts with chest held high . . . and storms withstood with courageous and stoic stomach]'. Marie reminded her father – as he had no doubt often reminded her, when she had been the one in need of comfort – that 'tein and troubill baith ar transitorie [suffering and woes are both transitory]'. She also made much of how he should take great comfort from the fact that he still had one son – clear proof, she maintained, of God's favour.

Indeed, although he was being held captive, Sir Richard's last remaining son had somehow managed to avoid execution for his Queen's Party loyalties. In obvious reference to John's narrow escape with his life, Marie observed how the Lord did with 'greit care . . . conserve and keip . . . your onlie sone, wha semed a slauchter scheip [a sheep earmarked for slaughter]'. What's more, she reminded her father, the house of Maitland had survived against the odds with only one male heir before. She drew parallels with one illustrious ancestor in particular, in the form of her father's namesake – a much older 'Richard Maitland' who had lived centuries earlier, back when the Maitland name was still being made. Marie wrote of how:

Him self was aged, his hous hang by a hair	*He, too, was aged, his house hung by a thread*
Doull and distress almost to deid him drew	*Sorrow and distress almost drew him to death*

However, 'burdalane, his onlie sone and air . . . his hous upheld [an only child, his only son and heir . . . his house upheld]'. The evocative historical Scots word 'burdalane' – literally, 'bird-alone' – has fallen out of modern use. Although technically gender neutral, in practice it was used to refer to a single male (the useful type) child. Sir Richard, at this point, of course still had five living children: four daughters, and one son. But he had only one meaningful heir: a burdalane. Marie used the word again in the next stanza, labouring the similarities between her father's present situation and that of his ancestral namesake: 'Richard he was, Richard you are also . . . burdalane ye have behind, as he . . . He will your hous in honour yet uphauld . . . from hence further ay, as it has bene of auld . . . [Richard he was, Richard you are, too . . . an only son you have left, as did he . . . He [John] will yet your house in honour uphold, from here on in and always, as it has been in times past].'

Marie ended the poem by urging her father to believe in God's mercy, including in the final line a tender reference to his 'gray heid [grey head].'

> Thairfoir rejoyis in him and tak your rest
> Be merry for his mercie manifest
> He your hous, your self, and sone will send
> Mair solace shortlie nor [than] ye can consave [conceive]
> Helthe, joy in hairt, honour, and in the end
> Your gray heid sall with glaidnes go to grave.

As well as this poem for her dejected father, around the same time, Marie also wrote a poem addressed to her imprisoned brother – her father's 'burdalane'. Recorded in her manuscript directly after the consolatory ballad to her father, the theme of its six stanzas is that, even if you find yourself imprisoned, if you know in your heart that you are honest and have done no wrong, then you remain spiritually free and should take comfort in this. It offered words of solace to her brother, sibling to sibling, but its sentiments also strongly suggest that Marie shared his Queen's Party political sympathies and believed in the righteousness of that cause.

'For gif thow doe not staine thy treuth and honestie, How can thow be in paine? No, suirlie thow art frie [For if you do not blemish your truth and honesty, how can you be in pain? No, surely you are free],' wrote Marie, in the first stanza. And 'gif thow . . . has done none offence, Thocht in captivitie Thow suffer violence, Yit suirlie thow art frie [if you . . . have committed no offence, although in captivity, you suffer violence, yet surely you are free]', she further comforted her brother, while also conveying that she did not consider his actions, in supporting the deposed Queen, to have been an 'offence'.

Marie rounded off the poem by urging her brother to remain stoic in the face of his misfortune, and to trust that his righteousness will be proven in the end: 'Thocht Fortoun be thy fo, Hir frowning sall not lest . . . For tyme thy treuth sall try [Although [Dame] Fortune is your enemy, Her frowning will not last . . . For time your truth shall prove].' The concept of 'Dame Fortune' being an enemy to be endured, in particular, is a poetic theme to which Marie would return, in describing her own romantic fortunes.

Not all family relationships were characterised by the evident tenderness and concern that Marie had for her father and brother. Granted, not all women had the means or time to console their male relatives through verse in times of strife. However, that Marie chose to use her unique position to write these particular verses tells us that she genuinely cared for these men, who continued to loom large in her life, in the absence of any others, while they had long since faded into the background for her married sisters, now occupied with their husbands and children.

Although intended as intimate and personal poems, these verses by Marie also inadvertently function as commentary on the political developments convulsing the nation at this time, from the fall of Edinburgh Castle and the death of William Maitland, to the confiscation of Lethington and the imprisonment of John Maitland. It is rare that we get such firsthand human insight into high politics. However, the stories of Marie's family and the Scottish nation are inextricable and, as a result of Marie's unique life, we have here the emotional response of an educated woman, a daughter and sister, in her own hand, to events that we generally have to reconstruct from (predominantly male) political sources and diplomatic dispatches.

Marie's father reflected in a poem on how, in his blindness, he had the words of his 'Goddis buik [his bible]' read out to him: 'Thocht I be auld and may not sie, I sall it gar be red to me [Although I am old and cannot see, I shall have it read to me].'[4] Along with verses from the Bible, Marie would also have read aloud to her elderly father from books of history and poetry, as well as some of her own poetry, written especially for him and his son. Although this no doubt offered the old laird welcome comfort, times were undeniably tough for Marie and her family. And there were several years more hardship yet to endure before things would start to look up.

*

The civil war may have ended in 1573 but John Maitland, the 'burdalane', would remain imprisoned until 1578, first languishing at forbidding Tantallon Castle, atop a cliff of the East Lothian coast, and then held under close confinement throughout the years of Morton's regency. Worse still, despite the fact that the civil war, in which Marie's father had never taken any side, was now over, the vindictive Regent Morton continued to withhold from him his rightful property of Lethington Castle. Morton had always hated William Maitland, and as scholar Joseph Bain later observed, he very much appeared 'to have transferred his enmity from the dead son to visit it on the head of the aged and unoffending father'.[5] Certainly, there is nothing to justify such enduring, extreme hostility towards Marie's blameless father.

Marie and her father both adored their beloved castle home of Lethington, and their unjust extended banishment from it, far beyond even the end of the civil war, took its toll. In August 1574, they found themselves in Edinburgh, where, in desperation, Sir Richard decided to dictate a letter to Elizabeth I, the Queen of England, beseeching her to intervene against his treatment at the hands of the despotic Scottish Regent. Amid the necessary formalities and flattery, the desolation of Marie's father is laid bare. His world-weariness at this point in time must have been a source of deep sorrow for Marie: he had almost given up. The words of this letter might well have been one of the hardest pieces of dictation she'd ever had to deal with, in her years of acting as her father's amanuensis.*

At the beginning of the letter, Sir Richard set out the context of the 'late trobles [troubles]' – the civil war – which are now 'most happelie putt end unto'. He then immediately threw himself upon Elizabeth's mercy; or, in his words, upon 'your hienes most godlie and vertuous inclinatioun, wherof so long your majestye hathe gevin so good and assured proufe'. Trusting in the Queen's 'continewall ayding of all soche [such] . . . as craveth your majestyes help in ther honest and juste actiounis', he went on to express his woes:

> I am dryven to Lament vnto your hienes my great and havie troubill, who nevir having offended agains the king his majestie, nor none of his graces Regentis, hathe notwithstanding, by the space of foure yeiris past, bene debarred and putt away frome my Leving, to my gritt hurte and skaythe.
>
> *I am driven to lament unto your highness my great and heavy trouble, who, never having offended against the king his majesty, nor any of his grace's Regents, has nonetheless, for the past four years, been debarred and banished from my lands and property, to my great hurt and damage.*

* Preserved among the state papers of Elizabeth I in England, this letter was written in neat lines of secretary hand. Marie had been supporting her father for years by this point and remained in his household. She is a clear candidate for the individual to whom Sir Richard dictated it. Although professional secretary hands tend, by their nature, to be fairly consistent and thus tricky to tell apart, it is notable that the hand of this 1574 letter exhibits considerable similarities to later examples of writing in secretary hand from the first part of the 1580s, which are more conclusively Marie's.

The next lines are also worth quoting at length, as they afford rich insight into the emotional state of the father to whom Marie was devoted and in whose household she lived. The task of comforting his wearied soul must have been a tough one.

> And now being a man well nere the age of foure scoir yeares, your majestie may considdir what dolour and displeasour it is to me to be kept frome my native hous of ledingtoun (which altho but mene in respect of the grandeur of utheris, yet inferiour to few for the ancientnes therof) as I have said befoir never having offendit . . . I am assured ther is none . . . within Scotland can accuse me of ony point or jote wherin I have mereted ony pairt of so extrame dealing, except it may be undiscreitlie alleged that for the sounes offence, the father deservethe puneishment, which is aggreable to no law, nayther of god nor man.
>
> *And now being a man very close to the age of eighty years, your majesty may consider what sadness and displeasure it is to me to kept from my native house of Lethington (which although mean compared to the grandeur of others, is inferior to few in its ancientness) given that, as I said before, I have never offended . . . I am certain that there is none . . . within Scotland who can accuse me of any point or jot wherein I have merited any element of such extreme treatment, expect that it may be uncivilly alleged that for the sons' offence, the father deserves punishment, which is agreeable to no law, neither of god nor man.*

The anxiousness of Marie's father to distance himself from the actions of his sons, and his strong sense of injustice at his punishment for their actions, is palpable. He also made explicit his disapproval of the alleged actions of his one remaining son, who was, he said, as good as dead to him, while noting that his fall from grace naturally saddened him as a father:

> Verrey displeasand hathe bene to me the late procedingis of my sone, if thai had bene as wes alleged, whois fall my naturall affectioun behuvit to mouve me to Lament . . . I have bene the father of mony sonnes, and now leife the destitute of thair conforte, having but onlie one remanyng on lyve, who is as it wer deid vnto me, in respect of the foirfaltour led agaynst him . . . as also his being yet detened.
>
> *Very displeasing have been to me the late proceedings of my son, if they were as alleged, whose fall my natural affection necessarily moves me to lament . . . I have been the father of many sons, but now live destitute of their comfort, having but only one remaining alive, who is as it were dead to me, in respect of the forfeiture led against him . . . as also his remaining detained.*

Having painted such a bleak picture of his circumstances, and pled his innocence, Sir Richard then set out his asks of the Queen of England, begging that she intervened 'with the regent his grace on my behalfe' on two counts: first, to have restored to him his 'house and landis'; second, and despite his fatherly disappointment, to secure the 'libertie' of his only son. Queen Elizabeth's help was his only hope, wrote Sir Richard; it was the only thing that could transform his 'misreabill estate [miserable state]' and ensure that he might 'ressave [receive] sum comforte befoir my ending, wherin I doubt not bot [but that] your maiestie shall doe a most godlye just and lovabill [laudable] deed, befoir god and the world'. If, however, Elizabeth did not act to assuage his 'greif and anguishe', then he would be 'yet moir miserabill', and death 'a thowsand tymes welcomer unto [him] than ony longer lyfe'.

How these words must have pained Marie, with her father wishing death upon himself, rather than have to endure more of his life as it was. Around the same time, he also composed a simple poem – doubtless dictated to Marie – lamenting the confiscation of Lethington, especially in his 'infirmitie' and his great age.[6] Each stanza ends with a similar refrain about his being so 'auld'. The following is representative:

> Sum now by force of men of weir [war]
> My house, my landis, and my geir [goods]
> Fra me they hauld
> Thocht [Although] I be auld

In echo of his letter to the English Queen, this poem also includes the line of plaintive protest: 'Sa weill is kend [so well is known] my innocence'. But if Marie and her father had genuinely hoped that Elizabeth, in her fabled grace and mercy, would be moved by Sir Richard's innocence, and his emotive letter, they must have been left sorely disappointed. Although it definitely reached her – it is preserved among the state papers of England – their desperate plea for help went entirely unanswered. Lethington would not, in fact, be returned to the Maitlands for almost another decade, until well into the 1580s, when the balance of power in Scotland shifted once again. Happily for Sir Richard, he would still be alive to see that day, and would get to spend his final years at his ancestral home. However, neither he nor Marie could possibly have known that in exile, in the depths of the 1570s, with no idea of when or whether they would ever get to return home.

*

Like father, like daughter, Marie once again turned to poetry as a form of comfort and occupation in these tough times of exile, penning a moving love poem to her castle home, which she was missing greatly.[7] Although – like the consolatory poem that she wrote for her father – left unsigned in her manuscript, this verse was also evidently written by someone who was very proud to be a Maitland, knew all about Maitland family history and, in this case, also had intimate knowledge of Lethington Castle, presented as the poet's ancestral home and a place they had spent many happy years but were currently banished from.

Showcasing her learnedness, Marie begins this poem by listing examples of famous bards who lauded their place of birth in poetry, including Virgil and Ovid. 'So every poet has some place to praise and to commend,' she declares. For Marie, that place was, of course, Lethington. And, as a poet, she could no longer hold her silence, but was compelled to praise it in verse:

> I can na mair [no more] my silence hauld,
> But maun [must] put furth my mynd
> To speik of thee, O Lethingtoun,
> Which standis fair on Tyne

Marie tells us of its 'lairge and lang . . . tour [tower] and fortres', its 'wallis, thik and strang [walls, thick and strong]' and its impressive vaulted features ['greit and fair . . . voltis']. She reminisces fondly on the pleasure of watching the sun rise in the morning and set in the evening, bathing the beautiful surrounding woodlands, fields and meadows ['wod and fieldis fair . . . meadowis fair and grene'] in different textures of light. She also dwells on Lethington's enchanting 'arbour' and 'orchard grene', which offered a 'maist plesand place to mak repair, thairin to sit or gang [a most pleasant place to spend time, whether sitting or strolling]'. We also learn that Lethington had 'knottis' – elaborate ornamental flower beds – and 'alleis' for playing bowls. Marie gushes about Lethington's 'buttis' – marks for practising with bow and arrow – which made for the 'maist pleasant place of archerie that ever I yet could find'; Marie, like Mary, Queen of Scots, was clearly a keen archer. The castle itself, Marie tells us, was furnished with 'beddis soft and tapeis fair [soft beds and fine tapestries]'. Perhaps most movingly, she records her memories of the 'treitting and guid cheir [discussions and conviviality]' that echoed around the tables and within the walls of the Lethington she knew and loved.

As challenging as Marie and her family's exile must have been, its prompting of this poetic outpouring affords us intimate insight into the first decades of Marie's life at Lethington, where she would have grown from a small child into a young woman. She should have departed her castle home when she came of age, and taken up residence with a husband. But, instead, Marie had remained with her parents, serving her father and continuing to enjoy the familiar luxuries and comforts of Lethington.

Through her own words, we can picture how she would have retired each night to a comfortable bed, enfolded in rich and luxurious sheets; how sumptuous tapestries graced her eyes before she closed them to sleep and when she opened them in the morning. A fire, diligently tended by a servant, would have kept her bedroom warm during the bitterly cold winter months; in summer, crisp fresh air, with a hint of North Sea salt, would have freshened the room. Around the dinner table, Marie would have engaged in animated conversation about the events of the day with her father, mother and siblings, as well as any illustrious guests they were hosting, from royals to preachers. Marie would have taken the air in pleasant grounds, delighted in honing her archery skills and playing at bowls, and strolled in beautifully cultivated gardens and orchards, perhaps plucking an apple fresh from the tree to crunch on. The oldest tree in the grounds of Lethington today is a sweet chestnut. Estimated to be around six hundred years old, it would already have been more than a century old when Marie knew it.

Marie devotes the next section of the poem to the praise of her ancestors who first dug the ground and lay the foundations, ready to build the family fortress:

> Greit was the work to houke [dig] the ground,
> And thy fundation cast . . .
> Michtie was that man in deid,
> That first thee tuik in hand
> And in his worke did so proceid
> That he thee maid upstand

Then, in lines so provocatively proud they can only have been penned by a Maitland, she declares:

> Wha dois not knaw the Maitland bluid
> The best in all this land

Indeed, Marie goes on, what distinguishes Lethington Castle above all is not anything to do with its architecture or gardens, but the simple fact that it belongs to the Maitlands. Its inextricability from the family's history and sense of identity must have made their banishment from it all the more difficult. It wasn't just a property that had been confiscated but their family's very embodiment in stone.

Marie makes clear at several points that this poem was composed in exile. After several stanzas of waxing lyrical about Lethington's many charms, towards the end of the poem she reflects sadly on how she is presently reduced only to reminiscing about the joys that once she found there: 'And only I rehers the joy, that I did in thee find.' Soon after, she refers to the 'troubill' currently keeping her from it: namely, the recent civil war and Lethington's continued confiscation, as a casualty of it.

At the poem's end, Marie invokes the 'triumphant nobill fame' of 'auld Sir Richard' – the same Maitland ancestor that she lionised in the consolatory ballad written for her father. In her father, Marie declares, she sees an equal to this legendary 'auld Sir Richard'. And, with no concerns about modesty, she states that she also sees an equal to their illustrious ancestor's offspring, in all the 'bairnis [children]' – not just 'sonnis [sons]' – of her father, which included, of course, herself.

And gif I dar the treuth declair,	*And if I dare declare the truth,*
And nane me fleitschour call,	*And none call me a flatterer,*
I can to him [auld Sir Richard] find a compair	*I can to him find a comparison,*
And till his bairnis all	*And to all his children*

As Marie read out these stanzas to her father, it surely caused a smile to pass over his tired old face, her words painting vivid images in his mind, behind his no-longer-seeing eyes, as she conjured happy memories of better times at their beautiful family home of Lethington. As heavy-hearted as he was, he must have felt gratitude at having at least one of his bairns right by his side throughout these difficult years, and very proud of his youngest daughter's learnedness and blossoming poetic confidence, which he had nurtured in her. This would, of course, result most strikingly in her magnificent manuscript – whose origins are most likely to be found here, during the distressing exile years of the 1570s, when the neat recording of their poetry for posterity would have offered both Marie and her father a source of comfort in an unjust and unsettling world.

Marie's father was an individual who devoted great time and energy to the careful creation and curation of records, from his collecting of older Scottish poetry, to his summaries of court judgements, his tables of the kings of Scotland, England and France, and his histories of the houses of Seton and Douglas. Some of his poetry was already preserved within an existing manuscript compilation belonging to the Maitland household (known today as the *Maitland Folio*, on account of its larger, folio-sized pages), which would continue to be added to by various scribes. However, the recording of his poetry in that manuscript was incomplete and, at times, inaccurate. It is also a messy and unwieldly manuscript, more a haphazard scrapbook, and the verse of Marie's father within it is greatly overshadowed by that of other poets, including Gavin Douglas, Robert Henryson and William Dunbar, the great Scots Makars of the Middle Ages.

As a man very concerned with the orderly recording and preservation of texts, legal, historical and poetic, it is easy to imagine how he would have been dissatisfied with this partial and problematic extant record, and instead anxious to gather his own poetry together into one place, fully and accurately. And who else would he have asked to undertake the task, who else could possibly have been better placed, than his devoted daughter Marie? She had spent her entire adult life by her father's side, giving her unparalleled knowledge of and access to his works; indeed, many of his poems will have been dictated directly to her in the first instance. Living with her father, in seemingly interminable exile, and unencumbered by the duties of wife and mother, Marie also had the time and space, not to mention the unique education and scribal skillset required, to produce such a book.

Alternatively, it might have been the case that Marie, driven by genuine fondness for her father, along with a desire to flex her calligraphic skills, took it upon herself to create a pristine collection of his poetry, knowing how much peace and comfort this would offer him, and that it would give her something productive to occupy herself with during this difficult period of prolonged exile. Marie might also have been inspired by the thought that, in creating a manuscript in honour of her father, she might also embrace the opportunity to record some of her own verse for posterity.

However the manuscript was first conceived of, as the years of banishment from Lethington dragged on, Marie found herself sitting at a table, the exciting promise of a pile of paper in front of her. Of good quality, thick and vertically lined, the sheets were folded, then folded again, to give pages that were quarter-sized. Marie was ready to begin work on her 'quarto' manuscript.

When she first embarked upon the creation of her manuscript miscellany, Marie might have been at Dundas Castle, or perhaps in the more humble surrounds of her father's lodgings in the capital. Wherever she was, with her father's reassuring presence nearby, and older papers with some of the poems she'd be copying into this new compilation scattered around her, so it was that she dipped her quill into the pot of ink and first began work on the literary undertaking of her lifetime, one that would occupy her for many years to follow.

Leaving some empty sheets at the front, to perhaps later fill in with a title page, the first words that Marie inscribed onto paper at this point, at the very birth of the manuscript, were the opening lines of an early poem by her father.* The next thirty-odd poems that she recorded are also by her father, chronologically ordered and carefully attributed to him, as the manuscript began to take shape. Then, after this opening series of poems by her father, Marie began to include some poems by others. First, she added several by Alexander Arbuthnot, a prominent kirk figure and poet, followed by a few by her brother John, an accomplished poet himself.

Significantly, now that it was officially a miscellany, Marie also began to add a few of her own. At this early point in the manuscript's journey of creation – and whether opportunistically or planned from the start – she first included her consolatory poems to her father and brother, anxious, perhaps, to record her response to the momentous political events of the time and their impact on those she held most dear.

But it was another momentous event that lay behind a poem she recorded soon after. For it seems that it was around this time, in the years leading up to the birth of the manuscript, that Marie fell life-changingly in love – with a daughter, not a son, of a fellow elite family.

---

* This is poem 2 in the finished manuscript. But it was the first poem to be committed to paper. What is now poem 1 was added much later.

Chapter Four

You wield me wholly at your will

When Marie first composed the forty-ninth poem in her completed manuscript, she was deeply and intensely in love.* This poem is not the literary expression of a new romance but the enshrining in verse of a well-established relationship between her and the woman who had her heart. More recently, it seems, that relationship had experienced a severe blow, with that specific event prompting Marie to produce a poetic statement of unwavering commitment in the face of that new adversity: a set of vows in verse. But Marie didn't address their harsh reality until midway through the poem's nine stanzas. Much of it was devoted simply to the gushing praise and erotically charged adoration of the woman she was in love with, and the unbreakable bond between them.

Marie might have first met the woman she would later exalt in poetry prior to her family's exile from Lethington. Or their paths might first have crossed later, during the early years of exile. Either way, she was most likely the daughter of a neighbouring landed family, whether of East Lothian, or the environs around Edinburgh or Dundas. While we might not, and may never, know the name of the woman who set Marie's heart ablaze and transformed her life, or the precise circumstances of how she and Marie met, it was Marie's ferocious love for her that drove her to first pen her most

* Although often referred to as 'poem 49' today, Marie would not have conceived of it as such. She recorded it with no title in her manuscript. What's more, at the point at which she did so, it would, in fact, have been poem number 48, as poem 1 would be added much later.

powerful love poem, and that also compelled her to include it in her manuscript.

Positioning her quill at the top of the page she'd just turned over to, the first strokes that Marie etched onto the fresh sheet created an ornamental capital '*A*', one she deployed frequently throughout the manuscript, with swirling flourishes looping out to the left, marking the first letter of the first word. Marie then recorded the rest of this first word, and, indeed, the rest of the poem, in secretary hand: the same script in which she had already recorded so many of her father's poems. She also positioned this poem such that it blended in with a series of poems by her father, perhaps to avoid drawing any particular attention to it.

But if there is little in *form* to distinguish Marie's poem 49 from the work of her father recorded directly afterwards, its *content* could not be more different. Typical of Marie's father's poetic output, his poem 50 is a lament on the lack of justice in the world: 'Lord God, how lang will this law lest, by quhilk [which] sum trew men are opprest' it opens. The first stanza of Marie's poem 49 offers a most stark contrast. Charged with the hyperbole of the madly in love, and replete with female references, we are in a woman's world from the off, in this poem of love from one woman to another.

As phoebus in his spheris hicht	*As Phoebus in his sphere's height*
precellis the kaip Crepusculein	*Surpasses the cloak of twilight*
And phoebe all the starris licht	*And Phoebe the light of all the stars*
Your splendour so madame I wein	*Your splendour so madame I believe*
Dois onlie pas all feminine	*Does only surpass all womankind*
In sapience superlative	*In sapience superlative*
Indewit with vertewis sa devine	*Endowed with virtues so divine*
As leirned pallas rediviue	*As learned Pallas brought back to life*

And as by hid vertew unknawin	*And as by hidden virtue unknown*
The adamant drawis yron thairtill	*The adamant draws iron thereto*
Your courtes nature so has drawin	*Your courteous nature so has drawn*
My hairt youris to continew still	*My heart yours to continue still*
Sa greit Joy dois my spreit fulfill	*Such great joy does my spirit fulfil*
contempling your perfectioun	*Contemplating your perfection*
Ye weild me holie at your will	*You govern me wholly at your will*
and raviss my affectioun	*And ravish my affection*

(stanzas 1 and 2)

The 'splendour' of the woman she is in love with, her 'madame', surpasses that of all womankind, Marie declares in its opening lines. The woman is like Phoebus, the sun, who outshines the cloak of twilight, and Phoebe, the (female) moon, who transcends the light of all the stars in the sky. Marie gushes about the woman's superlative 'sapience' (the feminine embodiment of divine wisdom), and wonders at the 'virtues so divine' she has been endowed with. It is, Marie writes, as if the Greek goddess of wisdom herself, Pallas Athena, has been brought to life! Marie's severe infatuation for this woman – who is more beautiful, more intelligent and more virtuous than any other – is already palpable. She is comparable only to a goddess, and even then!

What's more, 'madame' was a form of address commonly used by servants to their mistress, or subjects to their Queen. But Marie and her 'sapient' and 'learned' lover are highly likely to have been of the same social status; certainly, socially elite Marie was not employed as the woman's servant. Marie's addressing her as 'madame' thus appears to be sexually charged self-subordination as opposed to social decorum – and this sets the tone for what follows. For if the intensity of the opening stanza already strongly suggests that Marie's affections for this woman go beyond the simply platonic, any lingering ambiguity as to the nature of their relationship is swiftly dispelled in the second stanza, which shifts us unequivocally into the realms of the erotic.

Just as adamant (a naturally occurring magnet) attracts iron through forces invisible and not fully understood, Marie writes, her heart is forcefully drawn to this woman – not, ultimately, by choice but by an inexplicable natural pull: by 'hidden virtue unknown'.* The workings of this love may be mysterious and hidden; however, notably, there is nothing sinful or wrong about it. On the contrary, Marie says that it is rooted in 'virtue', in moral goodness. Indeed, there is no sense, anywhere, of Marie struggling to reconcile herself internally to the fact that she loves another woman; any conflicts she faces are purely external, with the world outside.

With breathless infatuation, Marie describes how her spirit is filled with 'sa greit Joy [such great joy]' as she contemplates the woman's 'perfection'. Her helpless if highly willing abandon in the face of this magnetic attraction then gains even more explicit voice, as Marie declares to her that 'Ye weild [govern] me holie at your will and raviss my affectioun'.

It is impossible to read these lines as anything other than erotic in the highest degree; they could be straight out of a fragment of Sappho. Marie has just set out how she is drawn to the woman by

* This poetic image was used in literature of the era to describe the pull of romantic attraction. 'You draw me, you hard-hearted adamant', as Shakespeare would have Helena declare to Demetrius in *A Midsummer Night's Dream*, for example.

forces beyond her understanding or control. Now, she reaches for a word normally reserved for describing the violation of a woman – 'raviss' – to convey how at the mercy of her lover she is; how she is governed wholly at her will. The verb 'to ravish' has its etymological roots in the Latin verb 'rapere', meaning 'to seize'. In historical Scots, the verb most commonly referred to the crime of the rape of a woman by a man; it is the very word that Melville used, for example, in his contemporary memoir to describe Bothwell's rape of Mary, Queen of Scots: 'the quen culd not bot mary him, seing he had ravissit[1] hir and lyen with hir against hir will'.

Although Marie clearly consents to these sapphic encounters, the force of passion behind them feels overwhelming: for there can be little doubt that Marie's impassioned references to her lover 'governing her wholly at her will' and 'ravishing' her affection were inspired by anything other than direct experience. When Marie talks of things that are only imagined or fantasised about, she abundantly employs the subjunctive and the conditional voice. In later stanzas, when Marie shifts into the mindset of 'if only', it is clearly marked through her use of the verb forms 'wald [would]' and 'sould [should]' and the conjunction 'gif [if]'. Here, by contrast, there is no sense of conditionality or wishful thinking. Marie doesn't *wish* to be at the mercy of her lover's will, or *dream* about being overcome by her. These acts are straightforwardly described, in the present continuous: the woman *wields* Marie wholly at her will and *ravishes* her affection. This was at a time when the God-given requirement was that sexual intercourse was to take place only between a man and woman, and only within wedlock. And yet, Marie exalts intoxicating sexual bliss, derived from acts between two, necessarily unwed, women.

Your perles Vertew dois provoike	*Your peerless virtue does provoke*
and loving kyndnes so dois move	*And loving affection so does move*
My Mynd to freindschip reciprocot	*My mind to mutual friendship*
That treuth sall try sa far above	*That truth shall prove so far above*
The auntient heroicis love	*The ancient heroes' love*
as salbe thocht prodigious	*As shall be thought prodigious*
and plaine experience sall prove	*And plain experience shall prove*
Mair holie and religious	*More holy and religious*
In amitie perithous	*In amity, Perithous*
To theseus was not so traist	*To Theseus was not so faithful*
Nor Till Achilles patroclus	*Nor to Achilles Patroclus*
nor pilades to trew orest	*nor Pylades to true Orestes*
Not Yit achates luif so lest	*Not yet Achates' love so lasting*
to gud Enee nor sic freindschip	*To good Enee, nor such friendship*
David to Ionathan profest	*David to Jonathon professed*
nor Titus trew to kynd Iosip	*Nor Titus true to kind Josip*
Nor Yit Penelope I wiss	*Nor yet Penelope, I say*
so luiffed ulisses in hir dayis	*So loved Odysseus in her days*
Nor Ruth the kynd moabitiss	*Nor Ruth the kind Moabite*
Nohemie as the scripture sayis	*Naomi as the scripture says,*
nor portia whais worthie prayiss	*Nor Portia whose worthy praise*
In romaine historeis we reid	*In Roman histories we read*
Wha did devoir the fyrie brayiss	*Who did devour the fiery coals*
To follow brutus to the deid	*To follow Brutus into death*

(stanzas 3, 4 and 5)

Marie describes how the woman's 'peerless virtue' and 'loving affection' move her mind to 'mutual friendship' – one which, as she has already established, is not merely platonic. Marie's use of the straightforward, present tense ('does provoke', 'does move') again stands out, as does her underlining of the mutuality of their feelings for one another. This poem is not a pining lamentation born of unrequited love, or a pained reflection on what once was, but rather the literary expression of a very live, and very much two-way, love affair. It is also in this third stanza that Marie first introduces the theme of the 'ancient heroes', whose famed love pales into insignificance compared to that between Marie and her beloved. The truth, she says, will prove that their love ranks 'so far above' anything that has been seen before, and 'plain experience' will prove it 'more holy and religious'. All her adult life, Marie had been exposed to the severe culture of Calvinist Scotland, with its low regard for the female gender in general, and abhorrence of any and all forms of 'sodomy'. And yet here, Marie boldly frames the love between two women as holy and religious – indeed, as *more* holy and religious than any other.

Marie then goes even further, elevating their example above a series of celebrated heroes from both classical mythology and history, and significant figures of biblical scripture. By the time Marie composed this poem, she had been a devoted student, rather than a devoted wife, for years. Now, she marshalls all the learning and erudition at her disposal and throws it at the feet of her same-sex lover. She draws on her rich classical education, along with her Christian faith, to honour the love between the two women, in a truly astonishing fashion.

Not even Patroclus was so devoted to Achilles, Marie claims, showcasing her knowledge of the classics. Nor was the friendship that David professed to Jonathan as steadfast as their own, she goes on, referencing the Old Testament. Of course, it will not have been lost on Marie, or her lover, that the stories of these illustrious male companions very much blur the boundaries between deep friendship and homoerotic love.

The tradition of Achilles and Patroclus, heroes of the Trojan War, as devastatingly devoted lovers, was already millennia old when Marie invoked their names in her poem. In the *Iliad*, written around the eighth century BCE, we read of how Achilles was driven senseless with grief following the slaying of Patroclus, who he professed to love 'beyond all other companions' as well as beyond his 'own life', and who he wanted to be buried alongside.[2] Achilles and Patroclus are similarly presented as lovers in the surviving fragments of Aeschylus's fifth-century tragedy *Myrmidons*, and in Plato's *Symposium*, written not long after. Their story was certainly well known to real-life warrior hero Alexander the Great (d. 323 BCE), who framed his love for his male companion Hephaestion in the image of the ancient example of Achilles and Patroclus. The two men even went on pilgrimage to the site believed to be the grave of the mythological lovers, where they placed garlands in their honour. And when Hephaestion died, Alexander wept as vociferously as had Achilles for Patroclus. As learned women of the European Renaissance, intimate with the classics, the tragic love story of Achilles and Patroclus would have been just as well known to Marie and her contemporaries, their naming in this same-sex love poem richly suggestive.

Key figures in the kingdom of ancient Israel, the relationship between David (of Goliath-defeating fame; later King of Israel) and Jonathan (the son of King Saul) embodies a similar deep romance and eroticism. The Geneva Bible of 1560 – the version most likely to have been read by Marie – describes how Jonathan swore himself to David in a 'bond' because he 'loved him as his own soul'. Later, it records David's proclamation to Jonathan that 'Thy love to me was wonderful, passing the love of women'.* In referencing the 'friendship' that David professed to Jonathan, Marie would immediately have called to mind for the sixteenth-century reader these evocative, homoerotic lines of scripture. Just as what David experienced with Jonathan was more wonderful than anything he had ever encountered with a woman, so is the experience of love between Marie and her lover more wonderful than anything a man could offer, Marie implies, in a sapphic inversion of the sentiment recorded in the Second Book of Samuel. Formalised through a bond, David and Jonathan's relationship reads as more akin to a marriage than a friendship. And their love is mutual: it is Jonathan who says that he loves David more than his own soul; but it is then David who declares the superiority of Jonathan's love to him. Mutual and marriage-like, erotic and transcendental, this was a same-sex pairing that Marie could relate to: and she read about it in her Bible, the word of God.

Marie's invocation of such highly homoerotic male friendships is already sexually and symbolically loaded. But she is nowhere near done. The next stanza takes things to a whole new level. It begins and ends with a renowned husband–wife couple, Renaissance household names, whose love is eclipsed, Marie claims, by the devotion between her and her beloved.

---

* 1 Samuel 20:16–17; 2 Samuel 1:26. Later versions of the Bible, including the influential 1611 King James Version, tend to translate that Jonathan swore himself to David in a 'covenant'. But Marie would never have seen the King James Version, and the 1560 Geneva Bible that she most likely knew notably translated the underlying Hebrew word ('berit') as 'bond' – which becomes 'band' in Marie's Scots – with its clear connection to the bond of marriage. Reading about Jonathan swearing himself to David in a 'bond' must only have further coded that relationship as one akin to a marriage for Marie.

Odysseus was gone from his kingdom for a total of twenty years: ten years during the Trojan War and ten years on his epic journey home. Through these entire two decades, as described in *The Odyssey*, his wife, Penelope, faithfully awaited his return, cleverly avoiding the advances of many suitors. And yet, says Marie to her lover, Penelope did not love Odysseus as much as I love you! From Greek mythology to Roman history: Marie also invokes Brutus (the most famous of Caesar's assassins) and his wife Portia, who, according to legend, dramatically took her own life by swallowing burning coals, in order to follow Brutus into death rather than live without him. But not even Portia, declaims Marie to her lover, whose worthy praise we read of in Roman histories, was as devoted to her husband as I am to you!

It is staggering enough that Marie is framing her love for a woman with reference to the love between a wife and a husband. But it is right in the middle of this stanza, about idealised marital devotion, that Marie also includes *two women*: Ruth and Naomi, another pair from the world of the Bible.

The Book of Ruth records how Ruth, a Moabite, became so devoted to her mother-in-law, Naomi, an Israelite, that she refused to leave her side, even after she became widowed.

> And Ruth answered, Intreat me not to leave thee, nor to departe from thee: for whither thou goest, I wil go: and where thou dwellest, I wil dwel: thy people shalbe my people, and thy God my God. Where thou dyest, wil I dye, and there wil I be buryed. The Lord do so to me & more also, if oght but death departe thee & me.[3]

These are Ruth's deeply moving words as they appear in translation from the original Hebrew in the 1560 Geneva Bible; they are thus likely the precise words that Marie would have known, probably by heart, and that she invokes at this point in her love poem to another woman, when she says that not even 'Ruth, the kynd moabitiss', so loved 'Nohemi [Naomi] as the scripture sayis'.

The language of lifelong devotion to another soul, until death and only death does you part, is highly evocative of the covenant of marriage. And, just as Achilles' dying wish was to be buried next to Patroclus, together even in death, Ruth wished to be buried alongside Naomi. While she remained alive, she was willing to worship Naomi's God: she would do anything, to stay with her.

Notwithstanding the relationship between Ruth and Naomi on paper (which, in any event, tells us very little about their bond, in practice, at a time when heterosexual marriage was so transactional), Ruth's fervent promise of ever-lasting fidelity to Naomi, until death do them part, has long resonated with romantic couples, such that this powerful, emotionally charged verse has long been used in heterosexual marriage ceremonies. Marie, too, read their story as one of quasi-marital devotion, and so positioned Ruth and Naomi as the centrepiece of her stanza showcasing (otherwise opposite-sex) married couples.

Marie, of course, would not have been overwhelmed with role models for her love for another woman. But in the devoted love between two women depicted in the Book of Ruth, Marie saw the bond between herself and her female lover reflected back at her positively; it was in the pages of her Bible that she caught a rare glimpse of herself. And ironically, Marie seems to have had the otherwise socially stifling Reformation to thank for this revelation.

Scotland had broken with Rome in 1560, when Marie was on the cusp of young womanhood. From that tender age onwards, it was in the culture and teachings of the reformed Scottish Church that Marie became steeped, which was defined, in large part, by its strict emphasis on scriptural authority.

The 'Scots Confession of Faith' was the document that underpinned Scottish Presbyterianism. In a radical departure from what became, by contrast, Catholicism, this founding document of the reformed faith formalised the supreme authority of scripture, emphasising the importance of a person having a direct, personal, unmediated relationship with God, through the reading and study of the Bible in their own language, and on their own terms. And, from the poetic testimony in her manuscript, it would seem that Marie truly took at least this aspect of the new faith to heart. In one of the anonymous poems of her manuscript, likely written about her by a woman who knew her, Marie is presented as the proud owner of a much cherished Bible, which she has had adorned with gold and silver, with no expense spared:

> A cot [coat] bedect with gold
> And sylver streamis it weiris [wears]
> As just rewaird the maistres gave [it]
> For [the] love to it scho beiris [she bears][4]

In another, she is praised in the same breath as Italian reformer Olympia Morata (1526–55),[5] a near contemporary of Marie's, who was derided by her critics as a 'Calvinist Amazon'.* Together with Marie's multiple invocations of scripture in her own poetry, this all combines to paint a picture of a woman with a sincere Presbyterian faith, rooted in a belief in scriptural authority and the importance of personal study of the Bible.

---

* In Greek mythology, the Amazons were fearsome female warriors. Excitingly, there is increasing evidence that the myth is based on real historical women.

Marie would have read her Bible, diligently and daily. Its gold and silver decoration would have glistened in the morning sunlight, and by candlelight in the evenings. The pages of the Book of Ruth may have been a bit more worn, a bit more ink-smudged than others, for Marie would have turned to it again and again, absorbing this story of devotion that, no matter how many times she read it, always seemed to be a story of love between two women; always seemed to be her God, speaking to her.

A Scottish Presbyterian who regarded the Bible as the basis of her personal, unmediated relationship with her maker, and a highly educated and independently minded woman, not only was Marie able to *read* her holy book for herself, she was also confident in her ability to *interpret* its words for herself – just as her faith told her she should do.

In the figures of David and Jonathan and, even more so, Ruth and Naomi, Marie saw her love validated in scripture. In the story of the two women, in particular, Marie found a powerful and precious precedent for her own ferocious love for another woman. In this poem, Marie invokes the very scriptural authority that was a central tenet of Scottish Presbyterianism and uses it to validate her sapphic love. With the striking words, 'as the scripture sayis', Marie repackages the vow made by Ruth to Naomi, and gifts it to her lover as her own.

Wald michtie Jove grant me the hap	*Would mighty Jove grant me the fortune*
With you to have your brutus pairt	*With you to have your Brutus' part*
and metamorphosing our schap	*And metamorphosing our form*
My sex intill his vaill convert	*My sex into his veil convert*

No brutus then sould caus us smart	*No Brutus then would cause us to hurt*
as we doe now unhappie wemen	*As we do now unhappy women*
Then sould we bayth with Joyfull hairt	*Then we would both with joyful heart*
honour and bliss the band of hymen	*Honour and bless the bond of Hymen*
Yea certainlie we sould efface	*Yea certainly we would eclipse*
Pollux and castoris memorie	*Pollux and Castor's memory*
and gif that thay desservit place	*And if they deserved place*
amang the starris for loyaltie	*Among the stars for loyalty*
Then our mair perfyte amitie	*Then our more perfect amity*
mair worthie recompence sould merit	*More worthy recompense would merit*
In hevin eternall deitie	*In heaven eternal deity*
amang the goddis till Inherit	*Among the gods to inherit*

(stanzas 6 and 7)

Marie believes that their sapphic love surpasses any other, and is more holy and religious than any other. Now, she states unequivocally her desire to marry the woman that she loves. If only this dream could come true, she writes, then the two women would be free of the pain that they are both currently suffering. For, in reality, her lover is not married to Marie but has a 'Brutus', or husband.

Marie pleads with God, or 'Jove', to intervene so that she can play the 'pairt' of her female love's 'Brutus' instead. As well as meaning simply 'part' or 'role', in historical Scots, 'pairt' had a secondary meaning of 'penis'. Ironically enough, one of the sources for this secondary meaning of the word is none other than John Knox, recorded as criticising a promiscuous individual for having his 'parte . . . in the pott'. And Marie would have well understood that, without the relevant 'pairt' (in the sense of a penis), she could never play the 'pairt' (in the sense of 'role') of her lover's husband: any marriage between a man and a woman had to be consummated through penetrative sex, and could be annulled if it was not.* Marie knew that simply loving the woman, however intensely, meant nothing: romantic devotion was no prerequisite for marriage, but consummation was non-negotiable. So, in order to marry and, crucially, consummate a marriage to the woman she loved, Marie knew that she would somehow have to take on the form of a man, 'pairt' and all.

Marie further spells out the idea of physical transformation – already implied in the double meaning of 'pairt' – when she states plainly her wish to 'metamorphose' her 'sex' in order to be concealed behind the 'veil' of manhood. One of the tales in Ovid's *Metamorphoses*, popular during the Renaissance, tells of how Iphis, born female, was miraculously physically transformed into a man, just in time for their wedding to Ianthe, the girl that they loved. Marie would have been familiar with the story, and seems to have been inspired by it, when she similarly wished for her visible 'schap [form]' to be transformed into that of a man, so that she and her lover could legally marry. No longer, then, would any 'Brutus' cause the two 'unhappy women' to hurt, as they do now, Marie writes; instead, they would both 'with joyful heart, honour and bless the bond of Hymen': that is, the bond of marriage, Hymen being the Greek god of marriage.

---

* This remains the case in the UK for opposite-sex marriages today.

On the one hand, this is Marie at her most breathtakingly bold. A pious Presbyterian woman, living in a newly reformed Scotland, she here gives explicit voice to a lesbian love so deep and impassioned that she longs for it to be formalised through marriage. At the same time, though, the only way that Marie can imagine this ever being possible is for one of them to become a man. As independently minded and critical thinking as she was, even Marie was not arguing, in the sixteenth century, for the right to marry a woman, as a woman. Her mind was, ultimately, limited by the strictures of the society in which she lived, such that she could conceive of marriage only in heterosexual terms, as between a man and a woman. Equal marriage, two women living openly and validly as wife and wife, in the eyes of the kirk, society and the law, would never have occurred to her as a possibility, even in her wildest dreams. Divine intervention and supernatural metamorphosis, like in the myths she had read, seemed to her the only plausible solution to her dilemma of wishing to marry another woman, as a woman herself. Given the severely limiting laws and customs of Marie's Calvinist world, however, it remains astonishing that she recognised and honoured her desire to marry another woman at all, even if the only way she could really conceive of doing so was with reference to mythically inspired metamorphosis into a male body.

These lines also contain the strongest clues as to the specific impetus behind Marie's composition of the poem. There is palpable animosity towards her lover's husband, who Marie powerfully resents and wishes that she could replace. This 'Brutus' is mentioned twice in the space of a few lines and is, Marie tells us, causing the two women pain. None of this feels abstract; quite the contrary, it feels immediate, and very much rooted in Marie's reality at the time of writing. This is not Marie expressing the sentiment 'I love you so much, I wish I could marry you' in generic terms; it is her saying, very specifically, 'I love you so much, I wish that I could be married to you *instead of your husband, whose existence is causing us both to suffer pain.*' This makes it seem likely that the event that inspired these passionate yet pained stanzas from Marie was the marriage of her lover to a man: a fate that she, unlike Marie, had been unable to avoid.

Marie has so far paid poetic tribute to an intensely mutual, sexual and very much live relationship between the two women. And there is a strong sense that they had been in love and enjoying an intimate relationship for some time at the point at which Marie was moved to compose this poem. If their great sapphic romance had, as it very much seems, just been ruptured by Marie's lover being married off to a man, we can imagine the ensuing emotional storm of jealousy and pain, love and devotion, that might have driven Marie to sit down at her desk, pick up her quill and first pour out these words onto the page.

Marie knew that she loved this woman more than anyone else ever would or could: indeed, more than anyone had ever loved another, in the entirety of recorded history and mythology. She knew that it should have been her, and nobody else, pledging herself to her lover until death, and only death, do them part. And yet, there she was, the love of Marie's life, married off, against her meaningful will, to some man who would never know or love her like Marie did.

But where Marie remained shielded from marriage by her unique role as her father's secretary, her lover had no such convenient opt-out. She and Marie might have enjoyed months, even years, of unsuspected intimacy, with the relative freedom of two unmarried, elite young women. Whether they first met while

Marie was still at Lethington or during the exile years, their lives and hearts could have become ever more intertwined: right up until the spell was broken by Marie's lover's arranged marriage to another. And the clock would, of course, have been ticking from the moment their worlds collided. It could only ever have been a matter of time before Marie's lover, if not Marie herself, would have to wed. It had been transcendental while it lasted, but their time was up. Marie's lover was newly married to some 'Brutus', Marie was bereft – and her poem 49 was, perhaps, the outcome.

Whatever the precise context to Marie's penning of this poem, the woman whom she loved had a husband, and Marie would have done anything to change this reality, even take on the shape of a man herself. But Marie knew, deep down, that there would be no divine intervention; that they could not change their fate. The ultimate hopelessness of their situation is reflected in Marie's shift to a voice (in only these two stanzas) that is wishful and conditional, where the rest of the poem is not. The pivotal sixth stanza begins with the historical Scots 'wald', leading to two 'sould' clauses. In modern English, the construction flows as follows: if only a divine force *would* intervene to metamorphose Marie's form, then the two women *would* no longer hurt but instead *would* be joyfully married. Poignantly, the only sentiment conveyed in the simple present tense here is the fact that the two women are in pain: 'as we do [hurt] now, unhappy women'.

The next stanza remains similarly rooted in the realms of longing for the impossible, both emotionally and linguistically. It turns on a 'gif [if]' clause, and also contains a conditional 'sould [would]'. Marie once again draws on her knowledge of the classics, declaiming that, if only they could be married, their loyalty would eclipse the legendary devotion even of Pollux and Castor. A more powerful symbol of loyalty than these mythological twins, Marie could hardly have conjured; Zeus had even transformed them into anchor stars of the constellation of Gemini, granting their wish to be joined together as one forever. But if Pollux and Castor deserved a place 'among the stars for loyalty', Marie contends, then *their* even more perfect bond would merit even greater reward. Marie's hyperbole when it comes to the love between herself and another woman truly knows no bounds: if Pollux and Castor were the ultimate symbol of devotion, it was only because the world hadn't heard of Marie and her beloved – and would never get the chance to. They would have no opportunity to prove what Marie believes to be their unmatched romantic devotion.

Yea certainlie we ~~eff~~ sould efface

Notably, the first line of this seventh stanza happens to contain one of the few instances of scribal error in the manuscript. Marie first skipped straight to the word 'efface', forgetting to write 'sould'. She committed the first three letters to the page before realising her mistake; then neatly struck through her premature 'eff' before continuing.

If Marie's manuscript were replete with such minor issues, this might not be noteworthy; however, it is not. On the whole, the manuscript is defined by its pristine and immaculate nature. A showcasing of Marie's calligraphic prowess, in multiple scripts, such mistakes and crossings out are few and far between. In this context, it seems odd that one of Marie's rare mistakes should occur in poem 49, of all poems – one whose recording was quite so important to her. It could be a simple coincidence, but it could also be a Freudian slip from a Marie who simply didn't want to write in the conditional when it came to her and her beloved, and could barely bring herself to. 'Yea certainlie we efface' is what she wanted to write, without any caveat; a reflection of what she felt in her heart.

And as we ar thocht till our wo	*As we are, though, to our woe*
nature and fortoun doe coniure	*Nature and fortune do conspire*
and hymen also be our fo	*And Hymen is also our foe*
Yit luif of vertew dois procuire	*Yet love of virtue does procure*
freindschip and amitie sa suire	*Friendship and amity so sure*
with sa greit fervencie and force	*With such great fervency and force*
Sa constantlie whilk sall Induire	*So constantly which shall endure*
That not bot deid sall us divorce	*That nothing but death shall us divorce*
And thocht adversitie us vex	*And though adversity afflicts us*
Yit be our freindschip salbe sein	*Yet by our friendship shall be seen*
Thair is mair constancie in our sex	*There is more constancy in our sex*
Then ever amang men has bein	*Than ever among men has been*
no troubill, torment, greif, or tein	*No hardship, torment, grief or pain*
nor erthlie thing sall us disseuer	*Nor earthly thing shall us sever*
Sic constancie sall us mantein	*Such constancy shall us maintain*
In perfyte amitie for ever	*In perfect amity forever*
finis.	*the end.*

(stanzas 8 and 9)

In these last two stanzas, Marie abandons her fantasy of marriage-permitting metamorphosis and concedes, however reluctantly, the totally insurmountable barriers to their love. Even if her lover *didn't* have a husband, the reality was that Marie couldn't marry her because she was a woman. And several enemies were lined up against the cause of the two women in love: 'nature' (their shared female sex), 'Hymen' (the institution of marriage) and 'fortune' (fate, or the accident of human affairs by which they had both been born women).

Marie's longing to be wed to the woman she loves remains as intense as ever, but she now admits freely its hopelessness. This small but mighty army of foes – Dame Nature, Dame Fortune and the marriage god, Hymen – simply cannot be taken on, let alone defeated. As two women in love in sixteenth-century Scotland, 'friendship' was the only real option open to them, and so it is to that 'friendship and amity so sure' that they will devote themselves, pledges Marie.

Even at this point, though, Marie only half concedes that their relationship is one of just 'friendship', only half lets go of the idea of marriage. For theirs is a 'friendship', Marie goes on, to which they will commit themselves with 'such great fervency and force' and 'such constant endurance' that 'nothing but death' will ever 'divorce' them.

> 'if ought but death depart thee and me' – Book of Ruth
>
> 'not bot deid sall us divorce' – Poem 49

The parallels with the til-death-do-us-part devotion of the bond of marriage barely require pointing out. This line of Marie's poem also echoes, no doubt intentionally, Ruth's similar declaration to Naomi that she wished nothing but death to sever them. Even as Marie describes their relationship as one of 'friendship', she leaves the reader in no doubt that the bond between them was, and would always remain, more akin to one of marriage.

With unapologetic boldness, in this final stanza, Marie moves from exalting the specific bond between her and her beloved to asserting the general superiority of the female sex when it comes to constancy and devotion. So unwavering will their 'friendship' remain, states Marie, it will prove that there is 'more constancy in our sex than ever among men has been'. At the time that Marie was writing, the virtues of male friendship had long been eulogised. Women, by comparison, were held to be inferior to men in every way, including emotionally. As a result of their assumed lesser capacity to feel, they were thought incapable of forming meaningful and enduring relationships in the same way. Contemporary French philosopher Montaigne (1533–92), for example, wrote that 'women are in truth not normally capable of responding to such familiarity and mutual confidence as sustain that holy bond of friendship, nor do their souls seem firm enough to withstand the clasp of a knot so lasting and so tightly drawn'.[6] In this context, Marie's jaw-dropping claim that there is 'more constancy' in the female sex has to be read, in the first instance, as a repudiation of the deep-rooted misogyny of her society. Her spirited championing of 'our sex' is an expression of a remarkably confident female identity, in an era that did not view women as equal to, let alone superior to men.

In Marie's experience, though, not only were women more than capable of forming deep and meaningful relationships with one another but these could be soul-shatteringly romantic and sexual, as well as platonic. Marie's insistence on the inherent dignity and equality – even superiority – of women is, of course, inextricable from her honouring of the love between two women: for it is not possible to respect romantic love between two women if it is not first fully accepted that women are serious thinking and feeling beings, as opposed to a lesser category of human, unworthy of the same basic respect, rights and privileges as men. The striking line about 'our sex' stands out, but the entirety of Marie's poem 49 is, ultimately, as much a celebration and honouring of women generally as it is of sapphic love specifically.

Marie also hammers home in these final lines the suffering that the two women – in love yet forced apart – must endure. She has already stated that the two women are in great pain, due to the fact of the woman's husband. Here, she opens the stanza by referring to the adversity that 'afflicts'* them, before proceeding to list no fewer than four evocative nouns of suffering: hardship, torment, grief and pain. Underlining their marriage-like bond to the last, however, Marie repeats that no such 'earthly thing' could ever actually sever them. Only death could ever divorce them. As long as they both draw breath, they shall live, defiantly and devotedly, in the spirit, if not the law, of marital devotion. 'Such constancy', declares Marie, at the poem's heart-stopping conclusion, shall maintain them 'in perfect amity, for ever'.

Unsigned by name, but straight from her heart, at the end of this most momentous love poem, Marie added only the Latin sign-off 'finis', in small, unadorned letters, followed by a full stop. But, as we will see in a later chapter, if poem 49 was 'finis', Marie's love story was not. And nor was her manuscript – although it almost was.

*

In Marie's poem 49, as in the poems of comfort that she wrote to her father and brother, what stands out is her stoicism in the face of adversity: whether her certain belief that the ill-fated love

* Note that 'vex' had a stronger meaning in historical Scots, where it denoted affliction or suffering, than it does in Modern English, where its semantic field has been diluted in the direction of mere 'annoyance'.

between herself and another woman would prevail, or her conviction that her Maitland family had come through worse before, that God was, ultimately, on their side, and that all would be well.

Stripped of his assets and deprived of his liberty, Marie's brother John might have found it difficult to share her upbeat mentality. Her elderly father, too, grieving the recent deaths of two adult sons, and unjustly banished from his home, seems to have lost all hope. But Marie's unshakeable optimism – at least in relation to her family's fortunes – was soon to be proven right.

As 1578 dawned, the Regent Morton, with his particular loathing of the Maitlands, remained in power. But things were about to change. In March, the Earls of Atholl and Argyll led a coup to oust Morton. They cajoled the now twelve-year-old King James VI, son of the desposed Mary, Queen of Scots, into assuming his legal responsibilities as an adult monarch.

Although he was now a ruling King on paper, in reality, it would be a while before James was fully in control of his fate and the country. Still, essentially, a child, he would remain at the mercy of whichever nobles were most powerful, and held most influence over him, for several years to come. Morton would, in fact, wrestle back a degree of standing within weeks of James's technical assumption of leadership, but his grasp on power had been loosened, and his days were numbered.

This was good news for the Maitlands. One of the immediate effects of this shifting in the balance of power was the liberation, in September 1578, of Marie's brother John, who had been in a state of captivity since the end of the Marian civil war, five years earlier. Although he remained deprived of his lands, he was now, at least, a free man, and able to begin the process of resuscitating both his political career and his family's standing through seeking favour and advancement at court.

Just months after her brother's release from captivity, Marie also achieved a significant form of freedom; perhaps the most meaningful type that a woman at this time could hope for, and one that had not been given to her lover: freedom from the need to marry.

Chapter Five

With my own hand

Over the years, Marie had watched as all three of her sisters and, devastatingly, her own lover were married off to men, as was expected of them, and as was, for most women, the only possible path. For Marie, though, life had presented her another option: in her early adult years she had instead been called upon to serve her blind father.

Back in 1569, when Marie had been in her late teens or early twenties, Sir Richard had set her up with an income of her own when he had directed 110 merks to be paid to her annually by local landowner, William Sinclair. However, this income was just a stop-gap, or allowance, while she remained in her father's service. At that time, although Marie was growing past the expected age for a first marriage, she still wasn't that old, and the prospect of her getting married (and thus a husband taking on financial responsibility for her) at some point in the future could still reasonably have been on the cards.

Indeed, a different Marie might well have become restless as she grew older, an ever less willing assistant, and begged her father to let her leave his side and establish her own household and family. Had this been the case, Sir Richard, who appears by all accounts to have been a kindly and caring father, is unlikely to have kept his daughter in his service under duress. Equally, Marie's already aged father could have passed away soon after the setting up of this stop-gap income. In either scenario, we might have found a standard contract of marriage for Marie within a few years of 1569, after a slight delay having spent some time serving as her father's secretary.

Instead, as the new decade of 1580 approached, Sir Richard, now in his eighties, remained alive and well – and Marie remained by his side. And, for the past few years, she appears to have done so without any clear income of her own. By June 1576, Sinclair had paid off the underlying debt due to Marie's father and thus became liberated from his obligation of interest payments to Marie. There are no signs that Marie had any other such formal income around this period; rather, it seems that, for the few years following 1576, Marie had simply been living in her father's household and at his expense. For her part, Marie therefore seems to have been more than content to continue in the role in which she had dutifully served for years.

But whatever Marie felt about her situation and whatever practical support her father continued to need at that time – while also no doubt deriving emotional comfort from his youngest daughter's presence – Sir Richard would not live forever, and Marie's future without him was looking increasingly perilous.

By the late 1570s, Marie was already long past the age at which a woman of her status would normally first marry. And, with each passing year, she was becoming an even less desirable marriage prospect. She had no secure income of her own (let alone one that she could live on), and no real plan for what she would do after her father's death. When that time came, his land and properties (heritable estate) would pass to his rightful male heirs, not to Marie, who would no longer have a father's household to reside in. At best, without a husband, Marie would find herself (precariously) reliant on the continued goodwill of male relatives to allow her the use of a residence or rooms.

Indeed, if there was ever a risk that Marie, the unmarried youngest daughter still at home, might have started to feel like an additional burden that her father could do without, then it was during these years of exile and hardship. Had that been the case, it would surely have been at this time that we might have expected to see Sir Richard put his powers of persuasion and diplomacy to good use in order to secure his unmarried daughter a husband, so that he had one less thing to think about.

But that is not what happened. Instead, a series of records from 1579 onwards tell us that Sir Richard resolved that Marie should remain at his side. And in anticipation that, by the time that she was released from his service by his death, she would no longer be a marriagable prospect, he would need to provide for her future as an unmarried woman for life.

*

On 5 February 1579, in Edinburgh, Marie signed her name to a contract through which she invested the sum originally intended as her dowry not in a husband but in an interest-earning loan. There were two parties to the contract, which was diligently taken for central registration at the Court of Session later the same day. The first party is recorded as 'Marie Maitland, dochter lauchtfull [daughter lawful] to Sir Richard Maitland . . . with avyse [advice] and consent of hir said fader [father]'. The second party comprised a group of landed men from Aberdeenshire: John Leslie of Balquhane (10th Baron), as principal, and Alexander Forbes of Pitsligo and William Forbes of Tolquhoun, as guarantors.*

In return for lending Leslie the sum of 1,200 merks – 'the soumm of tualf hundreth merkis all in silver of threttie shilling pecis twentie shilling pecis & ten shilling pecis' – Marie became

* 'Cautioners' in the original Scots, a term still used in Scots law today.

entitled to a payment of 144 merks a year in interest, or 'annualrent'. As security for the loan, Leslie pledged to Marie certain of his lands in Aberdeenshire.* In the terminology of the time, this sort of arrangement (a financial loan underpinned by the pledging of lands by borrower to lender, until the debt was repaid) was called a 'wadset'.[1] A 'wad' was simply a 'pledge', and so to 'set in wad' was to pledge something. In a turn of etymological irony, the verb 'to wed' and the related noun 'a wedding' (essentially, 'a pledging') have the same Germanic root. But instead of a 'wedding' – or 'wadding', in Scots – Marie got a 'wadset'; instead of pledging herself to a man, in return for financial security, she had a man pledging lands to her, as security for money that she was lending him.

The 1,200 merks in silver coins that Marie invested on 5 February 1579 can only have been the sum originally intended as her dowry. The amount itself is the first clue. In 1555, Marie's father had shelled out the same sum of 1,200 merks as a dowry for his eldest daughter, Elizabeth. In 1560, the dowry of his second-eldest, Helen, was 1,100 merks. Soon after, he paid out a dowry of 1,250 merks to the family of the husband of his third daughter, Isobel. A diligent and organised father, this same sort of sum seems to have been what Sir Richard had set aside in anticipation of his youngest daughter's marriage. But where the dowries of his other three daughters had been swiftly expended, Marie's had been gathering dust.

The fact that the express consent of Marie's father to this investment is confirmed is a further signal that this capital was originally intended as Marie's dowry, as it establishes him as the source of the money. In the normal course of things, a father would of course

---

* Those of Bonnyton, in the parish of Rayne.

duly pay his daughter's dowry directly to her husband's family; an ordinary daughter wouldn't really ever see the money put aside for her, and had no real agency over it.

But, in 1579, Sir Richard found himself handing Marie's 1,200 merks over to her. And it became entirely hers. By contrast, the first income that Marie's father had set up for her, a decade earlier in 1569, had remained, ultimately, his property. Marie had no right to transfer its benefits to anyone else during her lifetime, and a clause provided that, had she predeceased her father, it would simply have reverted to him. Back then, Marie had been merely the passive recipient of funds, at her father's pleasure. Now, she was the active owner and investor of her own money. She had the power to convey its benefits to someone else, if she wished, and it was for her to declare who should inherit this wealth upon her death.

Marie's newfound agency is apparent in the fact that she is named first, as the lead party to the contract. It is Marie who is described as negotiating the settlement, with the 'advice and consent' of her father. And the borrower of Marie's money was not an Edinburgh or Lothian local but rather someone based in Aberdeenshire. As well as illustrating the extent of the social and political connections of Marie's family across the kingdom, this also makes it noteworthy that the contract stipulates that payments to Marie are to be made twice yearly, in two equal amounts, within the burgh of Edinburgh; more specifically, at either 'the parioch kirk of Edinburcht now commounlie callit sant geilis [St Giles] kirk' or at a Maitland 'dwelling place' within the capital. Clearly, Marie did not want to have to travel up to Aberdeenshire to collect her money – and she had sufficient standing to dictate that Leslie, a landed man, come to her. Marie's name, though, does appear in a related document, which ended up far from her home territory of the Lothians. Contained within the legal papers of the Leslies of Balquhain, preserved in the north-east of Scotland, is a letter dated 6 February 1579, the day after the loan agreement was signed.[2] In it, Marie Maitland confirms the terms under which Leslie has the right to redeem his lands, pledged to her as security, once the debt had been repaid. Although a simple formality, underpinning the loan, it is also another example of Marie engaging in the legal system on her own terms, as an independent woman, including with landed men from the other side of the country.

*

From her dowry investment alone, Marie had secured herself 144 merks a year in interest payments. The substantial principal loan sum of 1,200 merks was also due to be repaid to her at some point in the future, which she could then reinvest as she saw fit. Even more significantly, though, in the months that followed, Marie was also furnished with a flurry of other income sources, resulting in annual income far too high to have been intended simply as an allowance while her father remained alive. Rather, this was about ensuring that Marie had sufficient funds to live independently as an unmarried woman, following Sir Richard's death.

First, in November 1579, Marie became entitled to 60 merks a year in interest, to be paid to her by a close family friend, the Laird of Dundas (underpinned by a loan of 600 merks). In July 1580, Marie added a further 100 merks in interest a year to her coffers, due payable to her by a powerful East Lothian laird, John Cockburn of Ormiston. Soon after, in October 1580, William 4th Lord of Ruthven, a dominant political player, became similarly obliged to pay Marie 100 merks in interest annually. Having already granted her the sum intended as her dowry to invest, it seems that Marie's father then also donated to her further pockets of money to lend to prominent and trustworthy individuals at interest, in order to generate a generous and reliable annual income for Marie. Although deprived of his main estate of Lethington, Richard Maitland remained cash rich and well connected.

By the autumn of 1580, then, Marie's known annual income totalled 404 merks a year, with the 144 merks in interest from her dowry investment swiftly supplemented by a further 260 merks, all underpinned by four principal loan sums. But Marie was still not done amassing her independent wealth. By the summer of 1582, we know that Marie had gained yet another source of income, as she had been granted rights to the teinds (tithes) of all or most of the estates of the parish of Bolton in East Lothian. This meant that Marie got to collect ten per cent of the produce of the land, or the cash equivalent. Originally a religious tax, derived from the Old Testament and paid towards the upkeep of the Church, since the grabbing of Church lands and associated incomes at the Reformation, teinds were now paid to the relevant secular superior, the teindholder. The underlying contract unfortunately hasn't survived, which means we don't know the identity of the superior who granted Marie these rights, or when precisely this took place. It also makes it difficult to say exactly how much income was involved. However, from a later record, we know that Marie was 'principal tackswoman of the teind sheaves of the parish of Bolton' (whereby a 'tack', in Scots, was a lease) and that, in July 1582, she subcontracted her rights to collect the teinds for the town and lands of Marvingstone, a smaller area within Bolton, to one John Cranstoun, in return for which he paid Marie duty of 10 merks per year. This contract was witnessed by Marie's brother John Maitland – who was doing a stellar job of re-establishing himself at court following his release from captivity – her brother-in-law James Heriot and one of her father's male servants. The entire Maitland network, clearly, was in on the efforts to ensure Marie's financial autonomy.*

Through this particular contract, Marie guaranteed herself 10 merks a year from the teinds of Marvingstone, without, crucially, having to concern herself with the actual practicalities of collection (it was literally a case of going round every year at harvest and collecting the tenth part of produce or cash equivalent). John Cranstoun, meanwhile, would get to keep what was left of what he had collected, once he had paid his duty to Marie. Similarly, Marie kept everything that she collected, once she had paid any required duty to her superior in the hierarchy, the teindholder who had appointed her principal tackswoman.

Marvingstone was merely one area of Bolton and Marie had the right to collect teinds from all or most of the entire parish. Thus, these 10 merks a year from Marvingstone can have been only the tip of the iceberg of the wealth that Marie had flowing in as principal tackswoman for the area. Marie may well also have had yet further income sources of which no formal record was ever made, or record of which has not survived, or is still yet to be found.

Based only on what we know at present of Marie's various incomes set up across 1579 and 1580, and her Bolton teinds, we can estimate conservatively that Marie's annual income by the early 1580s was somewhere in the region of 400 to 500 merks. Certainly, it was considerably more disposable income than a

* In terms of the identity of the teindholder who appointed Marie principal tackswoman, it is worth noting that Marie's late brother William had longstanding interests in the lands of Marvingstone, although ownership of land was distinct from ownership of teinds.

woman of Marie's social status would normally enjoy. As a direct comparison, 100 merks a year was deemed appropriate for her sister Helen, her bed and board otherwise provided through her marriage. Similarly, Marie had first been granted an allowance of 110 merks, while still comfortably living under her father's roof and at his expense. Around 100 merks a year was therefore an appropriate amount of income for a Maitland daughter who did not otherwise have to concern herself with paying for the fundamentals of accommodation, food and so on.

Marie found herself with four times this amount and more: enough to fund a comfortable lifestyle for herself as an independent woman, without being reliant on the goodwill of her relatives. Granted, it wouldn't quite afford her the luxuries of Lethington or Dundas Castle, but she could have rented a respectable dwelling in Edinburgh, with plenty change left over for the likes of servants, food and drink, clothing, jewellery, furniture and furnishings and, certainly in Marie's case, the essentials of books and writing materials.

As he set his affairs in order, Marie's father would have been able to rest easy, knowing that he had ensured that his youngest daughter, who had forfeited the social and financial security of marriage in order to serve him, would not want for a place to stay, food to eat or servants to serve her once he was gone.

Marie had been well provided for – and with the consent and support of her father, her wider family and wider elite society.

*

Marie, for her part, could have displayed little resistance to continuing in her long-standing role, and further relinquishing the prospect of marriage. Along with her no doubt genuine affection for her father, and the sense of fulfilment she would have derived from her education and role in assisting him, we know from the poetic record that Marie was also a woman who loved other women, and that she had fallen intensely in love with one particular woman. This insight into Marie's inner world can also be seen as going a long way towards explaining her embracing of her perpetually unmarried status, especially at the time, when marriage and the bringing forth of legitimate children were the primary societal and religious expectations of a woman. Indeed, this situation had only intensified in the years following the Reformation, when the previously sole alternative path of becoming a nun had been swept away by religious reform.

Of course, to the extent that Marie's love for another woman was a major factor in her jumping at the opportunity to sidestep marriage to a man, this particular motivation would have been kept close to her heart – a sapphic secret known about by only her lover and maybe a few close confidantes. It would not have been openly known about or supported by her father, her family or wider society. Far from it: 'sodomy' was a vile sin in the eyes of the kirk, a condemnable crime in the eyes of the state and nobody would wish to be tainted by any whisper of it. Instead, the ready willingness of the Baron of Balquhane, Lord Ruthven, the Laird of Dundas and however many other prominent and God-fearing landed men to enter into public contracts, supporting Marie's financial independence in her unwed state, reflects the legitimacy with which her situation was viewed. To the world outside, this was simply a case of the respectable daughter of a venerable and upstanding man sacrificing herself to the needs of her father. Indeed, nobody would have been more horrified at the idea of it being anything else than Marie's father himself.

Although a moderate, in relative terms, Sir Richard Maitland was, ultimately, a sixteenth-century male judge. And, although a loving and supportive husband and father, his worldview, as preserved in his writings, is, nonetheless, steeped in misogyny. One of his poems, for example, is a tirade against 'vain' and 'lustful' women, in which he urges them, morally weak as they are, to consider their reputations. There is also disparaging reference to 'harlots', whom he implores the reader to avoid at all costs, and several of his poems delight in crude sexual innuendos.

Sir Richard may have been content enough for his youngest daughter to receive an enhanced education and stay at home to serve him, instead of marrying, but we have to acknowledge the extent to which this was rooted in pragmatism and self-interest – about him, not her. Had Marie's father not gone blind, by contrast, it is simply inconceivable that she would have been permitted to stay at home and not marry. On what basis?

The stated case for Marie not marrying, the one understood by her father, family and wider elite society, must have centred solely on her role as a selfless daughter, who God had called upon to serve her father.

In Marie's world, women essentially had three boxes to chose from: virgin, wife or widow. Just as, in poem 49, Marie could see that the only way to publicly and legitimately marry her lover would be to adopt the veil of manhood, she would also have understood that the only way for her to exist as an unwed woman for life would be to adopt the veil of 'virgnity' and 'chastity'.

Indeed, in the contract of October 1580, which set up one of her incomes, Marie is introduced as 'ane chaist virgine, Marie maitland, Dochter Lawfull to Schir Richart Maitland of Lethingtoun Knycht'. That she is 'ane chaist virgine' is the very first descriptor of her that we read; the one that we are to take note of. Only after this do we read her name, and that she is the lawful daughter of Sir Richard Maitland of Lethington. 'Be it kend till all men' begins the contract – and what people were to know (or 'ken'), above all, was that they were dealing with a chaste virgin. Although references to 'virginity' and 'chastity' abound in documentary descriptions of women in this era, they were not, strictly speaking, necessary. Although formulaic, these phrases therefore served a purpose, and their inclusion was a conscious choice. This morally loaded descriptor vouches for Marie's reputation as a chaste and respectable woman, and for the legitimacy of the unique circumstances around her remaining unmarried.

However, even as she operated within the strictures of sixteenth-century Scottish society, aspects of how Marie used her newfound financial independence as an unmarried woman nonetheless emerge as remarkable.

*

Marie's sisters had all trodden the path expected of them. By the time that their youngest sister was giving up on the idea of marriage altogether, they had been married for years and had numerous offspring. By contrast, Marie's unwed status also meant that she would not be having children – that is, producing direct heirs of her own. In the contracts setting up two of her incomes, we see that Marie opted to name her nieces as heirs to her wealth. The July 1580 contract provides that, in the event of Marie's death without issue (children), the income was to transfer to her niece Elspeth Douglas, lawful daughter of William Douglas and her sister Elizabeth. Another niece, Elspeth Heriot, lawful daughter of James Heriot and her sister Isobel, is similarly named as Marie's substitute heir to her October 1580 income. It was a departure from standard practice to name specific beneficiaries, let alone women. Typically, such contracts simply made generic reference to a person's 'heirs', a commonly used and understood term that meant, in most cases, the person's spouse and children. This standard approach, however, was not suitable for Marie, who did not have – or plan to acquire – either. Had she left a standard 'heirs' clause in place, her wealth would have been divided among her siblings, as her nearest kin.

Marie could have chosen to bequeath her wealth to anyone she pleased, including her nephews; instead, she chose to use her own unusual financial autonomy to benefit two young female relatives. A special affection for and sense of protectiveness over her nieces is detectable in her unashamed favouring of these young relatives over anyone else. This was a woman who well understood the value of autonomy, and who used what agency she had to help other women. Her nieces must have felt lucky to have such an aunt: one who wanted them to enjoy even a small portion of the rare financial independence that she did, and one capable of having such measures written into contracts, and understanding the importance of doing so.

*

Marie also proved more than capable of pursuing action against anyone who failed to pay what was due to her – which, in 1583, one Sir William Lauder of Haltoun would learn the hard way.

When Marie was first set up with her October 1580 income, it was due to be paid to her by major political player William 4th Lord Ruthven. The following year, he was created 1st Earl of Gowrie by King James VI. Ruthven, or Gowrie, repaid the King for this honour by acting as the ringleader of the now infamous 'Ruthven Raid', to which his name has become indissolubly attached, and which saw the young King traumatically abducted and held captive by a group of Protestant Lords for ten months, from late 1582 to spring 1583. It is said that James started to cry when he realised he had been kidnapped, prompting the poignant remark from one of those present that 'Better bairns greet nor bearded men [rather children weep than bearded men]'. An overriding aim of the enterprise was to remove an impressionable young James from the influence of his much older French cousin, Esmé Stewart, 1st Duke of Lennox, who, since his arrival in Scotland in 1579 had groomed James, a young teenager, into submission and compliance.* It is difficult, based on the evidence, to avoid this disturbing conclusion.

The kidnappers of the King were successful in removing Lennox from the scene; with James held captive, he fled back to France, where he died. However, things didn't end particularly well for the kidnappers either. When the King finally managed to escape, and the rebel regime had been overthrown, Ruthven was,

---

* James was a young teenager at this point, while Esme was in his late thirties. There are suggestions that their relationship had sexual and romantic elements: there are contemporary reports of their brazen physical intimacy in public, alongside discussions of Lennox's endeavours to draw the King into 'carnal lust'. The child-King bestowed an extreme amount of wealth and titles upon Lennox, and his poem 'The Phoenix', penned in devastation and grief at the latter's departure, has strongly sexual overtones; or as David Bergeron, author of *King James & Letters of Homoerotic Desire* (University of Iowa Press, 1999), described it, 'compelling evidence' of 'homoerotic desire'. It is certainly inappropriate to subsume Lennox into the category of James's 'favourites', which should be a term reserved for his romantic interests when he was an adult king, with meaningful agency.

unsurprisingly, convicted of treason. He was executed and his lands (including those from which Marie's income was derived) were forfeited to the Crown and redistributed among the King's friends and allies.

Whatever his other failings, Ruthven had, since 1580, duly paid Marie her 100 merks each year, derived from his lands of Balerno and Kirknewton, near Edinburgh. Upon Ruthven's demise, these lands now made their way into the hands of Sir William Lauder of Haltoun, who failed to honour the existing burden on the lands that was Marie's income. Marie thus took it upon herself to raise legal proceedings against the offending Sir William for non-payment. This was a woman who knew how to use the law to protect her interests and who was not afraid to do so, even against wealthy and powerful men.

The records tell us that, on 5 August 1583, Marie Maitland, 'lawful daughter of Sir Richard Maitland of Lethington' had Sir William 'put to the horn' for 'non-payment of certain sums of money and annualrents from the lands of Balerno and Kirknewton, conform to a bond to her by William, sometime Earl of Gowrie'. 'Put to the horn' is a historical Scots term meaning 'to proclaim an outlaw', which was a consequence of failing to comply with a legal obligation at the time. The 'horn' element refers to the practice of the denunciation being read out publicly, followed by three blasts of the horn. Marie, thus, had Sir William declared an outlaw, until he repaid the debt. However, he must have remained unable or unwilling to pay the money due to Marie. A Privy Seal record tells us that by May 1584 the lands in question had been removed from him, and acquired instead by the Earl of Arran and his spouse – along with, crucially, express instruction to pay 'Marie Maitland, lawful daughter of Sir Richard Maitland of Lethington' the sum of 100 merks a year, as per the Earl of Gowrie's obligations to her, prior to the forfeiture of his lands.

So it was that, after a brief interruption, Marie had her rights to this income upheld by the authority of the Crown. If anyone else had ever considered not paying her, this very public and effective pursuing of Sir William no doubt gave them pause for thought: Marie Maitland was not someone you wanted to find yourself on the wrong side of, even if you were a powerful landed man.

Although Marie drove these proceedings, the resolution of the situation in her favour also can't have been harmed by her brother John's ever-increasing power and status at court. Since his release from captivity in 1578, he had deftly manoeuvred his way into position as one of the King's most valued and trusted advisors. Interestingly, one of the things that the two are likely to have first bonded over, during the early days of John's political revival, is a shared love of learning and poetry. Like the rest of his Maitland family, John was splendidly literary and intellectual, and these were most advantageous qualities in relation to as learned a King as James, who also styled himself a poet and philosopher.

In 1581, John Maitland had some of his lands restored to him, regained his seat on the bench as a Lord Ordinary and was reappointed Keeper of the Privy Seal (the office that his father had fulfilled back in the time of Mary, Queen of Scots, and later retired from in favour of his second son). Following the interruption of the Ruthven Raid, John Maitland's upwards trajectory under King James VI of Scotland very much continued.

On 29 August 1583, John was appointed to the Privy Council, where he quickly took on responsibility for handling the bulk of day-to-day governmental business. Then, on 18 May 1584, he was appointed Secretary of State for life to the King: the same crucial role that his brother William had fulfilled in relation to Mary, Queen of Scots, a political era earlier. It was just seven days later, on 25 May 1584, that a Privy Seal record stipulated that his sister Marie should continue to receive her income from Ruthven's forfeited lands; it paid, it would seem, to have a brother in high places. Marie was now the sister of the King's newly appointed and formidable Secretary, and behind this resolution no doubt lies a private conversation or two between the King and her brother, alongside Marie's effective public-facing litigation.

*

Marie had unusual agency as an unwed woman to dictate her successors and to act as a litigant to protect her incomes. What's more, it seems that Marie had the skills to not only sign but also draft legal documents herself – in the same confident combination of scripts that define her manuscript.

Although we don't have the original contract setting up Marie's Dundas income, what we do have are a series of eleven surviving acquittances, through which she confirmed, twice a year, that she had duly received the income due to her. Essentially a collection of receipts, covering the years 1580 to 1585, the eleven acquittances are formulaic and largely identical.

As is the case here, such legalistic texts were often drafted in secretary hand, then signed in italic. This practice was perhaps developed to clearly distinguish the authorising signature from the text of the document itself. It is noteworthy that Marie also reflected such practice in her manuscript. In similar vein, she often recorded the stanzas of (frequently very lengthy) poems in secretary hand, but then used italic script for their attribution to an author, or their title, when she included these. Marie's approach clearly visually distinguishes the text of poems from their titles and attributions, and poems from one another, throughout her manuscript.

The main body of each Dundas acquittance is written in secretary hand, in Marie's first-person voice, and they all conclude with her signature in italic. In each, Marie confirms that she has received payment due to her 'fra ane honorabill man george Dundas'; that is, from her father's friend, Sir George Dundas, 17th Laird of Dundas, at whose estate Marie's father and his household spent time during their exile. This was a man who will have known Marie since childhood, and someone her father could trust. And Marie's signing of each acquittance was witnessed by several other respectable and trusted men; the precise individuals differ across the years, but various of Marie's father's educated male servants are always named among them. As when she invested her dowry, Marie is centre stage; once again, she appears in the records as a woman exercising legal and financial agency, surrounded by men acting in facilitating and supportive roles.

The June 1581 acquittance begins as follows, in representative fashion, in an accomplished secretary hand script:

> I Marie Maitland, Dochtir lauchfull to Sir Richarde maitland of lethingtoun knycht grantis me to have ressavit fra ane honorabill man george Dundas . . . the sowme of twentie pundis money [I Marie Maitland, lawful daughter to Sir Richard Maitland of Lethington, knight, confirm that I have received from an honourable man George Dundas . . . the sum of twenty pounds (30 merks) money].

It then details the term for which payment has been made, the lands from which it has been paid, and so on. All the necessary practicalities covered, Marie declares that she thus:

> dischargis the said george thairof [. . .] for now & ever By this my acquyttance subscryvit with my awin hand AT edinburgh the Nyntene day of Junii the yeir of god foure scoir and ane yeiris [discharges the said George thereof . . . for now and ever, by this my acquittance signed with my own hand at Edinburgh, the nineteenth day of June, the year of god four score and one years].

This is followed by the names of the witnesses to the signing, then, at the very bottom, in a clear italic hand, distinguished from the text above, the words 'Marie Maitland, With my hand', repeating what has already been said in the secretary hand body of the text – that this is Marie's acquittance, signed with her own hand.

At this time, most women (and, indeed, men) could not write: literacy could not be assumed. Although some could at least scratch their initials or names at the bottom of legal documents when required to, very few could write confidently or in full sentences. In many cases, illiterate individuals would not sign their own name but would, instead, have a notary do so on their behalf. Nowadays, we don't usually need to follow up our signature with the clarification 'with my (own) hand' to confirm that we have literally done so: a signature on its own is sufficient to confirm that we, ourselves, have signed. In Marie's world, though, in writing 'With my hand' underneath her name in italic – in addition to the reference within the main body of the text to 'this my acquittance signed with my own hand' – she makes the fact of her having signed each document herself indisputable.

These assurances were, of course, intended for Marie's contemporaries, so that they would know that the signature was valid and that the payment had been duly received. For us, however, these signatures, inadvertently, provide proof positive of Marie's literacy in italic script, outwith the pages of her manuscript. And what's more, everything also points to the preceding neat lines of secretary hand having flowed from her quill, too.

All eleven of the acquittances, covering five years, are recorded in the same, well-executed secretary hand. Each begins 'I Marie Maitland' and continues in first-person voice, with multiple emphatic uses of 'my' throughout. Perhaps most tellingly, Sir Richard is referred to as 'my fader [my father]', along with the references to 'this my acquittance', signed by 'my own hand', in the secretary hand script. Further, although the ink colour varies from document to document, it is always the same within a given example; the text of the acquittance, and the italic signature at the bottom, are, in each case, in the same ink. If the text was drafted by someone else, and only signed by Marie, we could reasonably expect, over five years and eleven documents, to see evidence of different inks between the text and the signature, with the acquittance drafted earlier in time, and somewhere else, before being presented to Marie for signing. Instead, the consistency in ink would seem to further confirm that each acquittance was written and signed contemporaneously. Almost undoubtedly, what we have are eleven texts written by Marie, in a combination of secretary hand and italic script – just like her manuscript.

Marie writing both parts of these acquittances would, of course, be entirely consistent with a highly educated woman who had, by this point, served as her father's secretary for many years. Familiar with the wording of legal documents, Marie would have been more than capable of drafting up a straightforward acquittance, while writing in secretary hand will have been second nature to her. She was a woman who was not just functionally literate but who had spent decades honing her scribal talents far beyond the expected or strictly necessary.

As the 1580s wore on, Marie's scribal prowess, identity as a poet and status as an authoritative woman would be brought vividly to life in several stunning poems, preserved in the latter pages of her manuscript. And yet, the fact that Marie committed these particular verses to paper was, it seems, the result of another instance of sheer chance in her already astonishing life.

Chapter Six

Sapphic song so sweet

We left Marie and her manuscript just as she'd inscribed the last line of her poem 49. After she had recorded the nine stanzas of that momentous declaration of her love for another woman, Marie returned to recording the poems of her father: poems 50 to 59 are all by Sir Richard, with poem 59 the last of his poems preserved in its pages. An advice poem of ten stanzas addressed to the young King James, it begins, 'Our souverane lord, into thy tender age, Lerne to serve God, him luif above all thing.' However, just as Marie reached the last few lines of this last poem by her father, she ran out of paper. She already seems to have been worried that this might happen, and tried to avoid it, as her writing becomes increasingly cramped in the preceding pages. However, despite her best efforts to squeeze as many lines as she could onto each page, after she had written the half-line 'to thy leigis do justice equallie . . .', there was simply nowhere left to write. No doubt exasperated at the time, Marie procured and inserted some new paper: the thick, vertically lined paper that she had been writing on so far changes, at this point, to a thick, horizontally lined paper, with watermarks in the shape of a crown and jug. On the first sheet of this newly inserted, small batch of paper, Marie recorded the second half of her father's line of poetry – '. . . without respect to persone or pairtie' – then proceeded to record the remainder of stanza nine, and all of the tenth and final stanza, before dutifully attributing the verse to 'S. Richard Maitland of Lethingtoun knycht'.

Then, in a move completely out of keeping with her practice so far, Marie filled the remaining space at the bottom of the page with ornamental flourishes – in what seems to have been originally intended as the end of the manuscript. In the preceding pages, space had been very much at a premium; one poem often begins immediately after another, even on the same page, and lines are tightly packed together. And Marie had added only a small amount of new paper. Just enough, it would seem, to finish this last poem by her father, of which she had only a stanza and a half left to record. Certainly, the amount of paper she'd added was nowhere near enough to create the manuscript of more than ninety poems that it would, eventually, become.

If Marie had initially set out with a finite amount of paper, and the clear goal of creating a complete record of her father's poetry, plus a handful of other verse (including, crucially, her poem 49), she had now achieved this – even if she'd had to slip in some extra paper at the end to finish her father's final poem.

Marie's great task was, it seemed, done. But, as things would turn out, Marie was not yet ready to put down her quill.

*

We don't know for certain how much time elapsed between Marie finalising the page containing her father's last poem with ornamental flourishes and then deciding to turn the page and keep on writing, or what exactly might have prompted it. However, the first poems that Marie added, when she continued recording beyond her father's last verse, relate to the vindication of the Maitland family name in relation to past political events. And we know from her manuscript's earlier pages that she was always keen to record and put the Maitland spin on events of significance.

In any event, turn over the page and keep going she did. And, having made the decision to continue to add more poems, she soon found that the small amount of new paper she'd first inserted, to finish a manuscript ostensibly in celebration of her father, was no longer sufficient for what it was now evolving into. She, and the women around her, had a lot more to say, and they were going to need a bigger manuscript to do that.

So, midway through poem 66, Marie found herself adding yet another sheaf of new paper, and this time a substantial amount. The final lines of poem 66 begin at the top of a new page of a third and final distinct paper type, thin and vertically lined. The paper type does not change again, but now continues all the way to the end of the manuscript.

And it is in this latter part – after all her father's poems had been recorded, and with the fresh promise of much more paper – that Marie's manuscript really blossomed into a profusion of female-authored verse. It is on this paper that Marie recorded most of the 'anonymous' poems that first flowed from a female quill. Not only did the manuscript eventually nearly double in size, it also evolved, from this point, into something far more diverse – in both content and form. For in these later pages, Marie also made far greater use of italic script and decorative adornments. This development of the manuscript, which was underway by the early 1580s, seems to have coincided with Marie becoming generally more confident in her agency and creativity, and increasingly unapologetic about creating a record of her own voice, and the voices of other women. And one of those women we can even identify by name.

*

Poem 66 is the reworking in Scots of an original French elegy in the voice of an unhappy wife. Marie gave it the title 'Ane Elagie translatit out of frenche in English meter'* – and, tantalisingly, half-attributed it, by initials, to a 'G.H.'. These initials appear to have belonged to a young woman named Grizel Hay, the well-educated daughter of another landed East Lothian family, the Hays of Yester. This is not just because the initials of her name match up but because the known facts of Grizel's life also match the contents of the verse semi-anonymously attributed to her.†

Grizel, born around 1567, was betrothed by her parents as a girl to a man whom she really didn't want to wed – and this situation seems to be reflected in several unique lines that she worked into her Scots translation of the poem, words not present in the original French.‡ In one of the conspicuously new lines, for example, G.H. criticises the 'negligence' of her parents, asking, 'Why wald thay not at leist seik my consent?' Although 'consent' at this time did not mean the full and enthusiastic variety that we expect today, blatant coercion was still not acceptable. Even if she did not have meaningful free choice, the at least nominal consent of the woman to the marriage arranged for her was expected. Fortunately for Grizel, by the time she came of age, the betrothal contract would

* It was translated from French to Scots, but in an 'English' meter. The reworking is of the twentieth elegy in Clément Marot's 1533 *La Suite de l'Adolescence Clementine*.

† Credit is due to Dr Sajed Chowdhury for first suggesting Grizel Hay of Yester as the woman behind the 'G.H.' attribution attached to poem 66, and for identifying the additional lines in the Scots translation. See Dr Chowdhury's DPhil thesis, *Dissident Metaphysics in Renaissance Women's Poetry* (University of Sussex, 2012), pp. 88–9.

‡ Grizel's father, Lord Hay of Yester, betrothed her to Robert Home of Heuch, the young son of another local landed family, in 1576, when she was around just nine years old. The two being minors at the time, it was agreed that the marriage would take place when they had attained the age of eighteen.

be annulled, and the marriage would not take place.* But this poem seems to be the expression of a moment in time when she very much still feared that it would – and was powerless to prevent it.

However Marie came into the possession of Grizel's poem, she clearly felt that it merited inclusion in her manuscript.† Certainly, she would have been a very sympathetic pair of ears when it came to wanting to avoid a societally dictated marriage to a man, and was also supportive of women expressing themselves in poetry. Indeed, it was midway through the recording of this poem, by a woman, that Marie was prompted to add the third and final type of paper – from which the remainder of the manuscript bloomed, and in which Marie herself would come to the fore, in all her sapphic glory.

*

Swiftly after Grizel's poem, Marie recorded another 'anonymous' but female-authored poem, in which she herself is brought vividly and enrapturingly to life. Likely written by a woman who knew Marie well, poem 69 is set up as a dream vision, a well-worn poetic convention at the time, in which Marie appears to the dreaming author in a bucolic woodland setting:

Marie, I thocht, in this wod did appeir	*Marie, I thought, in this woodland did appear*

* In August 1585, the contract to marry was annulled. The Homes of Heuch found themselves in considerable debt to the Hays of Yester, and their inability to fulfil monetary aspects of the betrothal contract was likely a factor. In any event, the falling through of the contract must have come as a relief to Grizel.

† Marie was born in the 1540s, Grizel in the 1560s. It is therefore most unlikely that Grizel was the subject of poem 49.

Mait, land, and gold scho gave aboundantlie	*Mait [food], land and gold she gave abundantly*

There is no doubt who this poem is about. Marie is explicitly mentioned by both first and last name. The latter is a playful pun, with the reference to her bestowing of 'mait [food]' and 'land' also forming her 'Maitland' surname. As well as food and land, Marie is also described as dispensing 'gold . . . abundantly'. The picture painted is of an authoritative and wealthy woman, who is generous in her sharing of her assets with others.

Syne in hir hand ane flourishit trie did beir	*Then in her hand a blossoming branch did appear*
Quhairin wes writtin, with letteris properlie	*Upon which was written, in letters properly*
'This is in sign of trew virginitie,	*'This is in sign of true virginity,*
Quhilk I have socht and luiffit best of all;	*Which I have sought and loved best of all;*
Hierfoir I sall, with cair most diligentlie	*Therefore I shall, with care most diligently*
Sustein the same that it ressave no fall'	*Sustain the same so that it meets no fall'*

A blossoming branch then appears in the hand of the Marie in this dream. It is inscribed with a declaration, in Marie's own voice, saying that she has always 'sought and loved . . . true virginity best of all', and that she shall, 'with care most diligently . . . sustain the same so that it meets no fall'. The metaphorical 'sign' in Marie's hand is clear enough to be read at a distance of several centuries without squinting: in short, 'I will never marry, but remain a virgin forever.' In a formal document setting up one of her 1580 incomes, Marie was described as a 'chaste virgin'. Here, in this private, poetic record, the message is fundamentally the same, if a bit more tongue in cheek. And if Marie's commitment to 'diligently sustaining' her virginity alludes to her enduring unmarried status, her bountiful generosity with her 'gold' seems most likely to refer to actions such as her granting of high-value loans – such as through her dowry investment – and her naming of her nieces as beneficiaries. It is also in anonymous poem 77, which Marie recorded not long after this one in her manuscript, that she is presented as the doting owner of a highly adorned Bible, decorated in silver and gold. As well as Marie's religious devotion, this also, of course, underlines her material wealth, as a woman with the sort of assets at her disposal to have her Bible so opulently bound.

The fact that Marie's declaration of chastity is described as being written with 'letteris properlie', seems intended, on one level, as a straightforward nod to her prowess as a penwoman. Marie could certainly write in 'proper letters', in the sense of being 'accomplished' – and in several scripts. But 'properly' also had the meaning of 'in accordance with the rules', and so this can equally be read as a reflection of the fact that Marie's remaining unwed was formalised through all the proper channels. As we have seen, Marie's dowry investment, and her being furnished with further incomes, was certainly 'properly' implemented through above-board contracts, and consented to by her father, family and wider elite society.

The author of the poem goes on to describe Marie as a 'peerless . . . pleasant plant' – the word 'plant' was often used symbolically to depict someone full of promise and potential. This remarkable plant, the author continues, has a 'hairt . . . maid of faythfulnes' – which seems very appropriate, given the Marie we know from poem 49 – and solid and stable roots: a reference, it would seem, to the strong social and financial support of Marie's family, as well as to her proud Maitland ancestry.

the blomes quhyte and reid wes bewtie bricht	*the blossoms white and red were shining beauty*
the braunche and leifis wer all of propernes	*the branch and leaves were all of properness*
weill wrocht for till alluire all erdlie wicht	*well crafted in order to allure all earthly beings*

In an allusion to Marie's own beauty, the poet tells us how stunning white and red blossoms burst forth around her, and how the leaves and branches of the tree around her were of faultless proportion, perfectly crafted to allure and entice all earthly beings. Whoever wrote this poem, they were certainly enamoured of Marie Maitland.

Thrillingly, we then find out that Marie is not alone in this beautiful, blossoming tree but has company, and not just any. In this dream vision, Marie is sitting in its uppermost branches along with a whole host of goddesses and muses: Venus, Juno, Pallas, Minerva, Cleo, Terpsichore, Persephone and Diana.

In quhose crope ane plesand sicht thair wes	*In whose uppermost branches a pleasing sight there was*
Of ladyis bricht as Phoebus in mid day	*Of ladies as bright as the sun in mid day*
For thair wes Venus, Juno, and Pallas	*For there was Venus, Juno, and Pallas*
Minerva, Cleo and Tersiphone,	*Minerva, Cleo and Tersiphone,*
Prosperina, and Diana	*Prosperina, and Diana*

The symbolic suggestions are many. Their associations with wisdom and learning endow Pallas (Athena) and Minerva with obvious relevance for our highly educated Marie. However, along with Diana, they also rank as the most famed 'virgin goddesses' of Greek and Roman mythology, distinguished by their rejection of marriage and commitment to protecting their chastity. Normally, of course, such pledges to virginity could be made only by goddesses, in the realms of mythology: in the real world, women had to marry. And yet, when she invested her dowry, Marie had, to all intents and purposes, taken such a pledge herself. And here, the 'chaist virgine', who has always 'socht and luiffit . . . trew virginitie best of all', is situated alongside a trio of the most iconic virgin goddesses of lore. Marie must, indeed, have felt more affinity with these mythical women than with the women around her, whether her now-married lover or her three sisters.

Yet Marie was not the only real historical woman defying the expectations of her gender at this time. For all that Marie shared a name with the ill-fated Scottish sovereign, with her series of catastrophic marriages, in her commitment to 'virginity', Marie exhibited more similarities with the Queen of England, who was rewriting the royal rule book for women in live time. If a woman not marrying was questionable in general, it was utterly unthinkable for a queen, whose one role was to produce an heir (and ideally also a spare) to the throne. And yet Elizabeth I remained resolutely unwed, rejecting marriage in favour of autonomy all her days. Increasingly idolised for her projection of the image of chastity, the reputation of England's 'Virgin Queen' would have been well known to Marie. And as the cult of virginity that grew up around her intensified, Elizabeth was compared in portraiture to

Diana:[1] just as Marie was presented alongside that virgin goddess in poetry – and addressed her own poetry to her.

The goddesses invoked in this poem were famed for their wisdom and learning, talents and achievements, alluring charms and beauty, as opposed to their spouses and offspring. As well as symbolically highlighting aspects of Marie's own character – her own chastity, beauty and learning – the author might also have intended this gathering of goddesses around Marie to symbolise the poetic community of women she created around her. With certainty, we can identify at least Marie's lover – who was, of course, literally described as the embodiment of 'learned Pallas' in Marie's poem 49 – and the young Grizel Hay of Yester. But it would seem likely that other members of Marie's inner circle, even though their identities are lost to us today, are also represented among the thirty or so anonymous poems of her manuscript that suggest a female author; that Marie provided a space for numerous other women to write about their lives and faith, hopes and heartbreaks, and to have this recorded for posterity in an intimate family manuscript.

At the end of this fantastical poem, the cast of goddesses and muses begin to sing a song, sadly rousing the author from her Marie-inspired reverie, which awakening she laments with 'wofull hairt [woeful heart]'. Whoever wrote this dedicatory poem to Marie, shot through with familiarity and adoration, clearly admired her greatly; and, notably, she was moved to celebrate Marie's stunning physical beauty, as well as her generosity and literary talents.

It is not impossible that Marie herself is behind this verse, of course, given her obvious high self-regard, and her propensity for hiding herself in poetry, such as in the anagrammatic line of poem 1.

However, it seems equally plausible that it could be the work of Marie's lover. And, as well as presenting this fulsome, fantastical poetic image of Marie, the manuscript's new pages would also continue the great, real-life love story between the two women.

*

If Marie had, indeed, finalised the manuscript after her father's last poem, we would still have her poem 49. But all that we know of her love for another woman would have ended there. Fortunately, though, Marie's expansion of the manuscript means that her sapphic love story continued – at least on the page – with Marie commiting to paper not just one but two further poems documenting it.

Poem 72 appears uniquely in Marie's manuscript. The author of this anonymous love poem of just four stanzas is careful – unlike in the much bolder poem 49 – not to reveal their own gender, or that of their addressee, at any point. However, the main candidates for its authorship are both women: either Marie or her lover. The parallels with Marie's poem 49 are déjà-vu inducing, and so it could well be Marie again – still not over her lover's marriage, still pouring out her heart in verse. However, although poem 72 riffs on familiar themes to poem 49, it reads more like a response than a continuation, and the voice feels different, less confident in clarifying the nature of her love. It is, therefore, equally tantalising to speculate that this might be the work of Marie's educated 'madame', her reply to Marie in verse.

This poem is all about faithfulness and constancy in love, symbolised through the bond of marriage, and the idea of loyalty in love being deserving of recompense. It is replete with the exact same words and concepts as Marie's poetic declaration of til-death-do-us-part devotion in poem 49.

Gif faithfulnes ye find,	*If faithfulness you find*
And that your mynd content,	*And that pleases your mind*
Ane band heirby I bind	*A bond hereby I bind*
Of firme fayth and fervent	*Of loyalty steadfast and fervent;*
And to be permanent,	*And to be unwavering*
For ocht that may befall,	*In the face of anything that may transpire*
My hairt heir I present	*My heart here I present*
In pledge perpetuall	*In eternal pledge*
Quhilk simplie I resing	*Which simply I resign*
As hostage in your hand,	*As hostage into your hand*
And willinglie it bring	*And willingly it bring*
To bind it in sic band	*To bind it in such bond*
As plesis yow command	*As pleases you[r] command*
To lest till I may leif,	*To last as long as I shall live*
Quhilk is the gadge and pand,	*Which is the pledge and security*
Maist suir that I can geif	*Most sure that I can give*

(stanzas 1 and 2)

The poet begins by acknowledging how much her addressee values 'faithfulness'. This being the case, she pledges herself to her in a 'band [bond]' of steadfast and fervent loyalty. Immediately, we are transported back to Marie's invocation of the 'band of Hymen [bond of marriage]' in poem 49. There, Marie described how they would devote themselves to one another with great 'fervencie', 'for ever'. Here, the poet stresses how her loyalty is 'fervent', her commitment 'perpetuall'. If this is, indeed, a response to poem 49, what could possibly have caused Marie's heart to sing louder? If poem 49 was the proposal, poem 72, if by Marie's lover, reads as the 'I do'.

In guarantee of her commitment to their everlasting bond, no matter what may befall them, the author of this poem symbolically offers her 'hairt [heart]', which she resigns 'willingly . . . as hostage' into her lover's hand. What's more, she pledges it for as long as she may live ['till I may leif'], a commitment rooted in the vows of marriage, and echoing Marie's declarations in poem 49. Further underlining that it is the bond of marriage being implied, she writes that her heart is the 'gadge and pand [pledge and security], maist suir [most sure]' that she can give. While 'gadge', in historical Scots, referred to a pledge in general terms, the term 'pand' more frequently denoted the specific security 'payable by betrothed persons, returnable on orderly completion of the marriage'.[2]

Just like in poem 49, the sexual energy and mutality of feeling is also palpable in these stanzas. The author emphasises that she pledges her heart 'willingly', underlining the enthusiastically consensual nature of the bond being entered into. And her statement that she does so 'as it pleases your command' feels like a consciously playful echo of poem 49's erotically charged 'You weild me holie at your will'.

Resave it then, and treit it,	*Receive it, then, and honour it*
As treuth sall try my part;	*As truth shall prove my part;*
Gif I be fals, forleit it,	*Should I be unfaithful, forsake it*
And let me suffer smert;	*And let me suffer pain;*
Deil efter my desert	*Treat me as I deserve*
Than dreid I no disdaine	*Then I dread not your disdain*
Bot houpis to have ane hairt	*But rather hope to have a heart*
In recompence againe	*In recompense in turn*

Gif loyaltie may love	*If loyalty can love*
Ane recompence procuire;	*A recompense procure*
Or honest mening move	*Or honest intentions cause*
Your favour to induire;	*Your favour to endure;*
Gif lawtie you alluire,	*If integrity allures you*
Or constance mak yow kynd,	*Or constancy makes you kind*
Firme faith sall me assuire	*Steadfast loyalty will inspire me*
And treuth content your mynd	*And the truth will content your mind*

(stanzas 3 and 4)

The theme of marriage is also present in the second half of the poem. The verb 'to treit' – meaning, in general terms, 'to show respect to; to honour' – also had a specifically marital dimension at this time, used to describe how a husband should treat his wife, or a wife her husband. The author here implores the recipient of her heart to 'treit' it, in the way that spouses should honour one another.[3] In this, and other regards, the parallels with poem 49 continue. There, Marie claimed that the truth would prove their love superior to that of the ancient heroes: 'That treuth sail try sa far above . . . the auntient heroicis love'. The author of this poem expresses her commitment to playing her part in proving that truth, urging her lover to accept her heart, in the secure knowledge that 'treuth sall try [prove] my part'.

If her lover should ever find her unfaithful, she continues, she should forsake her heart and leave her to suffer pain ['smert']. But it is clear that she has no intention of ever acting in such a way, clear that she never expects this relationship to cause either of the two women 'smert' – unlike the Brutus of poem 49. Far from it. The author of this poem hopes and intends to secure her lover's heart in turn, in 'recompence' for her faithfulness – a word that she repeats in the final stanza, along with reference to 'constance [constancy]'. In poem 49, Marie wrote that their 'mair perfyte amitie . . . mair worthie recompence sould merit', that it would 'constantlie . . . induire', and that their 'constancie' would maintain them, forever. The sense that we have seen this before is overwhelming. Whoever composed poem 72, they very much shared the same sentiments, if not the same sapphic boldness, as the woman who authored poem 49 – who, fittingly, in another of these later anonymous poems, is compared to no less than Sappho herself.

*

In anonymous poem 85 – potentially written by a woman who knew her, or perhaps written by Marie herself – Marie is named alongside two renowned female writers: the near contemporary Italian reformer and scholar Olympia Morata, as well as the original lesbian poet, Sappho. Marie is urged to follow in their footsteps and make her name as a poet, by completing her nearly finished manuscript.

that lustie ladie rair	*That beautiful and excellent lady*
Olimpia o lampe of latin land	*Olympia, o lamp of Latin land*

Although dying from fever aged just twenty-nine, Olympia Morata made a huge impact in her short lifetime. Her rich classical education and fervent Protestant faith meant that her name was praised across Europe.[4] In being held up alongside Olympia, Marie's own religious faith and learnedness is underlined.

If sapho saige for saphic songe so swiet	*If wise Sappho for sapphic song so sweet*
Did pleid for prais & place amangs the nyne	*Did plead for praise & place among the nine*

The Ancient Greek poet Sappho – 'the Tenth Muse', 'the Female Homer', 'the Poetess' – meanwhile, has long been just as (in)famous for her love for other women, immortalised in several surviving poems and fragments, as for her general poetic prowess.* And as part of the Renaissance-driven revival of interest in Greek and Latin literature, Sappho's works, including some of her most explicitly lesbian lyrics, were in circulation and enjoying renewed popularity during Marie's time, not least through the various editions published by French printer and scholar Henri Estienne between around 1550 and 1560.[5]

Marie is likely to have known, for example, the 'Ode to Aphrodite', in which Sappho appeals to the goddess of love, passion and lust to intervene to help her gain the affection of a woman – and not for the first time. So begins Aphrodite in response to Sappho's plea:

> Who is it this time I must persuade
> to take you back and love you? Sappho, who does
> you wrong?
>
> If she's running away she'll be chasing before long . . .[6]

In another renowned surviving fragment, known as *Phainetai moi*, or 'Fragment 31' – and which we know was also printed and popular during Marie's lifetime – Sappho describes the debilitating bodily effects of her overwhelming desire for a woman.

> . . . I look
> for a moment at you and cannot speak,

* Harriette Andreadis sets out how the two main representations of Sappho in Marie's time were as an 'originary icon of female poetic excellence' and as an 'exemplar of female same-sex desire' in *Sappho in Early Modern England: Female Same-Sex Literary Erotics 1550–1714* (University of Chicago Press, 2001).

my tongue's broken, a quick thin
fire's run under my skin,
my eyes see nothing, my ears whirr,
a cold sweat runs down me, a tremor
all over has hold of me. I'm paler
than grass, and close to dying, it seems to me.[7]

In another, Sappho consoles a heartbroken female lover with memories of the beautiful times they had shared together, including their lovemaking. Sappho reminds her of the

many woven garlands
made of flowers
around your soft throat . . .

and of how

. . . with sweet oil
costly
You anointed yourself

And on a soft bed
Delicate
you would let loose your longing.[8]

It is all unmistakably erotic: Sappho's lyrics enshrine scenes of utmost sensual and sexual intensity between women. This is why women who love other women have long seen themselves in her words, and why her name is inextricable from lesbian love. When the author of poem 85 in Marie's manuscript gushed about Sappho and her 'saphic songe so swiet', these are precisely the sort of verses that she would have had in mind. To name Marie in the same breath as Sappho was to invoke not only her own poetic excellence, as a woman, but also her own love for other women: a veritable sixteenth-century Scottish Sappho.

A thrid, o Maistres Marie, maik I pray	*A third, O Mistress Marie, make I pray*

At the end of this poem, 'Maistres [Mistress] Marie' is explicitly named. Marie is also referred to as a 'maistres' in anonymous poem 77, where she is presented as the proud owner of a much cherished Bible. The title of 'mistress' not only conveys a general sense of authority but also has specific connotations related to learning, as the male form, 'maister [master]', was used to describe men with a university education. Its use seems intended to imply Marie's learnedness as a woman, like Olympia Morata, as well as her elevated social standing.

Marie is urged by the poem's author to join the ranks of these illustrious poets by completing her manuscript ['this buik'] – which she was, by this point, so very close to doing. If she does, the poem goes on, Marie will secure her legacy as a poet and be adorned with the 'croun of poesie [crown of poetry]'.

*

'To Your Self' – poem 85 title

'to your self maid ane immortall name' – poem 1, final line

Strikingly, where most of the poems of her manuscript appear with no title, Marie recorded poem 85 with the standout heading 'To Your Self'. This connects it to the very first poem of the manuscript, whose final line contains the anagram of Marie's name following the very words 'to your self'. Indeed, it would seem that Marie affixed the shameless literary appropriation that is poem 1 – in which she pretends to dedicate the manuscript to her father, but in fact dedicates it to herself – to an empty page at the front of the manuscript around the very same time that poem 85 was added at the other end.

The different inks used, apparent through differing colour, provides another clue that the order in which the manuscript's poems appear today does not necessarily reflect the order in which Marie recorded them. Poem 1 is recorded in a distinctly different, darker brown ink compared to what is now poem 2 – that is, the first poem by Marie's father, and the first thing that Marie herself had committed to paper back when she first embarked upon creating the manuscript.

Of course, by the time that Marie was recording poem 85 in its latter pages, her manuscript had evolved far beyond its original concept. By that point, it was as much (if not more so) about her own literary legacy as it was about her father's. And so, it seems, Marie also now turned back to the front and recorded what is now poem 1, giving it the title 'Ane Sonet to the Authour in Commendatioun of *his* Buik' – in full knowledge that, by this time, really, it was *hers*. In poem 85, meanwhile, the poetic subversion buried in an anagram in poem 1 is made explicit: Marie's completion of this 'buik' is about *her*, and not her father, achieving the 'crown of poetry' and joining the ranks of famed female poets before her.

And if Olympia Morata and Sappho were among the real-world women that Marie idolised and delighted in comparison to, we also know which particular goddess was her mythical idol – and to whom Marie turned as she neared completion of the now much expanded manuscript, seeking divine intervention to help her finish her scribal and poetic endeavours.

*

In the dream-vision poem, where Marie was situated among a whole gathering of goddesses and muses, only two were named twice: 'Dame Beawtie bricht' and 'Dame Chastitie', or Venus and Diana – who, the poet wrote, 'impyire abone the rest for ay [rule above the rest for ever]'. These are the luminaries with whom she most wanted Marie associated: Venus, famed for her dazzling beauty and associations with potent, even dangerous, desire; and Diana, the virgin goddess, who eschewed male company in favour of dwelling in the woods with her nymphs.

Ye heavenlie goddis and goddessis,
Ye most celestiall
Unto my muse your helpis doe bend,
And for your aydis I call.

And thow Diana, ladye bricht
With nymphes of chastetie,
Grant me your favours, I requeist
To end this worthelie

In 'anonymous' poem 86, Marie herself underlines her particular affinity with Diana once again, requesting her divine intervention to help her to 'end this [the manuscript] worthelie [worthily]' – which she was, at that point, so close to completing. In the first short stanza, Marie addresses herself to the 'heavenlie goddis and goddessis' in general. But it is the favour of 'Diana, ladye bricht' and her 'nymphes of chastetie' that Marie seeks most of all, a reflection of her sense of identity with the famous virgin goddess and her female-oriented world.

Diana did, of course, grant Marie her favours, and she did finish her manuscript – and in the happiest of places. By the time that she was adding the finishing touches (including, perhaps, these very last poems) to her work, Marie found herself back in her beloved castle home of Lethington. During the long and wearying years of exile, Marie had praised Lethington in verse, to prove her worth as a poet. She could hardly have hoped for a more fitting setting in which to complete her great literary work.

Chapter Seven

To end this worthily

While Marie had been busy falling in love and investing her dowry, expanding her manuscript and bolstering her wealth, her brother, John, had been hard at work affecting an impressive political comeback, firmly establishing himself as one of the most influential figures at the court of King James VI.

By 1584 – by which time he had been appointed Secretary of State – John Maitland's upward trajectory had resulted in the restoration of Lethington to his family. During the depths of their exile in the 1570s, when even a desperate plea to Elizabeth I by Sir Richard had gone unanswered, Marie and her family must have given up any hope of ever seeing their beloved castle home again. But, after more than a decade of pained separation, the Maitlands had, finally, returned.

Marie's parents, very much in their twilight years, must have been particularly overjoyed to find themselves ensconced within Lethington's walls once more, knowing that they would now get to live out their final days in peace and dignity in their ancestral home, instead of perishing in exile.

In the summer of 1584, after a long life of service and at the age of eighty-eight, Marie's father retired from all professional duties. Marie, for her part, may now have found herself with fewer professional commitments, but her life was full: she had her manuscript to complete and she tended most diligently to her independent incomes. Where Marie had recorded most of her Dundas acquittances as having been signed 'at Edinburgh', to what must have been her great joy, she now got to write that they were signed 'at Lethington' – a tiny, but poignant, change.

Marie also commemorated this return from exile in 'anonymous' poem 88, recorded late in her manuscript, and almost certainly composed with her own quill. Adorned with the italic title 'The Reid [Reed] in the Loch Sayis', in it, Marie employs the metaphor of the reed trembling and being overcome by water, but not breaking, during the storm, then rising up again in the calm, to reflect her family's dramatic and shifting fortunes in recent years.

> Thocht [although] raging stormes movis us to schaik
> And wind makis waters us overflow
> We yeild thairto, but dois not brek,
> And in the calme bent [determinedly] up we grow.

Just as the reed yields to the raging storm, but does not break, continues Marie, while the Maitlands have been 'baneist [banished, exiled]' and 'prisoners', they have not 'disparit [despaired]'. And now 'tyme', Marie writes in its final line, 'sic caussis has reparit [such matters has remedied]'.

*

In the spring of 1586, after nearly two years of peaceful life, 'in the calme', back at Lethington, Marie's father departed this world for the next. It was the twentieth day of March in the year 1586, and he had attained the advanced age of ninety, remarkable at the time. In a morbidly romantic turn of events, his wife, Mariota, died on the day of his burial. A person of the reformed faith would generally be buried within a day or so, particularly if their place of burial was close to their place of death; and so it was in Marie's father's case, as he was interred in the Maitland family aisle at St Mary's Kirk in

Haddington, close to Lethington Castle. If his burial did, indeed, take place promptly after his death on 20 March, then Marie's mother is likely to have died on or around 21 or 22 March.*

Married in 1522, Richard and Mariota had spent more than six decades together. By all accounts, they had genuinely cared for one another, and had remained devoted throughout their marriage. Over the years, they had grieved the loss of babes, nameless to posterity, and they had raised seven children who had survived infancy – two of whom, Thomas and William, they would later mourn. As to the five adult children they would leave behind, following the turbulent years of the 1570s, John was flying high at court; recently appointed Secretary to the King, he was still on the up. Their three eldest daughters, Elizabeth, Helen and Isobel, had long since been married off, and were successfully established with households, husbands and children of their own. As for Marie, their youngest and only still-unwed daughter, they had ensured that she would be more than ready to stand on her own two feet when the time of their passing came.

As Marie lamented the loss of both of her parents in quick succession, she must at least have found some solace and distraction in completing the great literary undertaking of her life, which she had been working on now for years. In the very final pages of her manuscript, Marie recorded – in a distinct, black ink – a series of poems eulogising her recently deceased father and mother, among which she also included a verse in celebration of her brother John, as her father's sole surviving male heir. Poems

* Calvin's *Ecclesiastical Ordinances* (1541), which Knox drew on significantly, stated that a burial should take place between twelve and twenty-four hours after a person's death, although no specific timeframe was set out in Scotland.

90, 91 and 92 are epitaphs to honour Sir Richard and poem 93 is a joint epitaph for Sir Richard and Mariota (to which there is also attached a short memento mori). Poem 94 is the verse in commendation of John Maitland and poem 95 is a final joint epitaph to the Maitland parents.

The first two elegies (poems 90 and 91) are attributed to Thomas and Robert Hudson respectively, brothers and writer–musicians at the court of King James VI, reflecting the stature and connections of Marie's father and his family. But the remainder of the elegies (poems 92 to 95) are unattributed, and to the last, likely to be by Marie. Preserved at the very end of her manuscript, these unsigned poems are shot through with intimacy and warmth, steeped in personal grief and love for Sir Richard and Mariota. They also revisit specific themes in Marie's earlier poems, namely, praise of her wise father and of their illustrious Maitland ancestors.

In 'anonymous' poem 92, Marie's late father is commended as a 'worthy knight, baith valiant, grave [dignified] and wyse', defined by his 'wisdome'. Here lies 'the maist unspotted [morally unblemished]', it tells us, a 'blamles [blameless] judge that justice did maintene'. It goes on, 'in his breist, quhilk [which] wisdome did contene, lay steidfast truth and uncorrupted fayth'. And so, although 'his feit, hands, breist lye buried in this grave . . . this, his saule, the heavens dois receave'.

Marie recorded 'anonymous' poem 93, meanwhile, with the title 'A Luid Of Him Self and his Ladyie Quho [Who] Dyed On His Burial Day' (which is how we know that her mother died on her father's burial day). In the verse itself, Marie both praises the 'noble birth and blood' of her parents and commemorates their many decades of loving matrimony: they 'lived long . . . in mariage-band . . . thrie scoir of yeirs and foure [sixty-four years], in honour maist contentedlye'. With palpable grief, she laments that 'now has Death thair aged dayes defaced by his dairt [dart]'. But neither, at least, will have to live long without the other, she writes, finding cold comfort in how quickly after her father's death her mother also perished. Although death tried to 'devyde' them, Marie's final thought is that 'love has againe, surmounting Death, the force of Death defyd'.

Poem 94 is the unattributed poem in honour of her brother John, her father's sole male heir, which Marie recorded with the title 'In Commendation of the Right Honourable Syr Johne Maitland of Thirlstaine Knight, Secretair to the King, his Majestie'. Also quite possibly by Marie herself, its author praises 'his worthye stock, baith valiant, stout and wyse' ('valiant' and 'wyse', in particular, being among her favoured adjectives to describe her father and their ancestors). This poem also includes reference to their 'father deir [dear father]' lying 'neir his buriall' – meaning that we can pinpoint its composition almost to the day in spring 1586. It seems that it must have been written at some point in the short period between Sir Richard's death on 20 March and his burial, a day or so after.

John and Marie's father is also praised in similar terms in this verse as he was in poem 92, as a 'judge maist just' with an 'unspotted name', who has been 'loved' by 'prences [princes]' – an allusion, it would seem, to his long decades of service to the Crown, from back in the time of King James V. His memory will live on in his 'learned' sons, the poem continues, reflecting Sir Richard's firm commitment to the cause of the humanist educational project of the Renaissiance. He is also described as 'ane Homer auld of everlasting fame', in a grandiose acknowledgement of his poetic output – preserved, most significantly, in Marie's manuscript, the very book in which she also recorded these words, upon his death. Marie concludes this poem with the optimistic reflection that, although John 'in presoun [prison] was detained', he is once again free – and thus able to honour his father's memory, through finding favour with the King.

Poem 95, the very last poem that Marie recorded in her manuscript, is another joint elegy for her father and mother. She curses 'cruell Deith', who has taken from her with his 'scharp huik [sharp hook]' not only the 'noble lord . . . of noble bluid' and 'perle [pearl]' that was her father, but her mother, too, that 'verteous lady excellent . . . quhom [whom] of he [her father] in his lyif sik plesour tuik [such pleasure took], so joyfullie'. Touchingly, Marie writes of how her parents will be missed by 'thair bairnes, kinsfolk and the puir [poor]' and 'thair faithfull servandis [servants]', for whom they shone, reliable and true, like a lantern: 'lyk a lanterne schynit . . . suir'.

That two of these elegies – including the very final poem that Marie chose to inscribe into her manuscript – honour her mother as well as her father, and the love that endured between them for decades, is suggestive of not only the work of a family member but, specifically, a woman's pen and perspective.

It would certainly be in keeping with all that we know of Marie – who, during her father's lifetime, wrote him poems of comfort, and praised the Maitland name in verse – for her to have also now marked her parents' passing via ink and quill.

*

This, it seems, had been the moment that Marie had been waiting for to conclude her life's literary work. The poems that appear immediately before these closing eulogies all convey the message that Marie's 'buik' is very near completion – all, that is, except one.

Poem 84 is a short poem in praise of 'ane buik' – quite possibly, the almost-finished manuscript. Poem 85 is the one that compares Marie to both Sappho and Olympia Morata, and anticipates her completing 'this buik' and becoming an accomplished poet. In poem 86, Marie appeals to the goddess Diana to help her to 'end this [the manuscript] worthily', and both poems 87 and 88 are short adages on transcending hardship. All of these verses signal that they were written at a point at which Marie had very nearly finished her project. It would seem that she had originally intended poem 86 – her appeal to Diana to 'end this worthily' – to be the final substantive poem of the manuscript, followed by the brief adages of 87 and 88, and then the elegies to her parents: a 'worthy' end to her great work, centred on her father's poetry.

However, as Marie awaited her father's death, in order to complete the manuscript, it seems that she found that she still had something that she desperately needed to say – even if it meant disrupting the carefully curated ending that she had had planned out.

Her great love story with another woman had accompanied, or haunted, Marie throughout her writing of her manuscript. Even at the eleventh hour, she found that she wasn't yet done with that story. And so it is that, immediately before her parents' elegies, we encounter poem 89: a lengthy and ornately adorned love poem of six stanzas. Awkwardly and conspicuously, it is sandwiched between poems anticipating the manuscript's completion, on one side, and the concluding poems about her late parents on the other.

To all intents and purposes, Marie had already written 'the end'. It certainly doesn't seem plausible that including this late love poem had been part of the plan.

Once, in the early pages of her manuscript, among her father's poetry, Marie's love for another woman had driven her to inscribe words of devotion. Now, whatever the precise circumstances, which are lost to us, Marie was moved again: this time to write words of pain. And so Marie left us a final record of her love story, and it confronts us with a truly tragic conclusion – Marie's palpable agony, her very last gasp of devotion, preserved forever in poetry.

*

In poem 89, the ferocious confidence in their unbreakable love that underpinned Marie's writing of poem 49 is no more. Although Marie remains as devoted to their cause as ever, she is now plagued by doubt as to whether her lover still feels the same. The themes of 'constancy' and 'recompense' in love, which dominated poems 49 and 72, remain prominent. However, they are overshadowed, in this poem, by the new theme of 'absence', which takes centre stage.

As absence is the greatest fo	*As absence is the greatest foe*
That Cupids clientis dois suspect	*That Cupid's adherents do fear*
Lang out of sicht engendris so	*Long out of sight causes*
To presence the contrair effect	*The opposite effect to presence*
And as oblivion dois deject	*And as being forgotten destroys*
The building of remembrance	*The building of remembrance*
So lak of memorie neglect	*So lack of remembering ignores*
The deidis deserving recompance	*The recompense deserved by the dead*

Of absence langour dois proceid,	*From absence proceeds suffering*
And langour breidis melancolie;	*And suffering leads to melancholy*
Melancolie procuiris the deid	*Melancholy brings about death*
By sindrie kyndis of meladie.	*Through diverse types of diseases*
Thus may I gatther easalie	*Thus may I gather easily*
That absence is ane homeceid	*That absence is a killer*
To martyre men maist cruellie	*That slays people most cruelly*
Except thair be found out remeid	*Except there be found a remedy*

(stanzas 1 and 2)

Absence is the 'greatest foe' feared by adherents of Cupid, Marie declares, in the opening lines. Immediately, it is clear that we are dealing with lovers ('Cupids clientis') and, straight away, we are transported back to poem 49 – but oh, how things have changed. In poem 49, the enemies that Marie identified were 'nature' (their female sex), 'Hymen' (the institution of marriage) and 'fortune' (fate); now, their greatest enemy is 'absence'. Being 'lang out of sicht' has the opposite effect to being in one another's presence, Marie expounds, just as lack of remembrance harms the dead.

Like poem 49, this first stanza begins with an eight-syllable 'As' clause: 'As Phoebeus in his spheris hicht'; 'As absence is the greatest fo'. It is also set up in the same way: 'As this . . . ,' says Marie, in the first line, 'so that . . . ', she goes on to explain. Marie must have had her earlier poem 49 in mind, as she inscribed the same ornamental 'A' at the start of the first word of this poem and set up the same opening gambit. Her emotional state when writing it, however, could hardly have been more different.

The popular notion that absence makes the heart grow fonder would not have resonated with Marie in the slightest. Absence leads to suffering, she continues here, which leads to melancholy, which leads to death.* Marie's painful first-hand experience is palpable as she writes how she understands all too well that absence is a killer: a condition that slays people most cruelly, unless they can find a remedy.

Now thocht the causer of thir thre,	*Now though the cause of those three,*
Langour melancolie, and deid,	*Suffering, melancholy and death,*
This present tyme dois threattin me	*Presently threatens to*
To pour thir plages on my heid	*Pour those plagues upon my head*
Laking that grace my cause to pleid	*Lacking the grace, my cause to plead*
At Bewteis bar to seek refuge	*At Beauty's bar to seek refuge*
Yit in your justice I confeid	*Yet in your justice I trust*
Absence my richt sall not prejudge	*Absence my right shall not prejudice*
Thocht other loveries doe alledge	*Though other lovers do make claims*
For to defend thair libertie	*In order to defend their liberty*
Sum other caussis to repledge	*Others still cause themselves*
Thame selfis from absence tyrannie	*To be removed from absence's tyranny;*
Yit into that securitie	*Yet into that security*
With thame I put na confidence	*With them I put no confidence*
Suppose in love my constancie	*Believe in love my constancy*
Deservis als great recompance	*Deserves as great recompense*
To find ane trew Penelope	*To find a true Penelope*
Quhair other sum hes wrocht in vaine,	*Where others have sought in vain;*
Yit I belief to find you sa	*Yet I believe to find you so*
And constanter for to remaine	*And yet more constant to remain*

* Note that 'langour' had a much stronger, and unequivocally negative, meaning in historical Scots. See: https://dsl.ac.uk/entry/dost/langoure

In easing thus your loveris paine	*In easing thus your lover's pain*
As scho was to be registrat;	*As she was to be registered;*
And sua thocht absence me disdaine	*And so though absence scorns me*
I shall induire the last combat	*I shall endure the last combat*

(stanzas 3, 4 and 5)

The centrepiece of the poem is an extended court metaphor, which could not be more reflective of Marie Maitland's private and public lives, in its combination of complex legalistic diction and classical allusion, in order to exalt her love for a woman. The daughter of a well-respected judge, Marie was both a legally well-versed and litigious woman, steeped in the language of the courtroom, and a woman of the European Renaissance, steeped in the world of the classics. Her last poetic plea to her female lover embodies her unique life and learning.

In this poem, for example, the word 'repledge', is a historical Scots legal term meaning 'to withdraw (a person) from (fra, furth of, out of) the jurisdiction of another court to one's own, on giving surety that justice will there be done'.[1] Marie deploys it here, in her imagined court of love, in a line that reads, literally, 'Some others cause the repledging (removal) of themselves from absence's tyrannie'. In poem 49, meanwhile, Marie invoked 'leirned pallas' – the goddess of wisdom, Athena Pallas. In poem 69, written in celebration of Marie, 'Dame Beawtie bricht' was conjured alongside 'Dame Chastitie', and a host of other female deities. In poem 86, Marie appealed to 'Diana, ladye bricht' to help her finish the manuscript. Marie's invocation of the court of Venus – 'Bewteis bar' – in this late poem rounds off the connecting thread of goddesses that runs through so many of the female-authored poems of the manuscript.

But Marie lacks the grace, she says with false modesty, to plead her cause before Beauty's court. Instead, her only recourse is to appeal directly to the justice of her lover, whom she here addresses directly. Before 'your justice', Marie says, I trust that absence will not be held against me ('absence my richt sall not prejudge').

Marie contrasts herself favourably with the inconstancy of other lovers, who give up when faced with adversity. She has no affinity with these other lovers and 'no confidence' in their misguided attempts to find release. Instead, just as when she wrote poem 49, Marie remains unwaveringly committed to 'constancie' in love, which she still believes deserves 'great recompense'. In another unmissable echo of that earlier poem, Marie spells out exactly what she believes her constancy in love merits: to find a 'true Peneleope, where others have sought in vain'. In poem 49, Marie had cited Penelope's famed devotion to Odysseus as a shining exemplar of faithful marital devotion, only to then exalt the love between her and the woman she wished to make her wife as deeper still: 'Nor yit Penelope . . . so luiffed ulisses in hir dayis', she wrote then.

Not only does Marie believe that she deserves *to find* her own Penelope – but, she declares in the next lines, she believes that she has *already found* her, in the woman to whom this piece, like poem 49 before it, is addressed. 'Yit I belief to find you sa [so]', Marie, again, addresses her directly.

In a brief return to the overblown confidence that so characterised poem 49, Marie states her certainty that her 'Penelope' will remain even more constant than the Penelope of legend, thus easing Marie's pain – 'your loveris pain' – as 'scho [she]' was to have been 'registrat', that is, registered or recorded in a legal setting. Here, Marie rounds off her court metaphor. Had she been able to plead her case before Beauty, it is implied, she would have been registered in the books of the court as a lover in pain, caused by her beloved's absence. As it is, Marie cannot plead her case before Beauty, but only before her Penelope – whose constancy and justice she trusts she can rely on to ease her pain. These lines also confirm that this poem, like poem 49, is unambiguously a love poem by one woman to another. It is, plainly, addressed to a woman: a Penelope. And, through one small but monumental pronoun, Marie lays bare that it is also *by* a woman. The lover who is in pain, which will be eased by the constancy of the 'Penelope', is a she – 'scho' – not a he.

The author of 'anonymous' poem 72 declared that, so loyal would she prove herself to her lover, she would never have any cause to dread her 'disdaine'. Marie uses the same word in this poem, but it has taken on a bitter edge. Although she is currently suffering the 'disdaine' of her lover's absence, Marie writes, she will, nonetheless, endure this 'last combat' and hold fast to their love. But the cracks are beginning to show. It would seem that the two women had been absent from one another for some time – how long, we may never know – and that Marie was becoming haunted by the idea that her lover, her Penelope, was perhaps no longer as committed as she once was.

The final stanza of this poem is perhaps most heartbreaking. Marie presented it as visually distinct from the preceding five stanzas of poem 89, composing it in short, simple lines, and placing it right in the centre of the page. It is also a mirror image of the final stanza of poem 49 – but a warped one.

And thocht adversitie us vex
Yit by our freindschip salbe sein
Thair is mair constancie in our sex
Than ever amang men has bein

Thocht absence be
The meladie
Tormenting me
With daylie greif

no troubill, torment, greif, or tein
nor erthlie thing sall us dissever
Sic constancie sall us mantein
In perfyte amitie for ever

(poem 49, final stanza)

Your constancie
May remedie
Gif not: I die
Without relief

(poem 89, final stanza)

Each final stanza begins by introducing a problem through an 'although [thocht]' clause – and, in each case, 'constancie' in love is presented as the solution. In poem 49, *although* the women are afflicted by adversity, their *constancy* will maintain them. In poem 89, *although* Marie is tormented by absence, her lover's *constancy* may yet save her. The parallels are clear – but, at the same time, things couldn't be more different.

In poem 49, Marie and her lover form a united front. The voice is plural and mutual, with 'us' and 'our' repeated throughout. It is also confident and declarative, with no conditionality: there *is* more constancy in our sex, such constancy *shall* us maintain. The theme of the final stanza of poem 89 is identical – the overcoming of hardship through constancy in love – but the perspective is entirely different. It is no longer Marie and her lover against the world, but Marie against her lover's absence. The voice is singular: Marie is apart from her lover, alone. Even more revealingly, the voice is also doubtful, unsure: her lover's constancy 'may' yet save her, Marie wrote, not 'shall'.

When she was writing poem 49, Marie believed in their love with all her heart and soul; that they would always be just as in love, just as committed to one another, as they each were then. Anything else was unthinkable. By the time that she came to write poem 89, however, she found herself confronted with the previously inconceivable: did her lover still feel the same? Or had she been abandoned? Although Marie still holds onto a glimmer of hope, it is clear that, despite her best efforts at her trademark stoicism, she is far from convinced that her lover *is* actually going to save her from her pain and doubt.

The last line of this poem is one of heartbreak: if you do not save me, Marie writes, I will die, without relief. It is this scenario that she seems, mentally and emotionally, to be preparing for. Not only does she give voice to the unthinkable, not only does she say the dreaded thought out loud, she gives it the final word.

After poem 89, there is nothing. Nothing to tell us whether Marie and her lover ever saw each other again, or exchanged letters or poetry, after Marie etched the word 'finis' at the end of this ode to absence. All that we have of their story is contained in the pages of Marie's manuscript. And what was meant to be the greatest love story of all time ended, it seems, in tragedy.

*

We don't know how much time might have elapsed between Marie's recording of poem 89 and the death of her parents, leading her to finalise the manuscript, once and for all. But, after she had recorded the concluding elegies, it seems that Marie turned, finally, to the very front, to add the title page.

On this page, she emblazoned her name twice, in two different decorative fonts, along with the year of completion, 1586, also recorded twice, along with two small decorative embellishments – inspired no doubt by the contents of calligraphic training manuals such as the popular *Excercitatio Alphabetica [Alphabet Practice]*.[2] Marie would certainly have had ample time, over the preceding years, to have practised and finessed her skills, such a manual open in front of her; and these were the final pages of her magnum opus, in which to showcase the results.

Marie Maitland . 1586.

Through this double stamp of authorship, Marie left no room for ambiguity as to who penned the pages that follow. Declaring her creative ownership on page one, Marie ensured that her name would be the first thing that any reader of the manuscript encountered – and twice. This title page, and the final memorialising verses at the very end, are alone preserved in a striking black ink, distinct from the brown ink of the rest of the manuscript's pages.

If this title page was, indeed, the very last page to be added, at the very end of the manuscript's journey of creation, then the last words in it that Marie wrote – and the first thing that we see today – were her own name, with her own hand.

*

Already suffering the grief of the loss of her parents, and the pain of her lover's absence, Marie must have thought that things could hardly get any worse. But, as she completed her manuscript with those final strokes of her quill in the spring of 1586, she was also marking the end of her entire life as she knew it.

Any idea of Marie marrying, or bearing children, had long since been discarded. It had been resolved many years ago that, following her father's death, she would live out her days as an independent woman. Her economic self-sufficiency had long since been provided for and her substitute heirs, her two nieces, had long since been named. Her commitment to everlasting virginity had been celebrated in poetry in private and also proclaimed to the whole of elite society in public contracts. Marie had no doubt planned where in Edinburgh she would rent a property. And yet, barely had the ink dried on the manuscript's final pages, barely had her father breathed his last, than Marie found herself married off. Her father had died in late March. Before June was out, she was wed, at her brother John's behest.

CHAPTER EIGHT

The Lord Secretary's sister

On 25 June 1586, in Edinburgh, a lengthy and complex contract of marriage was signed in front of a host of witnesses. There were three signing parties. The first party comprised the Maitland siblings, John and Marie Maitland, described in the original Scots as 'the ryt honourabill Sir Johnne Maitland . . . secretar to our soverane lord' and 'Marie Maitland his sister germane [legitimate]'. The members of the second party were Sir William Lauder of Haltoun – the very same individual who Marie had pursued for non-payment and had declared an outlaw in 1583 – and his young son, Alexander. The third party to the contract took the form of another branch of the Lauder family, namely, Sir William's brother, Gilbert Lauder of Balbardies, his spouse, Elizabeth Lauder, and their son William.

The contract stipulated that Marie and Alexander were to wed in front of witnesses in a 'halie [holy] kirk', between that day and the very next, without further delay: 'sall solempnizat and compleit the band of matremony with utheris godwilling in face of halie kirk betwix the dait heirof and the Day of nixttocum vnce forder delay'.

It was abnormal to specify that the ceremony must take place within twenty-four hours of the signing of the contract. There is a sense of tension, almost as if its negotiators wanted to ensure that it was done before anyone could change their mind. As it was, there was no delay; the marriage took place the very same day. We know this because another contract, this time between Marie and her brother, was approved by Alexander later that day, where he is described as 'now spous to the said marie'. All of this is our first hint that, even allowing for the generally businesslike nature of elite unions, the union of Marie and Alexander was particularly fraught and complex.

Of course, the fact that multiple parties were ready to sign on the dotted line in late June, agreeing to detailed terms relating to the movement of significant amounts of land, money and property, reflects weeks, perhaps months, of earlier preparations. The main terms must have been settled on at least three weeks prior, allowing for the commencement of the 'reading of the banns'. This was when the marriage was publicly announced in church on three consecutive Sundays, providing time for anyone to raise any objections. A core part of the marriage ritual, the reading of the banns was central to the community and Church's approval of any union. For the banns to start being read in early June at the latest, John Maitland must have leapt into negotiations for his sister's hand almost immediately upon becoming responsible for her, following their father's death at the end of March.

Although Marie lived a remarkably independent life for her time, she was still always, ultimately, defined in relation to a man. During all the decades of her life so far, that man had been her father, under whose auspices she had enjoyed a unique degree of personal and financial freedom. Upon his death, however, Marie found herself at the mercy of her closest male relation, in the form of brother John, who had other ideas, and promptly handed Marie over to a husband. In the space of a few months, in a game of patriarchal pass-the-parcel, she went from being Marie Maitland, *daughter* to Sir Richard Maitland of Lethington, to Marie Maitland, *sister* to the King's Secretary, to Marie Maitland, *spouse* to Alexander Lauder of Haltoun.

Only within the world of her manuscript could Marie exist, or at least pretend to exist, without male qualification. No reference to her relationship to any man follows her name, emblazoned twice and all on its own, on its title page. In its poems, too, she is just 'Marie Maitland', 'maistres marie', mistress of her own literary universe. Back in the real world, however, being just Marie Maitland, entirely on her own terms, as an unmarried, independent woman, was never an option. And her brother, at whose behest she now found herself, had decreed that she was to wed.

Testament to the fact that elite marriages are far better conceived of as a business deal between two families than as a love match between two people, the contemporary description of the contract in the records mentions neither Marie nor Alexander by name; rather it is a 'Contract of Mareage Betwix the lord Secretear, his sister, and the lairdis [lairds] of haltoun'. Marie, 'his sister', is simply one party among many, and subordinate to her brother, Lord Secretary to the King. Alexander is merely one of the 'lairds' of Haltoun involved in the arrangement. Alexander and Marie were also the last two people to sign their names on the contract, just as they were probably the last two people to find out that other people had decided that they would be getting married to one another. Only after Marie's brother, Alexander's father and the Lauders of Balbardies had agreed to the terms does Alexander sign his name – followed, last of all, by Marie.

Awkwardly flung together as a result of the machinations of others, the bride and groom would certainly have cut an odd couple. The average age of a woman of Marie's elite status upon her first marriage was around eighteen; for an elite man, it was a few years older, at around twenty-one. Alexander, in his early twenties, may have been the ideal age for a first marriage – but Marie, at this point approaching forty, was not. Alexander's bride would have been expected to be several years younger than him, not a woman nearly twice his age. And marriage between a mature woman and a much younger man was not just rare but socially outrageous. Such unions flew in the face of the main purpose of Christian marriage, in general, and elite marriage, in particular: for the wife to bear as many legitimate children as possible; the prospects of this naturally reduced the older the woman was. They also upset the whole social order: as a woman was 'subordinate' to a man, so a wife was meant to be subordinate to a husband, including in age.

On the uncommon occasions that such marriages took place, they attracted opprobrium. In 1567, for example, the Earl of Caithness wed his eldest daughter, Barbara Sinclair, to the young Earl of Sutherland, more than half her age, in a shameless attempt to enact political control of the earldom. This was lambasted at the time as, 'ane unfitt match indeid, a youth of fyftene [fifteen] mareid to a woman of threttie-two [thirty-two] yeiris!'[1]

A few decades later, another high-profile example was provided by no less than the widow of Marie's brother, who would die in 1595. Two years later, in 1597, John's wealthy widow, Marie's sister-in-law, Jean Fleming, then a woman of forty-three, married the twenty-three-year-old 5th Earl of Cassilis, raising her into the highest ranks of the titled nobility. Jean's previous marriage had been 'only' to a Lord, and she had accordingly been a Lady. Once she wed an Earl, she became the even grander Countess of Cassillis. If it's clear how Jean benefitted from the union, however, it made far less sense for the young Earl to scandalously marry a woman in her forties, considered well past child-bearing age. The Earl's main concern should have been producing legitimate heirs, and his decision to wed a woman almost twice his age provoked outrage among his kinsmen, and derision from King James VI himself, who regarded it as 'utterly irresponsible knowingly to marry a barren woman because of other attractions'.[2] The Earl and his older wife were brutally mocked at court. Caustic sonnets were penned about their union, with the King leading the charge. A near contemporary chronicle describes elite society's response to the match as follows:

> the Erll of Caissillis mareyis Dame Jeane Flemyng, wha was wyff to the last Chancellar, ane verry onmeit [inappropriate] matche, for scho [she] was past bairnis beiring [child bearing], and he was ane young man not past xxiii [23] yeiris or thairby, and his landis onairitt [uninherited]. The King and Court mokit [mocked] the same mareage, and maid sonattis in thair contempt ; and speciallie his Majesty tuik his pastyme of that sportt.[3]

Clearly, an older woman marrying a much younger man was absolutely not the done thing, and attracted the extreme social censure of elite society, with King James VI particularly intolerant of such unions. And yet, here we have Marie, a woman approaching forty, and sister to the King's Secretary, being wed to the much younger Laird of Haltoun.

What on earth was going on? Why was Marie, financially independent, and long past optimal marriageable or child-bearing age, being married off at all? And why especially was she being wed, in a rushed and urgent agreement, to Alexander Lauder of Haltoun, a young man around half her age *and* the son of the individual she had recently pursued legal action against, who would now become her father-in-law? Why was another branch of the Lauder family involved as well? What was her brother up to?

Records at the highest level, of the Parliament and Privy Council, help us to reconstruct some of the background to this unusual union – which appears to have been a Political marriage with a capital 'P'.

*

Like the Maitlands of Lethington, the Lauders of Haltoun were an ancient and important family of the Lowland elite, long enmeshed in Scottish political and court life. Their main residence was the grand fortified dwelling of Haltoun House, which had its origins in a medieval tower. Located near Ratho, a parish about eight miles west of Edinburgh, it was at Haltoun House that Bothwell slept the night before he abducted Mary, Queen of Scots. A generation later, King James VI was a frequent visitor to the Haltoun estate, where he enjoyed hunting.

In stark contrast to the apparent domestic harmony of Marie's Maitland family, however, the Lauder of Haltoun household was a very unhappy one. The head of the family, Sir William, seems by all accounts to have been a volatile and violent tyrant. The formal record preserves what must have been only the tip of the iceberg of his disturbing and abusive behaviour towards his wife, Jean, and their eldest son, Alexander. Sir William frequently acted in cahoots with his brother, Gilbert, head of another branch of the Lauder family (the same Gilbert who appears in the marriage contract).

A flashpoint occurred in 1581 when Sir William, encouraged by his brother, disinherited his own son and heir, Alexander, and instead pledged his patrimony to Gilbert and his eldest son, Sir William's nephew, also named William. And Sir William's animosity towards his own eldest son did not stop at denuding him of his rightful inheritance. Around the same time, Alexander was ambushed near the town of Inverkeithing, north of Edinburgh across the River Forth, and 'chasit and cruellie persewit [pursued] of his lyfe' by his father and his servants and accomplices. The records affectingly describe how Alexander 'pacientlie sustenit' this 'outrage and cruell and unnaturall persute . . . hoiping that his said fader sould have bene moved with tyme to the acknawlegeing of his dewetie'.[4] Unfortunately, however, for both Alexander and his mother, who sided with him, things were to get worse before they got any better.

The next year, in August 1582, Sir William and around thirty accomplices – Gilbert, and his three sons, among them – stormed Cringletie House in the Borders, where Alexander and his mother (who owned it jointly through the marriage) were staying at the time. The ambushers were highly armed, equipped with 'steilbonettis [steel armour caps], speris, lance, staffis, hagbuttis [portable guns] and pistolettis . . . and utheris wappynnis [weapons] invasive'. They also brought with them 'poulder [powder]' with the intention of 'blawin up the said place'. In what must have been a terrifying experience for Alexander and his mother, they proceeded to besiege the house, relentlessly shooting at all parts of it. The country folk who lived nearby were roused by all the commotion and rushed to try and help the poor individuals inside. Their assistance meant that Alexander managed to escape – but his mother, sadly, did not. She was repeatedly violently struck, forcibly put on horseback and transported to Haltoun House, where she was held captive. Even in their legalistic formality, the words of the original record are difficult to read: after 'lang assegeing', 'Alexander . . . eschaipit [escaped] by the cuming of the cuntre folkes to his relief'; however, 'they maist schamfully put violent handes in the said Jeane Cokburne, kaist hir on horsbak, and, efter many bla [blows], bauch [strokes] and bludy strekis gevin, they at last perforce cariit and transportit hir away to the place of Haltoun'.

Eventually, Jean must have managed to escape, as she and Alexander were able to appeal to the Privy Council for help in the face of their horrible treatment. It considered their complaints against their husband and father respectively when it met at Perth on 14 September 1583. Among the members of the Privy Council was Marie's brother John Maitland. He had been an ex officio member since 1581, as Keeper of the Privy Seal, and was then formally appointed in August 1583.

In the record of that meeting, we read how it was not unknown to the King and Council that 'William Lawder of Haltoun . . . has maist unnaturally and without onie deserving on his part' disinherited Alexander, depriving him of 'that leving whilk [which] he, of the law of God and man, sould succeid unto'. The inalienable right of the eldest son to inherit was a founding principle of elite society, and the disapproval of the Privy Council at Sir William's subversion of the natural order of things is palpable. We also learn that Jean appeared personally before the Council and, 'being sworne, declarit that she wes violentlie takin furth of the said place of Criniltie and perforce transportit to the said place of Haltoun, wharin she wes detenit aganis hir will'. The Lords of the Privy Council determined that, in the circumstances, Jean was 'to be fre and at liberty furth and fra [away from] the cumpany and societtie' of Sir William until 1 January – and also, significantly, permitted to sue for divorce during that period, a course of action that was newly possible, as a consequence of the Reformation. In practice, however, it remained rare, difficult and disapproved of, especially among the elite.

In the meantime, Sir William was ordered to pay his spouse sustenance payments equivalent to 20 shillings a day, 'under the pane of rebellioun'. That is, if he failed to comply, he would be publicly denounced as an outlaw – and not, of course, for the first time. It was just a month earlier, in August 1583, that he had been put to the horn at Marie Maitland's behest for his failure to pay money owed to her. The Privy Council now threatened him with the same, if he failed to pay his wife as instructed during this period of formal separation.

*

Unsurprisingly, given all that she had suffered, Jean jumped at the opportunity to pursue divorce, despite the scandal attached to it. By 1584, an action was in front of the relevant court in Edinburgh. However, before Jean could achieve the absolute severance that she wanted, King James VI swooped in. In a letter addressed to Edinburgh's commissary court, the King referred to the 'accions of divorsement dependand befoir you betwix the layrd of hatoun and his lady' and expressed his fear that such a divorce would 'tend to the greit dishonour, wraik [ruin] and skayth [damage] of thame bayth', as well as 'to the greit Inconvenient [trouble] of that howss [the house of Lauder of Haltoun] whilk [which] has bene in all tymes bygane [all times past] ane ancient & guide houss, ay [always] reddy to do work & our predicessouris service'.

Pertinently, the King informed the court that the unhappy couple were currently engaged with none other than John Maitland of Thirlestane, his newly appointed Secretary (as of May 1584), who, along with his friends, was committed to helping them reconcile. In the King's words: 'thay have well alliat [allied] with our traist [trustworthy] counselour and secretar Sir Johne maitland of thirlestane knycht wha has employit him selff & his friendis in reconceling of the saidis persones'. Marie's brother had a tough task ahead of him in the role of mediator: the King's letter also explains that, for all the 'greit obedience' that Secretary Maitland had found on the 'pairt of the said layrd [laird] of hatoun', he had thus far found nothing but 'greit stuburnes' on the 'pairt of the lady' (understandable, given the circumstances). That notwithstanding, the King went on, he remained hopeful that the couple could yet be encouraged to reconcile and avoid divorce, for everyone's sake. In the meantime, he instructed, the court was to refrain from progressing the action for divorce lodged by Lady Haltoun, while Secretary Maitland and other friends tried their best to reconcile them, writing: I 'discharge yow of all proceding in the saidis causis or makyng or grantyng of ony modificatioun to the said lady hatoun [. . .] whill freyndis tak sum ordour betwix thame'.

At the same time that he was tasked with preventing Jean from divorcing Sir William, John Maitland was also occupied with helping his sister Marie extract the money due to her from lands belonging to the same Sir William, which he had failed to pay her. It was in May 1584, supported by her brother's ever-increasing influence at court, that Marie was confirmed in her income – the lands in question having been removed from Sir William and granted instead to the Earl of Arran, along with express instruction to pay Marie her entitlements from them.

Secretary Maitland then turned his attention to another big Lauder problem, in the form of the unnatural disinheritance of Alexander, as the eldest son and heir. On 10 December 1585, when the Parliament met at Linlithgow, he would take a massive first step towards fixing that, too. Among the many acts it passed that day was one annulling Alexander's disinheritance, an action that has the fingerprints of John Maitland all over it.

As the original, helpfully straightforward, title reads, it was: 'Ane act annulland the infeftmentis [infeftments] maid to Gilbert Lauder of Balbardeis and his sone of the landis and leving of Haltoun', where 'to infeft' means to invest (in the sense of 'provide or endow') someone with heritable property. The act enumerates all the lands and properties that made up Alexander's considerable patrimony, which spanned the immediate Haltoun estate, as well as a whole host of other lands and properties around Edinburgh and in the Borders. It acknowledges that they had been in the possession of the 'ancient hous' of Lauder of Haltoun since 'lang befoir the said Schir William succedit thairto', and states that the debarring of Alexander from his rightful inheritance – 'the lyk whairof has nocht bene sene within this realme in na aige past', and which has been 'to the said Alexanderis utter wraik [ruin]' – cannot be allowed to stand.

As such, 'his hienes [highness] and thrie estaitis in this present parliament' declared any and all 'alienationis, venditionis [sales], chartouris, infeftmentis, preceptis and instrumentis of sesing [sasine*] whatsumevir maid by the said Schir William Lauder of Haltoun, knycht, to the said William Lauder, sone to the said Gilbert, his airis and assignais heretable, of the landis, baroneis and utheris particularlie abonespecifeit . . . to haif bene fra the begyning and to be in all tyme cuming of nane availl, force nor effect [to have been from the beginning and to be in all time coming of no value, force nor effect]'.

Alexander's disinheritance was thus overturned. Any previous pledging of his patrimony to the Lauders of Balbardies was deemed

* Sasine is a Scots legal term relating to the transfer of heritable property.

invalid, and he once again stood to inherit upon his father's death; things had, essentially, been returned to normal.

Marie's brother was deftly working his way through the Lauder of Haltoun shaped problems on his desk. However, could Sir William, or his brother, Gilbert – given their villainous track record – be trusted not to make another attempt to keep Alexander from his patrimony? On top of this, Secretary Maitland still also had the issue of divorce-hungry Jean Lauder to deal with. But then, in spring 1586, upon the death of his father, John suddenly found an extra card in his hand, in the form of an unwed sister – and he played it both immediately and effectively.

*

As the eldest son and heir, Alexander stood to inherit the lands of the ancient house of Lauder of Haltoun automatically upon his father's death – or, at least, he was set to again, following the act of Parliament annulling his previous disinheritance. However, through the mechanism of a marriage, he could be infefted in (endowed with) much of his inheritance while his father remained alive: that is, before Sir William could even think about trying to disinherit him again.

As in the case of Marie's sister's marriage to Douglas of Whittinghame younger, for example, when the couple were granted the estate of Langtoun, it was a common mechanism in marriage contracts at this time to endow a husband and wife in joint ownership (in Scots, 'in conjunct fee') of a property, in advance of the husband coming into his full inheritance. It was through this 'fast track' form of inheritance, 'in favouris of the whilk [which] mareage', that Sir William agreed to 'dewlie and sufficientlie infeft ... The saidis alexander and marie ...' – and in not just one property, but entire swathes of the ancient Lauder of Haltoun estate. Sir William retained some rights to reside in certain properties and to draw on certain income sources during his lifetime – he still had to live, after all – but he had been denuded of much of his power over Alexander through this marriage union.

The last time that we saw Jean, Alexander's mother, meanwhile, she had been doggedly pursuing divorce and stubbornly resisting the efforts of Marie's brother, on behalf of the King, to reconcile her with her husband. However, not long after Marie and Alexander's marriage (and Alexander gaining much of his inheritance), it was also recorded that he had taken 'the burding [burden] on him for Dame Jeane cokburne his mother', in his father's stead, and that Jean had agreed to drop her action for divorce, 'for grittar quyatnes in tymes cumming Betwix thame and removing of all sklander quhilk has rissin or may ryss thairanent [for greater peace in time coming between them and the removing of all slander which has arisen or may arise in relation thereto]'. While Jean may never have succeeded in formally divorcing her hated husband, following her son's marriage she did get to live her life entirely free of him. Under the terms of the separation, Jean and Alexander were to reside at one Lauder property – the manor at Bruntsfield, an area just outside the city walls of Edinburgh – while Sir William was permitted to reside at Haltoun House for the remainder of his lifetime, along with his other children. And Jean maintained her separation from her spouse even in death. In her testament, she expressed her clear wish that she be buried apart from William, and alongside her own forebears instead.*

* On 1 July 1600, Dame Jeane Cokburne, 'being seik in bodie, haill in spreit & memorie' left her soul to God and 'corps to be buriet by hir sones and freindis honorabillie in ormestoun kirk with hir foirbearis'.

So much for the Lauders of Haltoun: Alexander was secure in his patrimony, and the divorce of his parents had been avoided. But there were still the Lauders of Balbardies to deal with, who had interests in certain of the Lauder lands now being bestowed upon Alexander and Marie, and who had been heavily involved in Alexander and his mother's earlier persecution. For this marriage-based settlement to work, their consent also had to be obtained – which is to say, they had to be bought out. And so the Lauders of Balbardies were also a party to this three-pronged contract, in which 'Sir John Maitland of thirilstane knyt' agreed to 'thankfullie content [satisfy] and pay to the saidis gilbert elizabeth his spous and thair sone The sowme of aucht thowsand merkis'. That is, in return for the Balbardies surrendering any and all interest in the lands being assigned to the newlyweds, John Maitland obliged himself to pay them the handsome sum of 8,000 merks. This sum was made up of 2,500 merks in hard cash, due to them within two days of the marriage taking place, and Marie's brother granting them the enjoyment, during their lifetime, of various properties and lands of his own, worth 5,500 merks in kind.

Not only was John paying this dowry of sorts to a nefarious uncle rather than the father of the groom but he was also parting with a vast amount of his own personal wealth. Sir William may have been willing to forgo a dowry payment, and to prematurely transfer lands to his son (and Marie), in order to avoid a scandalous divorce and get the King and his Secretary off his back, but his brother, Gilbert, clearly required more persuading as to the benefits of this Maitland–Lauder union to him and his family. For his part, Secretary Maitland was obviously willing to do what needed to be done in order to close this multi-party deal. Satisfied with the price, the Balbardies were persuaded to renounce, publicly and bindingly, any interest in Alexander's lands (now jointly owned by

Marie) that any of them might ever have had, or 'may pretend to haif or clame in ony tymes cuming'. They also specifically committed to 'niver truibille the said alexander nor marie or thair airis in the peceable bruiking [enjoyment] of the saidis landis'.

Anything that Sir William may ever have promised or granted them, in relation to lands now transferred to Marie and Alexander, was absolutely null and void. Marie's brother left no room for doubt in this part of the contract. All eventualities were covered: for example, the next lines say that, if some old document should happen to turn up, purporting to testify to rights that they held, they had to take immediate action to surrender those rights in favour of Alexander and Marie: 'And gif [if] ony ryt be fund to remane in ony of thair personis thai sall mak speciall reversiounis thairof . . . In favouris of the sadis alexander and marie . . . and renew the samen [same] saoft [so often] as the saidis alexander and marie sall think expedient'. Once the marriage contract had been signed, the Lauders of Balbardies were firmly out of the picture.*

*

Through the marriage of Alexander and Marie, a persecuted eldest son was confirmed in his patrimony, a cruel father and his nefarious kin were neutralised, and a stubborn, albeit abused, wife was persuaded to drop her divorce action. By bartering away his sister's hand – an asset that had, of course, only recently become

* In the weeks and months following the signing of the 25 June 1586 contract, the parties duly drew up various charters, which were then formally confirmed, in order to implement the movement of rights to land and property that had been agreed on. One such charter received Great Seal confirmation on 9 August 1586, at Falkland Palace. The date on which this charter (which implemented elements of a contract signed in June) was confirmed is often erroneously given as the date of Marie's marriage.

available to him since his father's death – Secretary Maitland had solved, once and for all, the political headache of the Lauders that had been taking up the time of the Privy Council and Parliament, and causing concern to the King for the past years.

It was for precisely this sort of solutions-driven industriousness that John Maitland was so valued by the King, and for which he was well rewarded across his glittering political career. Just as he was arranging Marie and Alexander's marriage in spring 1586, John was, in fact, appointed Vice-Chancellor, in addition to his role as Secretary. The royal charter investing him with the office records that the King was 'induced to promote to the situation of Vice-Chancellor John Maitland of Thirlestane, Knight and Secretary of State, on account of his great judgment and experience, of his knowledge, both in the theory and practice of the laws, and of his eminent abilities as a scholar'.[5]

But if the King was happy that Marie's brother had solved the problems of the Lauders, he wasn't, it seems, about to celebrate his particular methods on this occasion. When it came to the marriages of the elite, King James was generally involved and interventionist, as monarchs often were. And this was a union involving the sister of his influential Secretary of State and Vice-Chancellor, and the eldest son and heir of another prominent Lowland ally, Sir William Lauder of Haltoun. In normal circumstances, such a wedding, involving two important elite families, both allies of the King, would have been celebrated with great fanfare, and graced by the presence of the monarch. A few years later, for example, in February 1591, the King honoured John Maitland by attending the wedding of his niece to the Laird of Lugton, riding through the snow to Thirlestane.

But these were not, of course, normal circumstances – and there is no known record of the King having been anywhere near this wedding. Nor is there any record of him having presented any sort of gift, such as a masque, as he usually would, as a token of his approval. Equally, there is no recorded criticism of it, which seems significant when we know that the King disapproved of unions involving a young man and a much older woman – and was not shy with his pen when he had something to say.

Given the absence of any record of public disapproval, it would seem that the King must have privately consented to this marriage going ahead. Secretary Maitland will certainly have made a persuasive case as to its political benefits in dealing with the many issues of the Lauders, including Jean Lauder's action for divorce, which the King was very keen to resolve and had personally intervened in. However, even if his Secretary made a good case for this course of action – which had only recently opened up to him, now that he had his unmarried sister, Marie, at his disposal – it was still a union of a much older woman, way past optimal child-bearing age, to a younger man, and so not one that the King could enthusiastically celebrate or endorse. Secretary Maitland was left to quietly get on with it, it seems, just like he ran most of the business of Court on the King's behalf. Then they could all move on. But what about Marie?

*

If it is clear what Marie's multi-party marriage contract *was* about, it also seems clear what it was *not* about. None of it was really about Marie, who simply found herself an unwed sister in the wrong place, at the wrong time – or in the right place, at the right time, from her brother's perspective.

And, given all that we know about Marie and the life that she lived up until this point, it is difficult to imagine her having been anything other than devastated at how events unfolded following the death of her parents. All the evidence, from both the formal and the poetic record, tells us that any intention for her to marry and produce heirs had long since disappeared. She was dangerously beyond optimal child-bearing age, and scandalously past the normal age for a first marriage. With no expectation of children of her own, she had gone out of her way to name nieces as her substitute heirs.

There was also no financial reason for her to marry: she was more than self-sufficient in that respect, thanks to the investment of her dowry in 1579, together with her range of other independent income sources. Even when her father had formally retired from court and public life in 1584 and technically needed Marie's support less – a point at which, if there were suddenly to have been an abnormal late-stage marriage, we might have expected to see it – there had been no whisper of a wedding. What's more, the establishing of Marie's unmarried independence all took place in the public sphere, with the consent and participation of her family and wider elite society. At the same time, in the private sphere, we know that Marie was a woman who loved other women in the image of Sappho, and who strongly identified with the virgin goddess Diana.

For years, Marie had managed to remain unwed, as if some goddess of ancient myth herself. But that time was over. She had come so close to escaping the fate she had been born to, but she had run out of luck. Marie would now take the path that all the women in her life – including her sisters and her own lover – had trodden before her. Still reeling from the grief of losing both her parents at once, Marie must have been aghast when she was informed by the King's Secretary – for it seems, in all of this, that John Maitland was acting not as a brother but as a politician – that she could stop whatever she was doing to set up her own household as he had other plans for her: she was to marry, and he had already arranged her match.

If obtaining a good spouse for an unwed sister had been her brother's aim, the young Alexander Lauder – even with his newfound infeftment – could hardly have been a less appealing prospect to Marie. As well as obtaining a live-in mother-in-law, and the father-in-law from hell – whose shameful behaviour was the talk of the court, and against whom she herself had pursued legal action just a few years ago – the Haltoun properties that Marie gained in joint ownership were creaking under the pressure of many and considerable debts.

Indeed, whether driven by her brother of his own accord or at Marie's shrewd urging, substantial parts of the marriage contract were about protecting Marie from the burdens of debts on her marital property. Infeftment in joint ownership was typically a mechanism to protect the wife, as being endowed in this way afforded her more security than 'terce', a widow's standard entitlement to a liferent of one third of her late husband's heritable estate. However, Marie's on-paper substantial gains through her marriage to Alexander seem very much to have been more about him being protected from future disinheritance than Marie being protected in the event of his death. The marriage contract provides, in some detail, that while the couple were to receive the Haltoun lands, 'speciallie anenttis [anent/regarding] all and whatsumevir annuelrenttis whairin it may appeir the said marie in lyfe rent is or may be burdenit eftir hir said spoussis deceis The whilk said contractis vnderstandis that sche salbe fre dureing hir lyfetyme'. That is, as concerned all the property given to Marie and Alexander in joint ownership, where it may appear that Marie would otherwise be burdened with their debts, Marie 'shall be free during her lifetime'.

What's more, as well as all the enumerated lands and properties (if not their debts) to be jointly held with Alexander, as extra protection, Marie was also personally assigned, among other things, the exclusive right to use and enjoy, during her lifetime, a townhouse in the centre of Edinburgh owned by Sir William but not otherwise forming part of the Haltoun estate. This was for Marie's 'grytter securitie [greater security]', in order to ensure that she would have secure possession of a home as a widow, in the event that Alexander predeceased her. Given the state of both the Lauder family and the Lauder finances, this seems a sensible move. However, as Marie's liferent to the Edinburgh townhouse did not just kick in on Alexander's death but took effect immediately, the practical effect was that Marie was provided with a residence to stay in, apart from her husband, if she wanted to, throughout the marriage. Marie had a place of her own.

The property that Marie was assigned was described in the marriage contract as 'lyand withein the burgh of edinburgh on the north syde of the streit thairof foiranenttis [opposite] the salt trone'; that is, opposite the burgh's large weighing beams ('tron') for measuring salt, which stood for centuries on the High Street, just down from St Giles.* As well as being a practical marketplace at the heart of the city, it was also a site of ceremonial significance, central to processions such as the symbolic entry of monarchs. For example, during James VI's entry to the capital in 1579, at the beginning of his adult rule, a contemporary account describes

* Today, that places Marie's townhouse across from the tellingly named 'Tron Kirk', built after her lifetime, but whose name preserves the traces of the historic beams that stood outside it in Marie's time. Marie's house must thus once have stood somewhere amid the short row of buildings facing the modern kirk, now occupied at ground level by a tourist shop selling cashmere, tartan and tweeds and a branch of the chain restaurant Bella Italia.

how part of the ceremony took place at the 'mercat place of salt, wharupon was payntit the genealogie of the Kings of Scotland, and a nomer of trumpets sounding melodioslie, and crying with loud voyce'.[6]

Had Marie remained unmarried, this is just the sort of townhouse she would likely have rented and lived in, with her own household of servants, and supported by her own money. Even upon her unexpected marriage, she still gained a liferent of such a townhouse, allowing her to live apart from Alexander, should she wish, and to cling on to some vestige of the independent life she had originally planned to live. Marie had plenty of experience in negotiating with powerful men, and this townhouse, just for her, as well as the watertight protections from Lauder debts, might be one final example of her shrewd and stoic character, even as she found herself married off by a man to a man. In any event, although Marie was gaining a husband, it did not mean that she would necessarily reside with him (and his mother) at a marital residence. While Marie might eventually have been married off, this arrangement was still nothing like the marriages of her sisters.

*

John Maitland had expended 8,000 merks of his own money to secure this marriage, but it was not out of the goodness of his own heart. As well as reaping the political rewards in the form of favour with the King, he was also intent upon recouping what costs he could from his sister. Once, he had helped to ensure Marie's financial independence as an unwed woman. Now, he wanted to claw back all the cash that he could by claiming her independent income sources for himself.

And so there is not just one but two contracts relating to Marie's union with Alexander preserved in the records: a main marriage contract, followed by a supplementary contract 'Betwix the Lord Secretar and his Sister'. At its most simple, this second contract compelled Marie to repay her brother every last penny that she could, even though she was not able to repay him the full sum of 8,000 merks that he had spent. Through it, Marie relinquished to her brother three specified income sources: her annual income of 100 merks, established in July 1580, her annual income of 100 merks, established in October 1580, and her annual income of 60 merks, established in November 1579. There is no mention of Marie's teind collection rights, as principal tackswoman of the parish of Bolton, in this contract. There is also, markedly, no mention of the income related to her dowry investment, which she may have been permitted to keep (however, it's unclear how likely this would have been, when this contract is all about her brother reclaiming as much of the 8,000 merks he had parted with as he possibly could).

As well as the three specified incomes, the contract also stated that Marie must relinquish to her brother 'all & syndry soumes of money . . . that be ony maner of Way may fall or appertene to hir by deceiss of hir said vmquhile [late] fader & vmquhile [the late] dame merioun cranstoun hir moder or athir of them . . . And all assignations maid to hir . . . by hir said vmquhile fader for ony purport'. That is, any and all sums of money she might have received from either of their late parents, as well as, specifically, 'all assignations made to her . . . by her said late father for any purport'. No further information is given about these assignations, but this reference points, tantalisingly, to Marie's father having made yet further, potentially valuable provisions for her. But whatever these other assignations might have been, her brother had snatched them away before she had the chance to enjoy them.

The contract recorded Marie's 'understanding' that, in arranging her marriage to Alexander, her brother had not only gone to 'gret trubell & cair [great trouble and care] . . . for hir furthsatt and weill [interest and wellbeing]' but that he had also incurred 'larger expensis & expensis'.* As set out in the main marriage contract, this contract similarly went on to detail that, 'for the performing and completing of the said marriage', John Maitland 'has allreddy debursit the sowme of fyve thousand & five hundreth merkis of his awin proper money' and 'maun [must] pay the sowm of Twa thousand & five hundred merkis mair to certane persouns to whom the samyn is appointit to be payit extending to the full to the sowme of aucht thousand merkis'. Although they are not named here, it is clear from the connected marriage contract that the 'certane persouns' to whom John was due to pay all this money were the Balbardies, who had been bought out. Therefore, the contract continued, the said Marie, being 'willing to satife & repait [satisfy and repay] ane part of the sadis grit sowmes [the said great sums] of money debursit & to be debursit by the said Sir jhone upoun hir . . . tochir [dowry] and mariage' but 'not able to satife for the haill [whole amount]', duly handed over to him all that she had to her name.

In the above extracts, as throughout the contract, notably, Marie appeared only in the third person. It was all written from her brother's perspective, framed around the great efforts he had gone to and the large expenses he had incurred, in order to secure, in his words, Marie's interest and wellbeing. Marie, meanwhile, was recorded only as passively 'understanding' or acknowledging

* It seems to me that the double mention of 'expensis' is to be read as follows: larger expensis [the 5,500 merks in kind] & expensis [the 2,500 merks cash].

the situation, not as being grateful for his efforts, or actively supporting or consenting to them. We might contrast this with a near-contemporary contract between another elite brother and sister, Annas Campbell and her brother, Duncan, signed just months earlier, in April 1586.

Duncan had been responsible for his sister since their father's death, and had recently arranged her a marriage, for which he paid out a dowry of 4,000 merks. The contract in question served the practical purpose of Annas and her new husband obliging themselves to provide Duncan with certain lands, in return for his support of their marriage; Annas also pledged to support his own daughters' marriages, in due course. That is, it is also a contract in which a sister is repaying a brother for his money and efforts in securing her a marriage. However, this is where the similarities with the contract between Marie and her brother end. For not only is this contract written in Annas's voice, in the first person, it is also almost nauseatingly gushing about her appreciation for her brother, whom she describes as having 'sen the deceiss of umquhile my fader and mother . . . borne the burdene of me and has in all things not as ane broder but as ane loving fader to me honorablie intertenyit [since the death of my late father and mother . . . borne the burden of me and has in all things not as a brother but as a loving father honorably maintained me]'. She goes on to refer to his 'greit kyndnes' to her, in contracting her in marriage to James Campbell, and to how she has 'greit respect to the said Duncanis gude intentiounn to this my honorabill provisioun in mariage . . . And greit burdene whilk [which] he has borne of me in tyme past as alsua [also] of the sowmes of money to be pait be him by occasiounn of my mariage'.[7]

There is none of this rhetoric in the contract between Marie and her brother, which is devoid of Marie's voice at all, let alone any such affection for her brother. Marie is emotionally absent; there is (unsurprisingly) no sense of genuine gratitude for his efforts to secure her marriage to Alexander.

Marie was perfectly capable of writing in her own voice and of dealing with her own financial affairs: 'I Marie Maitland', began all the Dundas acquittances. And this contract with her brother was all about her money. Yet she does not write or even dictate it. Instead, it was drafted and framed by her brother, who played up his great efforts and the great sums he had expended, all driven, he claimed, by his 'care' for his sister. Marie's brother got his spin across, but he did not push it when it came to describing his sister's feelings on the matter. The contract recorded only that Marie 'understood' what was going on.

In his darkest days, as he had languished in captivity, powerless, Marie had written this brother tender and comforting poetry, which she recorded in the early pages of her manuscript. Later, amid the elegies of its final pages, she had recorded a poem praising his honour. And this was how he repaid her.

Marie's carefully amassed, and diligently tended, independent wealth was intended to support her, in her unwed state, following her father's death. It was not meant to be handed over to her brother, in partial repayment for an unnecessary marriage, when their father was barely cold in the grave. And yet, that is what happened.

At the end of the contract between Marie and her brother, it was confirmed that they both signed with their own hands in front of witnesses: 'bayth . . . subscryvit this present contract with thair handis'. And so Marie signed away, literally, her financial independence – and, symbolically, her life as an independent woman, with the last strokes that we know to have flowed from her quill.

But even in this tragic, final act, Marie did not get the last word. Following her signature, we see that Alexander affixed his own, approving the terms that his new wife had just agreed to.

> Sir Johne Maitland
>
> Marie Maitland
>
> I Alexander lawder feare [owner] of haltoun and now spous to the said marie Maitland Ratefeis and approveis the contract abovewrittin

Alexander is not a meaningful party to this contract; his role here is simply that of spousal rubber-stamp, 'ratifying and approving the contract above-written' – but this was a necessary technicality. Upon marriage, a woman became subsumed into her husband's legal persona, and she required his express consent for any contract she entered into to be lawful. This was the doctrine of 'coverture', a term deriving from a Latin root meaning 'to cover': a woman was, essentially, 'covered' by her husband's legal identity. And Marie was now 'covered' by Alexander. In her previous life, Marie had signed documents with her own hand; now, she could sign them only with the consent of her husband.

*

As part of the Calvinist clamp-down on pleasure that followed the Reformation, the feasting and festivities that had previously attended weddings had been banned in favour of a strict focus on the sermon and the word. However, the elites often turned a blind eye to this injunction and continued to party, the disapproval of the Church notwithstanding.

On the day of this Maitland–Lauder union, however, the kirk would have had little to worry about; no rules are likely to have been broken on that day in June. Neither the normally party-loving King nor the individuals being wed and their fractured families were in the mood for celebration. Dealt with as quickly and as efficiently as possible, it was simply a set of contracts that had to be signed, a deed that had to be done. By the end of the day on 25 June 1586, it had been.

> In presens of the lordis of counsale comperat personalie . . . Marie Maitland...and gave in this contract...and desyreit the samyn to be insyrt and registrat in the buikis of counsale.

Marie later appeared personally before the Court of Session, then housed at St Giles, to submit the contract between her and her brother for central registration. She had been here before, as an independent woman, protecting and enhancing her autonomy. On that day, though, she appeared as a wife, who had signed her freedom away. After this point, Marie does not appear in the records during her lifetime again.

This is the last firm image that we have of her, and the last location that we can securely place her. Her face might have been as stony and as grey as the looming edifice of Edinburgh's central kirk, her mood as sombre as her dark Presbyterian dress, but her head, surely, would have been held high, in dignity and strength; her demeanour as stoic as ever.

CHAPTER NINE

If not: I die, without relief

Despite the unusual circumstances of their marriage, and the undoubted lack of enthusiasm on both sides, Marie and Alexander would have understood what had to be done. Bound to lie together by decree of kirk and state, the marriage had to be consummated in order to be valid – and, however reluctantly, it was. Despite her advanced age, soon enough, Marie found herself with child. Each of her three sisters – whose marriages had taken place decades earlier – had first missed their monthly blood, then watched their bellies swell, many years ago. Since then, they had all gone through the motions of pregnancy and childbirth many times more. Marie, so knowledgeable in other ways, would have known nothing of this world herself.

Not only had Marie, our 'chaste virgin' (in the heterosexual sense, at least), never anticipated being with child, she would also have been acutely aware of the dangers that attended childbirth. Around one woman died for every forty births in this period,* with the risks only compounded the older the woman was. Marie would have known, and known of, many women and girls who had not survived childbirth; she was thus aware of the dangers of her condition. And if women in their prime childbearing years could be

* Scottish-specific figures are lacking, but we can extrapolate from comparable English data. In the 1600s, 'in London and other cities and larger towns, about one woman died for every 40 births'. We can expect similar numbers for Edinburgh and bigger Scottish towns, around the same time. Louis Schwartz, '17th-Century Childbirth: "exquisite torment and infinite grace"', *The Lancet* 377:9776 (2011): 1486–7.

so afflicted, what could it mean for someone of her own advanced age? She must have been terrified.

As Marie was left to face the consequences of the political marriage her brother had thrust upon her, John Maitland reaped the rewards of his dutiful service to the Crown. In 1586, at the time of Marie's marriage, he been appointed Vice-Chancellor, in addition to his role as Secretary. The next year, in 1587, he was elevated to the yet more prestigious post of Chancellor, heralding the years of his greatest dominance at the court of King James VI. This was a higher position than his late brother William had achieved, who was only ever Secretary at the court of Mary, Queen of Scots. Although well born, John was also the first person to be appointed to the position of Chancellor who was, at the time, neither a bishop nor a nobleman. However, three years later, in 1590, he would also be ennobled, at least in part for his role in the arrangement of another marriage, this time that between King James VI and Anna of Denmark, even accompanying the King on his voyage to Scandinavia to collect his royal bride.

When they were all safely back in Scotland, in May 1590, Anna was formally welcomed to her new country by a splendid, seven-hour long coronation ceremony in the capital. In front of the Queen, in the procession to Holyroodhouse, walked Chancellor Maitland, holding the cross, clad in red robes, and flanked by knights.[1] Later, during the ceremony, it was to none other than Marie's brother that King James VI handed the crown to be placed on the Queen's head.[2] It is as part of these same coronation festivities that John Maitland was ennobled, created 1st Lord Maitland of Thirlestane. As Chancellor, Marie's brother had gone as high as he could go politically; now, he also became the first in his family to be ennobled. The successful negotiation of political marriages –

whether of his sister or the King – was, clearly, a very good way to win royal favour.

From prison to the highest political office in the land, from laid low to created a lord, it is difficult not to admire the scale of the political comeback affected by John Maitland. But it ended up being really bad news for Marie. It had been useful for her to have a brother close to the King in the past, such as when she had benefitted from his influence as she faced off against Sir William. It was a different story altogether, however, when the same brother decided that his political needs dictated that she now had to marry her enemy's son. But Marie's brother did not go from being powerless prisoner to right-hand man to the King by always being virtuous, or by letting feelings get in the way of politics. He got to where he was because he could be relied upon to do what needed to be done – even if that meant marrying off his own sister, at the expense of that sister's own independence, lifestyle and incomes, to which she had become accustomed. Marie was not exempt from the machinations of the King's man.

*

As King James VI of Scotland was coming into his own as an adult ruler in Scotland, with Marie's brother at his side, it was finally the end of the road for the mother he had never known, in England. Mary, Queen of Scots had fled to the south back in 1568, seeking refuge with her cousin, Elizabeth I; instead, she found herself imprisoned. Now, nearly two decades later, on 5 February 1587, Mary was beheaded on the orders of the English Queen, for her implication in a plot to assassinate her.

These two female monarchs had dominated the backdrop to Marie's life. She shared a name with one of them, and aspirations with the other. Marie had hoped, like Elizabeth I, to remain boldly unmarried – and, for a long time, she had. Eventually, however, she had to follow in the footsteps of the Queen of Scots, succumbing to the fate of the vast majority of women, royal or otherwise: marriage and childbearing.

As news of Mary's shocking execution reached Marie's ears in Scotland, she may have remembered how bonfires had lit up the streets to celebrate the Queen's first wedding, in Paris, all those years ago, and the great excitement that had gripped the nation when Mary had first returned to Scotland in 1561, when Marie was just a girl. It was around the very same time that her father, Sir Richard Maitland, had gone blind, Marie would also have recalled, setting her own life on its unique path – one that she had so hoped to stay on. But that was now the past: Mary was now dead, and Marie was married. The execution of the Queen of Scots no doubt also caused Marie's thoughts to turn to her eldest brother, William. He had given his life for that Queen – and for what, at the end of the day? Her life had ended, like his, in tragic failure.

Where one life ended, though, another began. For it can't have been too long after the execution of Mary, Queen of Scots that Marie gave birth to her first child, a son, named Alexander, for his father. Marie must have felt a huge sense of relief that she had made it through the pregnancy and given birth to a healthy child – a desirable male heir, no less.

Any newly birthed little Lauder heirs were likely to have been fed by a wetnurse, not Marie herself, and brought up by servants in the Lauder nursery. But if Marie had looked forward to some respite, as she handed over her newborn, she was in for a nasty surprise. Barely had she survived the roll of the dice of birthing one child than she found herself being impregnated by Alexander again. Her unavoidable role, as a wife, was now to regularly copulate with her spouse and bring forth as many children as possible.

Evidently fertile, even in her advanced years, in 1589, Marie gave birth to a second son.* When it came to his naming, his still-living paternal grandfather, William, was passed over, as was his mighty politician uncle, Chancellor John Maitland. Instead, this second son was named Richard, surely in honour of Marie's beloved father, the grandfather he would never meet. Not, of course, that Sir Richard would ever have expected a grandchild by his daughter Marie, but things had changed, dramatically, since his death.

Alexander continued to exercise his conjugal rights and, as the 1580s gave way to the 1590s, Marie was pregnant and giving birth again. Next came a daughter, named Jean, likely for Alexander's mother. The fact that Marie was conceiving and birthing children is, unfortunately, all that can be reconstructed of these final years of her life with any certainty.

She may have lived out much of her days in her townhouse on Edinburgh's High Street, her personal right to which was protected in the marriage contract. She would also have been familiar with Bruntsfield Manor, where Alexander and his mother resided, and where Marie is likely to have gone into confinement ahead of giving birth.

Although without her own independent income, Marie would have lived a comfortable life as the wife of Alexander. She jointly owned with him various lands and properties (whose debts she had been protected from), and had various places to reside. As a woman of the social elite, she would have been attended by a

---

* Richard had a portrait of himself painted when he was eighty years old, in the year 1669, which gives us a secure birth year of 1589 for Marie's second son.

gentlewoman and other servants, and adorned in expensive clothes and jewellery. She would have eaten fine foods – cooked for her, of course – and drunk fine wine, which would have come ashore at the port of Leith, imported from lands across the sea.

But despite the relative comfort of her lifestyle, it is difficult to imagine that Marie was content, emotionally, as a married woman. She was in a near constant state of pregnancy or recovery, following requisite intercourse with a male spouse who seems to have cared little for her (a feeling that was no doubt mutual). She would not have wanted for somewhere to reside, or servants to attend her, but no amount of material wealth could have made her as fulfilled as she might otherwise have been – and nor could it protect her from the perils of pregnancy and childbirth.

If Marie continued to write poetry after her marriage, there is no known trace of it. If she ever saw or spoke to her lover again, there is no known record of it. If she wrote any letters which survive, they are yet to be discovered.

*

While Marie had continued to produce offspring, John Maitland had continued on the up. However, as the 1590s progressed, Chancellor Maitland came to face challenges at court. His success made him the target of many jealous and powerful nobles, and he did not get on well with Queen Anna. Alongside his political troubles, he also became physically unwell, languishing under some sort of fever. Eventually, he retired to Lauder, where he had built himself a fine seat in the form of Thirlestane Castle. The King wrote with his best wishes, even sending him the royal physician, a German by the name of Dr Martin Schöner, who had attended both James and Anna for years.

But it was to no avail. On 3 October 1595, at the age of around fifty-one, John Maitland died at Thirlestane. He must have known that the end was near as, around a month earlier on 31 August, being 'seik in body' but 'haill in mynd & spreit [spirit]', he had made his last will and testament. In it, he instructed that his body be buried beside his late father in the Maitland family aisle at St Mary's kirk in Haddington. He was later honoured with a magnificent tomb there, and King James himself composed an epitaph in his memory.

John stressed in his testament how he had been a faithful and true servant of his sovereign lord, along with his belief that the King would be 'ane cairfull protectour and defender' of his 'wyf and twa bairnes' and 'nawayis [in no way] suffer thame to be wrangit'. He also commended the wellbeing of his spouse and children unto a series of noblemen whom he trusted would also maintain and defend them. He appointed his wife, Dame Jean Fleming (the same Jean who would go on to scandalously marry the young Earl of Cassilis), as his only executor, and as tutor to their children, John and Anna. In the case of his widow's premature death, the role of tutor was to be fulfilled by his nephew, Sir Richard Cockburn of Clerkington. A son of the Maitland sister Helen and her spouse, John Cockburn of Clerkington, Richard was now Secretary of State, having succeeded his Uncle John in that role. The signing of John's testament was witnessed by, among others, the royal physician, Dr Schöner.

There is no reference in John's testament to Marie, just as there is no reference to any of his other three sisters. They all had their own husbands (i.e. male guardians), and he had no need to mention or provide for any of them. Once Marie had been handed over to Alexander in 1586, he didn't need to give her a further thought.

If Marie attended John's burial, in the same place that she had buried her parents nearly a decade earlier – just before that self-same brother had turned her life upside down – it was surely only out of a sense of propriety, as opposed to affection. The brother she'd once thought so fondly of had changed the course of her life, taking away her freedom.

*

In any event, Marie did not outlive her brother by long. Less than a year later, in June 1596, she also breathed her last. The day of her death was not recorded, nor was the cause. However, after surviving their childbearing years, following their marriage at 'normal' ages, Marie's mother and sisters all lived into old age. They got to watch their own children grow into adults and lived to meet their grandchildren.

Marie, by contrast, died in her late forties, and left behind four children under the age of ten, whom she would never see grow up. The youngest child she might not have meaningfully met at all. For it seems most likely that Marie died giving birth to her final surviving child, a daughter named Helen, perhaps for Marie's sister.

Although Marie had found herself able to conceive upon her marriage, her body was nonetheless well past its prime for childbearing, with the risks increasing with each passing year. Since her marriage in the summer of 1586, she had been in a relentless cycle of pregnancy and childbirth, with no meaningful respite. Alexander must have been born around 1587 or 1588, as we know that Richard was born in 1589. And, although we don't know their exact years of birth, Jean and Helen must have been born sometime between 1590 and Marie's death in June 1596. As well as the four children we know of, Marie is also likely to have suffered who knows how many miscarriages and stillbirths, unrecorded but awfully, painfully real.

If, as it seems, Marie found herself taking to the birthing bed once again, in June 1596, she would have been both exhausted and vulnerable. This time, it seems, her hardworking body and womb were unable to take any more; while young Helen lived, Marie was gone, not long after her birth.

Death through childbirth was, tragically, far more common in Marie's time than it is in Scotland today. It was a harsh reality of life, against which being of the social elite offered no protection. When reference to Marie's death formally appears in the sources, some years later, the cause was not deemed worthy of mention.

Marie did not leave behind a testament written with her own hand. As well as denying us one last meaningful record of her, this is a further sad sign that her death was unexpected and unplanned for: the tragic result of a traumatic birth as opposed to, say, a prolonged illness, in which case Marie would have had time to set her affairs in order. For a woman so fluent in the language of the law, so conscious of the importance of legally binding documents, it would certainly have been out of character for Marie, even while under the 'coverture' of her husband, not to have written a will, on her own terms, without good reason.

*

Following Marie's death, at some point in the month of June, in the year 1596, she would have been buried within a few days, according to Protestant rites – but there is no record of where that might have been.

Had Marie had the opportunity to write a will, it feels likely, given the unique circumstances that defined her life, that she would have expressed her wish to be buried in the Maitland family aisle at St Mary's kirk in Haddington, by Lethington Castle, alongside her parents and Maitland kin, rather than anywhere connected with her family by marriage. Indeed, had Marie remained unmarried, she would almost certainly have been laid to rest there, as she would never have left the sphere of her family of birth. As it is, however, she was married off by her brother, and she didn't leave a will. There is also no known record of her having been buried there.

Marie could well have been buried somewhere in Edinburgh. After her marriage, it seems likely that she would have opted to spend as much time as she could at her townhouse in the city. Certainly, it's difficult to imagine Marie living together in domestic harmony with Alexander and his mother; Marie and Alexander are more likely to have crossed paths only for the purposes of copulation, otherwise living largely separate lives. When it was time for her confinement, however, Marie probably retreated to Bruntsfield Manor, the home of her husband and mother-in-law, outwith the walls of the noisy and disease-ridden city, for her own wellbeing and comfort, as well as to give birth to a Lauder heir in an appropriate setting. As a resident of Edinburgh, who most likely died in the capital, or just on its outskirts, at Bruntsfield, Marie could thus have been buried at Greyfriars Kirk, which had taken over as the main resting place for distinguished inhabitants of Edinburgh in the mid-1560s, replacing the burial yard to the south of St Giles, which had reached concerning levels of over-capacity. However, any precise resting spot is unmarked today.

Equally, upon her late-stage marriage into the house of Lauder of Haltoun, Marie technically became a woman of the parish of Ratho, by the family's ancient and main residence of Haltoun House. It's unlikely, of course, that Marie would have spent much time at Haltoun during her lifetime, as the place where her hostile father-in-law had the right to reside, while her spouse and his mother dwelled at Bruntsfield. On paper, though, the kirkyard at Ratho would have been both Marie and Alexander's proper local burial place. When Alexander came to write his own will, much later, however, he stipulated that he was to be buried not at Ratho, by his ancestral home, but at Holyrood Abbey in Edinburgh. His testament expresses his wish for his 'bodie to be buriet amongis the faithfull in the kirk of halirudhous gif it sall pleis god', and its signing was witnessed by a Mr John Dunbar, minister at Ratho Kirk. Alexander, of course, had a difficult relationship with his father and his patrilineal ancestral house, and so may have had little desire to be buried there. Family loyalties aside, being laid to rest at Holyrood Abbey, among royals and nobles, was also simply the more prestigious resting place.

Likewise, Marie is unlikely to have borne much affection for the parish of Ratho as her final resting place. However, there is little to suggest that Alexander cared enough about his first wife to have made any such similar special arrangements for Marie.

*

As Marie died without having written her own will, various documents had to be retrospectively produced in order to deal with her affairs. It fell to Alexander, as her surviving spouse, to do this. A 'testament dative' was one registered after the person's death (in contrast to a 'testament testamentar', written by the individual during their lifetime). Normally, testaments dative were registered within weeks, or months. For example, Marie's eldest son, Alexander junior, would die in his thirties, on 29 October 1623; his widow registered his testament dative on 14 November 1623, a matter of weeks later. By the time that Alexander senior got around to dealing with his spouse Marie's death, however, she had been dead for nearly three years – and he had already remarried and had a son by his new wife.

Alexander's second wife, whom he wed swiftly after Marie's death, was Annabell Bellenden, daughter of John Bellenden of Auchnoull, Lord Justice-Clerk. In 1598, even before the formal registration of Marie's death had taken place, Annabell gave birth to their first son, Lewis.[3] It wasn't until the next year, in February 1599, that Alexander had a short administrative document, totalling about five lines, registered at Edinburgh's commissary court, which saw the young Maitland–Lauder children appointed as executors to 'umquhile [the late] Marie maitland thair mother'. Because they were minors, the record went on, their father, Alexander Lauder of Haltoun, produced the inventory of Marie's movable goods in court and attested to its veracity.

Although Marie died in June 1596, this document, from February 1599, is the first reference that we get to her passing in the records. Even then, the month and year, if not the day, of her death is mentioned only in her full testament dative, registered a few months later, on 14 July 1599. It is this record that tells us that 'umquhill [the late] Marie maitland sumtyme [former] spous to alexander lauder of haltoun . . . deceist in the moneth of Juni the yeir of god 1596'. It was registered by Alexander, as 'hir spous' and 'fader & lawfull administratour' of their children.

As well as the fact that it took Alexander several years to get round to registering these documents (more pressing, evidently, was his second marriage), the contents of his own later testament only add to the sense that he had never had, or developed, any warmth of feeling towards Marie.

Following Marie's death, as well as swiftly remarrying, Alexander pursued a successful political career. By 1621, he was both Sheriff Principal for Edinburgh and Member of Parliament for 'Edinburghshire', as it was then termed. He died on 14 November 1627, likely in his sixties. In his testament, drawn up in his very final days – he signed it on 10 November – he referred to Annabell as his 'onlie beloved spous annabell ballendeine'. Although terms such as 'beloved' were formulaic, they were by no means a requirement. Their inclusion, or lack of, was an active choice, which can be taken as reflective, or not, of genuine affection.[4] In this case, the use of 'beloved' to refer to Annabell is compounded by the word 'onlie'. Alexander had been married twice, but he seems to have been at pains, in his final words, to convey that Annabell was his 'only beloved' spouse. There is no mention of Marie, who is, at best, only gracelessly implied.

*

Marie's sister Isobel, by contrast, seems to have been genuinely cherished by her husband, James Heriot of Trabroun, just as Alexander seems to have been genuinely fond of his second wife, Annabell.

James undertook to write his testament in 1612, in respect of, in his words, his 'great aige'. He in fact lived another six years, but died on 4 June 1618. In his testament, he refers to Isobel repeatedly as his 'wellbelovit spous'. He also nominated Isobel as his sole executor, entrusting her fully with the administration of his estate, and leaving all that he had 'to be usit [used] at hir discretion'. He also went out of his way to praise her in gushing terms, writing that: 'scho [she] has bene to me ane honest verteous godlie guid wyf and helper, and brocht up hir thrie dochters in vertew and knawledge of gods word'. None of this was required, and so it can all be read as a reflection of his sincere love and appreciation for his beloved spouse. Unlike Marie's, Isobel's marriage seems to have been a happy and healthy one by early modern standards.

Isobel's husband's testament also included his request that his body be 'honorlie buriet in the buriall place of my father at hadington kirk and the south eist syd'. The Heriots of Trabroun were of East Lothian, like the Maitlands, and so had the same local church in Haddington. Isobel herself would live until 1621. In her own testament, she requested that her body be buried alongside that of her late husband. Isobel's specific bequests, meanwhile, included 600 merks left to her servant, Elizabeth Douglas, 'as reward recompence to hir of hir guid thankfull & dewtifull service' to both her and her late husband over many years, and 'for hir furtherance to ane honest and competent mariage'. She also left 'all my Frenche buikis' to her nephew, John (the son of her late brother John) and 'all uther my buikis' to her grandson William.

This provides us precious insight into Isobel's personality, and into who and what mattered to her. She loved her husband, whom she wanted to be buried alongside. A generous and fair woman, Marie's older sister left a substantial sum to her servant, in reward for her loyal service and so that she might marry well. A woman who loved reading, including in French, she had a whole library of books, and strong relationships with younger male relatives, two of whom she singled out to receive specific volumes.

If we had a will in Marie's own hand, we would know so much more about her: we would likely learn of things like particular items of clothing and jewellery, and which books she had in her library. We'd have a sense of which of her possessions, and which people, meant most to her, based on who she left things to. We'd also likely know where she wished to be buried. As it is, we are left with pretty much only her bank statements, pulled together after her death as an administrative necessity. Essentially an inventory, the purpose of the testament dative was to enumerate Marie's goods and finances upon her death in order to ensure that any debts were paid, and her remaining wealth fairly distributed. As well as the month and year of her death, and the names of her children, we learn from her testament dative, that upon her death, Marie owned, together with her spouse, eight oxen, worth £10 each; five cows with calves, worth £8 each; 40 sheep, at 26 shillings and 8 pence a piece; 20 lambs, at 13 shillings each; 8 sown bolls of barley, estimated to yield four times that at harvest, worth thus £320 overall; and 30 sown bolls of oats, estimated to yield three times that at harvest, worth thus £600 overall. There was also farming equipment and domestic utensils, along with 'the abuilzementis [clothes] & ornamentis [jewellery] of hir bodie', valued at £133 6 shillings and 8 pence, but of which no further details are given. At the same time, Marie and her spouse, at the time of her death, owed £100 to John Fairlie burgess of Edinburgh, in interest on a loan, and £25 to Robert Livingston, baxter (baker). We know all this practical detail, yet of Marie's emotional landscape – of who and what were actually important to her – we have nothing.

We, today, might not know exactly when, where or how Marie died, or where she was buried, but those she left behind, those who knew and loved her, would have. If not particularly mourned by her spouse, Alexander, she would have been by her sisters and her grown-up nieces – especially those who, in her earlier life, she had named as her substitute heirs and was close to. She may also have been missed by her nephews, and by those of her children old enough to have grasped the sad news that their father, or their nursemaid, would have had to explain to them.

Marie would have been mourned, too, and perhaps most sincerely, by the women who had known her best and loved her most. By those who had cherished her secrets – her manuscript, her sapphic love – while she'd still had them to keep safe, those who had celebrated her in poetry as a real-world Diana, a Scottish Sappho, and who would always remember Marie the way she most wanted to be, in her unique and independent prime.

If she herself remained alive, the woman who was once Marie's lover might have clasped her hand to her heart, even shed a tear, when she found the privacy to do so, as news of Marie's premature death filtered through the channels of elite society to her ears – as it all came rushing back to her.

We know that, if they survived the perils of their childbearing years, the women of Marie's family tended to live long and rich lives. Marie's mother was likely in her eighties when she died. Although born before Marie, her eldest sister, Elizabeth, who wed in 1555, was still alive in August 1608 – when she was referred to in a charter – and Isobel wouldn't die until 24 December 1621, which we know from her testament.

Marie should also still have been alive, well into the 1600s. She should have lived long past her forties – maybe even reached the age of ninety, like her father. She should have lived to see the death of England's great 'Virgin Queen' in 1603, and to witness the son of Mary, Queen of Scots, James VI of Scotland, also accede the throne of England as James I, in Elizabeth's stead. She should have outlived King James VI and I, who died in 1625, having ruled both kingdoms for two decades and more.

Marie should have written yet more poetry, left yet more records, made even more of a mark than she did. But she perished before the sixteenth century was out, leaving us only the poems preserved in her one known manuscript.

When Marie had written 'finis' underneath poem 49, which she had inscribed within its pages all those years ago, she had been certain that nothing but death could ever divorce her and her beloved, that their unwavering constancy would prove the truth of their devotion to one another, forever. 'Nocht but deid sall us divorce [nothing but death shall divorce us],' she wrote. Later, when Marie would have cause to question the woman's continued love for her, and to doubt the survival of their bond, she wrote in her poem 89 that her lover might yet provide her with salvation. 'Gif [if] not,' Marie concluded, 'I die, without relief.'

*

When Marie breathed her last, in the year 1596, we don't know whether she had received any reassurance, so desperately craved, of her Penelope's enduring loyalty – or whether she was left to die, without relief.

But we do know that, during her years on this earth, Marie experienced real and deep love, for another woman. And that, for a while, at least, she had been deeply loved by her, too.

Afterword

Only me and a woman called Sappho

Marie Maitland lived an astounding life as a woman in the Scottish 1500s.

At a time when most women, including her own three sisters, had no choice but to tread the path of wife and mother as soon as they came of age, Marie lived the majority of her life on her own terms, as a meaningfully independent woman. First stepping into the role of secretary to her blind father, by chance, in her teens, she remained unwed for decades. In her relative freedom, she embraced an enhanced education, developing rich calligraphic and literary skills, and she exerted great social, legal and financial agency, as she increased, protected and bequeathed her substantial wealth.

In 1579, in full view of elite society, Marie proclaimed her commitment to everlasting virginity, and invested what should have been her dowry in an interest-earning loan. Proudly and publicly, she eschewed the financial security of marriage, instead engaging in cash and property networks with powerful landed men from across the country.

Not a woman you would want to cross, in 1583, Marie did not hesitate to have Sir William Lauder of Haltoun, a ruthless man who owned vast swathes of the lands around Edinburgh, declared an outlaw for his failure to make payments due to her. He ended up losing the lands in question, while Marie got her money back. At the same time, she was drafting and signing her own acquittances, in a combination of 'male' secretary hand and italic hand, to confirm when she had been duly paid what was owed to her.

Aware of her own good fortune in getting to sidestep the inevitable fate of most women, she used her status to bolster those around her as much as she could. In the absence of her own direct heirs, she named her nieces as inheritors to her wealth and she offered support to a young woman who faced the distressing prospect of an unwanted marriage, also recording her poetry for posterity.

And all of this in early post-Reformation Scotland, with its puritanical enforcement of gender norms: where women were meant to be only demure wives and mothers, not confident, independent agents, operating as if they were a match to the men around them, and as if the rules of the man's world in which they lived did not apply.

But not only was Marie a female trailblazer with financial firepower and legal know-how, scribal skill and poetic prowess, she also emerges from the past as a woman who loved other women, and as the author of among the earliest known explicitly lesbian love poetry in Europe since Sappho herself. She wrote at a time when 'sodomy' was a transgression of the highest magnitude, severely punishable by kirk and society, and conflated with witchcraft and the demonic.

Her poem 49, in particular, is a masterpiece of profound emotional force and fizzing eroticism, which still deeply moves, more than four hundred years after it was written. The feverish infatuation and sexual energy of the opening stanzas build up to Marie's staggering claims about the incomparable devotion between her and the woman that she loves. Marie roots the sanctity of their bond in a series of increasingly astonishing comparisons, and even invokes the supremacy of scripture, a central tenet of the newly reformed Scottish kirk.

At the poem's climax, Marie expresses her explicit, desperate desire to be married to her love, and her pained resentment of the man who is. In the end, Marie is forced to concede that 'friendship' is, ultimately, the only option available to them as two women. However, even this acceptance of reality is shot through with a disarming defiance, as Marie claims that only death could ever really divorce them and that they will devote themselves to their relationship with such intensity and constancy that it will prove not only the truth of their love for one another but the superiority of the female sex as a whole. It is doubly and deeply radical, celebrating not just women but women who love women. In giving powerful poetic voice to the soul-shattering love that raged between herself and another woman, centuries ago, Marie also elevated all women who love women, and all women generally, at all times and in all places.

In all of this, Marie's significance to not just Scotland's but the world's feminist and sapphic history cannot be overstated. Yet until now, Marie has been practically invisible. For more than four centuries, she has been overlooked, her momentousness unsung.

*

Marie's first-born son, Alexander, died of an illness on 29 October 1623, when he was only in his thirties. He was survived by his widow, Susanna Cunningham. They had no known children. Marie's second-eldest son, Richard, lived until 1675, having reached the age of eighty-six – nearly as impressive as his namesake grandfather – and after a successful career in politics. He married a woman named Mary Scot, with whom he had two daughters, Elizabeth and Jean. A contemporary portrait of him exists, painted in the year 1669, when he was eighty years old. He was buried at

Ratho. The lives, and deaths, of Marie's daughters, Jean and Helen, are more shadowy than those of her sons.

As to Marie's manuscript, we don't know what happened to it following her marriage in June 1586. However, it doesn't seem to have been well circulated or read by many of her contemporaries. Granted, the readership of an ink-and-quill manuscript, as opposed to that of a printed book, was generally intimate and small, restricted to the family and personal circle of the author.* Even then, Marie's manuscript exhibits next to no sign of handling or reader engagement; to this day, it remains in pristine form. It seems that it was only ever intended as a presentational manuscript, focused on the preservation of her father's (and her own) poetry, within the family – and, for several generations, it succeeded in that aim.

We know that, following Marie's death, her manuscript remained in the Maitland family through her brother John's line, into the next century, last belonging to Marie's great nephew – another John Maitland, the 1st Duke of Lauderdale.†

---

* As Priscilla Bawcutt noted on the circulation of a printed book versus that of a manuscript: 'A printed book's readership was potentially large, geographically dispersed, and mostly unknown to author or publisher. A manuscript's readership was likely to be smaller, close at hand, and more intimate. One might roughly analyse its components as the compiler; his (or her) family and friends; and later generations of the family.' ('Manuscript Miscellanies in Scotland from the Fifteenth to the Seventeenth Centuries', in *Older Scots Literature*, ed. by Sally Mapstone (Edinburgh, 2005).

† This John Maitland, the 1st Duke and 2nd Earl of Lauderdale, lived from 1616 to 1682. He was the son of the 1st Earl of Lauderdale, John Maitland, who died in 1645 (the nephew to whom Marie's sister Isobel left her 'Frenche buikis') – who was, in turn, the son of Marie's brother, 1st Lord Maitland of Thirlestane, John Maitland, who died in 1595.

In the years following the Duke's death, the manuscript appeared on a list of books for sale at an auction in London in 1692. From here, it was first purchased by influential Scottish politician and writer Andrew Fletcher of Saltoun (1655–1716), who lightly inscribed his name in the top right-hand corner of the title page.* He didn't hold on to it for too long, however.

By 1697, just over a century after Marie's death, it had found its way into the vast collections of famed English diarist and book collector Samuel Pepys (1633–1703), in whose private library – part of Magdelene College at the University of Cambridge – it remains to this day.

As was typical, when it became part of his collection, Pepys had the original cover of Marie's manuscript – now forever lost to us – removed, and its pages newly bound.† Its cover is decorated with gold-tooled adornments, including Pepys' coat of arms, and gold lettering on its spine describes the book as containing 'Maitland's Poems' (by which Pepys, of course, meant the poems of Sir Richard, not Marie, though it's pleasing to be able to read it either way).

From the outside, then, it no longer looks at all like the book that Marie would have known. The pages inside, however, would remain a lot more familiar – yet still not without their unpleasant surprises. Marie would no doubt be horrified to discover that, on the reverse of the title page with her iconic double signature, Pepys

---

* Fletcher of Saltoun is best remembered today as a vocal opponent of the Union of Parliaments of 1707. Incidentally, he was also from East Lothian, not too far from Lethington.

† The manuscript is bound in 'sprinkled' medium-brown calf leather ('sprinkled' being a type of speckled decoration).

slapped a great bookplate, almost the same size as the page itself, featuring his face. A case of a man, quite literally, imposing himself on to a woman's work.

Thus very much marked as the property of Pepys, for almost a century Marie's manuscript, newly bound and book-plated, lay quietly on the shelves of his library, its poems never seeing the light of day.

The first time that any of its poems appeared in print was in 1786, fully two centuries after Marie completed it, when Scottish antiquarian John Pinkerton travelled to Cambridge and published from it a selection of what he deemed to be its most worthy verse, under the title *Ancient Scottish Poems, never before in print. But now published from the MS. collections of Sir Richard Maitland, of Lethington, Knight, Lord Privy Seal of Scotland, and a senator of the College of Justice.*

In no way a true representation of Marie's manuscript, Pinkerton's edition contains only a selection of its poems, not its whole contents. And her poem 49 was not one that he deemed worthy of print. He wrote of his selection process that 'the Poems here given are mingled [in the manuscript itself] with a vast heap of rubbish; for the poets of these days did not know the art of throwing into the fire, which yet is the greatest art of poetry. To gratify the reader's curiosity, a regular list of all the contents . . . is added in the Appendix; so that he [sic] may himself judge of the reasons of rejection'.

In the appendix, Pinkerton tells us that Marie's poem 49 – which, he implies, should have been thrown into the fire by its author – did not make the cut because it is nothing but 'a poem of friendship from one lady to another of sufficient insipidity'.

The first time that all the poems of the manuscript appeared in print was not until 1920, more than three hundred years after Marie's death, when the Scottish Text Society published an edition entitled *The Maitland Quarto manuscript. Containing Poems by Sir Richard Maitland, Arbuthnot, And Others.*

This 1920 edition, overseen by William Craigie, is the closest to a faithful copy of Marie's manuscript that we have. Almost a facsimile, it contains the title page followed by all the poems, in the order in which they appear in the original. Different fonts are used to indicate the different scripts they were recorded in, with ornamental flourishes also included, 'to convey as distinct an idea of the appearance of the original as could readily be done in print'.

However, we still lose out on crucial clues left in the physical object of the manuscript itself. We can't discern when the paper type or ink changes, and we don't see things like scribal errors, or the copied-out line in poem 1 that contains the anagram of Marie's name.

What's more, Craigie followed Pinkerton in giving the poems titles that do not appear in the original. It is here that poem 49 is printed for the first time, but under the heading 'An Address of Friendship'. For the second – and far from the last – time, someone read the stanzas of poem 49, that most erotic and powerful poem of love, from one woman to another, and thought: 'good friends'.

And, despite literally printing the title page featuring Marie's name, twice, at the start of his edition of the manuscript, Craigie considered it too accomplished to have been the work of a woman, writing that 'it is more probable that it was written for her [Marie] by some expert penman, whose work well deserves the praise given to it'.

In 2015, the Scottish Text Society published another edition (edited by Joanna Martin) with the title *The Maitland Quarto: A new edition of Cambridge, Magdalene College, Pepys Library MS 1408* ('MS 1408' being the manuscript's reference number).

Although entertaining the idea more generously than Craigie, this latest edition also ultimately remains on the fence as to Marie's authorship of the manuscript: 'the possibility . . . cannot be ruled out', it states. Similarly, although open to the prospect that homoerotic poem 49 could be by Marie, this is caveated by the 'not impossible' alternative that it was 'composed by a male poet and ventriloquises the female voice'.

The 2015 edition also takes a very pared-back presentational approach. All the poems are presented in the same font, with no calligraphic adornments.

Once again, the copied-out line at the bottom of poem 1 is not printed. It also doesn't represent the title page with Marie's double signature. The first thing that you see when you open the real manuscript, the first thing that Marie wanted you to see, is simply not there.

*

To really engage with Marie Maitland, her life, love and poetry, clearly, you need to handle the original artefact, written with Marie's own hand, for yourself. None of the three print editions – 1786, 1920 or 2015 – get you close enough.

It is only by sitting with the original that you can discern changes in paper and ink, and linger over the repeated line of poem 1. It is also only by turning the pages of the manuscript itself that you can fully appreciate the extent of the scribal prowess on display.

So much of what is shared in this book is based on hours spent up close and personal with the manuscript that Marie created with ink and quill, that she also touched and held. But getting to see the manuscript itself is very difficult. Undigitised, the only way to lay eyes, let alone hands, on it is to visit Cambridge in person. Even then, access is tightly controlled, and at the discretion of the library. In its own words: 'The collection is carefully preserved and access is limited.'[1] You need special permission, confirmed long in advance. To obtain that permission, you need to prove that you have the right academic and research credentials and you need a letter of introduction from an appropriately respectable professional who will vouch for you.

Writing in 1830, in the introduction to a collection of Sir Richard's poems produced for the Maitland Club, its editor, Joseph Bain, reflected:

> It is unfortunate in every respect that two volumes* so precious in the regards of every lover of the early literature of his [sic] native country should be placed in a situation so difficult of access for literary purposes, as that where they have been entombed for more than a century. At the Pepysian Library, in Magdalene College, Cambridge, where the MSS. are, certain rules, imposed by the Founder, must be complied with, which render the consulting or examining the volumes, both irksome and difficult. By the politeness of the officers of this College, we believe that the task is made as agreeable as possible; still, however, the access to the MSS. is not such as an ardent admirer of the venerable Collector would require in consulting these literary treasures.

Nearly two hundred years later, nothing much has changed.

---

* Bain is referring here to the *Maitland Quarto* manuscript (Marie's manuscript) and the *Maitland Folio*, another manuscript related to Sir Richard and the Maitland family.

Marie had access to different worlds through books, which empowered her to rise above the expectations she was born subject to. She found validation and inspiration in reading of the lives of others, ancient and contemporary, mythical and real: from the poetry of Sappho and the story of Ruth and Naomi, to the writings of Olympia Morata, the myth of Diana and the tale of Achilles and Patroclus.

It is, therefore, a sad irony that her manuscript should be so inaccessible today, 'entombed' within the private library of a man.

*

> The extent of her role as transcriber [of the Maitland Quarto manuscript] is undetermined. On the assumption that the italic hand was traditionally taught to women, it is probable that Mary [sic] Maitland was responsible for transcribing the manuscript's poetry in italic as opposed to the other secretary hand in evidence. – *Oxford Dictionary of National Biography*[2]

To this day, there is no academic consensus that Marie wrote the manuscript, in its combination of secretary hand and italic, or that poem 49 (recorded in secretary hand) is genuinely a lesbian love poem with Marie, or even a woman, as its author.

In the manuscript itself, Marie's name is of course emblazoned twice on the title page. Multiple poems within its pages refer to her as its creator. One even names her as not only a poet but one in the image of Sappho.*

* Interestingly, despite Pinkerton's dubious take on poem 49, which he did not print, he did consider Marie's authorship of the manuscript as self-evident, a position rolled back on by later scholars.

To my mind, the evidence for Marie's authorship – of both the manuscript and numerous poems within its pages, including secretary hand poem 49 – has always been compelling, based even on just the manuscript alone.

But we don't have just the manuscript. We don't have to rely on its evidence in isolation. No. On top of the evidence in the text itself, we know of so many supporting details of Marie's life. We know, for example, that she remained unmarried until after her father's death – her acting as his scribe, in which role she would have acquired secretary hand, the only clear explanation for this otherwise highly unusual state of affairs. She also left behind traces of her early learning of secretary hand, scribbled in the margins – and, later, confident secretary hand records, signed off, literally, with her own hand and name: Marie Maitland.

We also know that Marie was at her father's side during his exile from Lethington and that she would have had the intimate family knowledge and genuine love and affection, plus the time and means, to pen the unattributed poems to both her father and brother. And yet the 2015 edition, for example, says of the consolatory ballad to Marie's father that it was 'possibly by Arbuthnot', a male poet, not Marie.[3] As to the verse of comfort to her brother, the same edition notes only that 'the poem has similarities of phrasing to works by Alexander Scott and Montgomerie', two other male poets.[4]

In 1579, Marie invested a dowry-sized sum of money, instead of getting married. And, as we know, poem 69 in Marie's manuscript praises her true and enduring virginity, and her vast wealth and generous bestowal of 'gold'. The editor of the 2015 edition, however, suggests that this poem 'may anticipate her forthcoming marriage on 9 August [sic] 1586 to Alexander Lauder', even while conceding that 'the poem also stresses Marie's continued commitment to virginity, which is less easy to relate to this context'.[5]

The biographical facts of Marie's decades-long role as her father's secretary, and her enthusiastic eschewal of heterosexual marriage, combine with the documentary evidence of her fluency in secretary hand in the Dundas acquittances. Add this to the evidence contained within the manuscript itself – from Marie's aforementioned twice emblazoned name on the title page, to her being compared to Sappho – and there is no need to seek or suggest any other author for the manuscript, or for its most powerful poem of lesbian love, poem 49, recorded in secretary hand script, in Marie's own hand, in her own manuscript.

And when we meaningfully accept poem 49 as a lesbian love poem, written by Marie to another woman, then our mind is open to, primed to see, the connections between that poem and poems 72 and 89 – which are both presented as sapphic poems for the first time in this book.*

It is only when we weave together the historical and the poetic threads that the full riches of Marie's extraordinary life and manuscript become clear.

*

* In his section entitled 'Poemes by Unknawin Makars', Pinkerton printed both poems 72 and 89, clearly as oblivious to their sapphic nature as he was to that of poem 49, yet finding them (unlike poem 49) at least poetically pleasing, and thus worthy of being printed. He gave them the titles 'The Faythful Luifar. A Sang' and 'Constance the Cure of Absence. A Sang' respectively. He also printed poem 69, which he gave the title 'The Visioun of Chaistetie, To Miss Marie Maitland', and poem 85, which he gave the title 'To Miss Marie Maitland'.

In 2017, my wife and I got married at Falkland Palace (a newly built Renaissance jewel during Marie's lifetime, and a favoured royal retreat of Mary, Queen of Scots).

It was a wonderful day, with a beautiful ceremony, but it is a source of enduring regret that our readings did not include any of the love poetry preserved in Marie's manuscript – poetry written by women of our country, in our historical language of state, which would have been so powerful and perfect.* But at the time of our wedding, neither of us had heard so much as a whisper of Marie Maitland, the woman whose biography I would, years later, find myself writing. As we said our vows to one another, at the beginning of the twenty-first century, we had no idea that a woman like us, who lived in the same city as us, four hundred years and more ago, had felt just the same way about another woman. In fact, it would be several more years before I first came across Marie Maitland, by chance, in 2020.

As a Scottish historian and Scots language specialist – who has always been particularly interested in the 1500s, when Scots was still the language of state – I found myself reading the *Maitland Quarto* as a significant record of historical writing in Scots from that period. I thought that, as the title of Craigie's 1920 edition told me, I would be reading '*Poems by Sir Richard Maitland, Arbuthnot, And Others*' – that is, poems by the male great and good of sixteenth-century Scotland. I was not expecting, when I opened the front page, to be confronted by the name of a woman, twice emblazoned. And I was definitely not expecting to find myself reading among its pages heart-stopping, passionate lesbian love

* Poem 72 would make for such a beautiful wedding reading, as well as some lines from poem 49 (if not the entire thing, which is sad in parts).

poetry, written by a woman more than four hundred years ago, concealed behind only the flimsiest cloak of 'anonymity'.

I could not believe that this most precious primary record of sapphic and women's history had been kept from me, and from so many others. From that day on, I made it my mission to share Marie's significance as widely as possible, and never let her name be forgotten

In February 2021, in a long-form blog for the National Library of Scotland published for LGBT+ history month, I wrote about poem 49 as a lesbian love poem in Marie's own hand, and first introduced her as our 'sixteenth-century Scottish Sappho'.[6]

Later that year, in a beautiful coincidence of timing, Scotland made history by becoming the first country in the world to embed LGBT+-inclusive education across the curriculum, following the indefatigable efforts of Jordan Daly and Liam Stevenson, co-founders and co-directors of Time for Inclusive Education.*

It was the personal and professional privilege of a lifetime to work with them on teaching materials focusing on Marie's poem 49 in its historical context, which formed part of Scotland's world-first launch of inclusive education in autumn 2021.

Together, we also commissioned an imagined portrait of Marie, to form part of those classroom resources.† There is no contemporary portrait of Marie that we know of. There are, how-

---

* Time for Inclusive Education (TIE) began life as a grassroots campaign. Following its success, it is now a charity of the same name, which delivers on inclusive education on the ground.

† The portrait was part-funded by TIE, and part-funded by the private contribution of me and my wife, Eilidh, who first suggested the idea of commissioning a portrait, and who also did not hesitate to put her hand in her pocket to support the realisation of the project. (Note, however, that the portrait is entirely copyright to me, Ashley Douglas.)

ever, surviving portraits of her brothers William and John. That being the case, we developed detailed instructions for an artist to create a portrait of Marie, basing her facial features on portraits of her brothers, and her dress on that of real contemporary female portraits. The result puts a plausible, historically rooted face to the name Marie Maitland. Symbolically, in the portrait, she holds a quill and a book. Echoing in style the lettering on a contemporary portrait of her brother John, the year that the manuscript was completed, 1586, appears alongside the invented epithet 'SCOTTIS SAPHO SAIGE'. Drawing directly on words that appear in her manuscript, it feels like a fitting title, which would have been recognised by Marie, and by those who knew and loved her best.

Over the years that followed, I continued to share the significance of Marie's poem 49 to as wide an audience as possible, while simultaneously embarking on further research into both her manuscript and her wider life.

When I first went looking for more information about Marie Maitland, having stumbled upon her manuscript and poem 49, there wasn't much to be found, beyond a brief entry in the *Oxford Dictionary of National Biography*.* But I wanted to know much more about Marie – indeed, I wanted to find out everything that I could about the astounding woman who, it was clear to me, had written poem 49. And, as it transpired, there were more records waiting to be discovered than I could possibly have hoped for.

---

* In this *Oxford DNB* entry, published in 2004, Marie is among other things incorrectly named as the mother of the poet George Lauder, who was born in 1603, several years after Marie's death, and who was actually a son of Marie's husband, Alexander, by his second wife. Marie's date of marriage, 25 June, is given as 9 August. (Accessed 17 November 2025: https://www.oxforddnb.com/view/10.1093/ref:odnb/9780198614128.001.0001/odnb-9780198614128-e-68146)

Many days spent in libraries and archives, two intense research trips to Pepys Library, in Cambridge, and countless hours of writing later, the result is the biography you are holding today, published in 2026, whose front cover features a detail of the imagined portrait, first shared with the world at the launch of inclusive education in 2021.

*

> 'As far as I knew, there was only me and a woman called Sappho.' – Judith Butler

It is true that, comparatively speaking, the histories of women who loved other women have simply gone unrecorded. This is the sad but inevitable consequence of the inequalities and oppressions of the past, which persist today. Put simply, you cannot deny women literacy and equal opportunity to write, and then be surprised if they write fewer books than men. You cannot vilify and criminalise people who love those of the same gender, and then wonder that there are far fewer records of such love than that of the heterosexual variety. The archive is not neutral.

However, this is only part of the picture. Increasingly, it is becoming apparent that far more records, in fact, survive than we have been led to believe – but that they have not been sought out or shared. That the same forces that conspired against many records being created in the first place now conspire to keep those that we do have suppressed, to keep them, and the stories they tell, from the people who need to hear them most.

At its most extreme, this takes the form of destroying records: Anne Lister's iconic diaries were, after all, very nearly burned. Who knows what other records might have been obliterated, before we even had the chance to find them.

Often, though, it takes the form of simply ignoring records, where they do exist, or explaining their contents away, when they become known of. The example of Marie Maitland lays this bare.

A woman of the social elite, Marie's story played out at the upper echelons of Scottish society, and alongside some of the best-known, best-researched and most written about people and events of Scottish history: from Mary, Queen of Scots and Secretary Lethington to James VI and Chancellor Maitland, and from the Scottish Reformation and the Ruthven Raid to the marriage of James VI and Anna of Denmark.

Marie's life is attested to in some of the key sources for Scotland's past – in places like the Register of Deeds of the Court of Session and the Register of the Privy Seal. Held at the public institutions of National Records of Scotland and the National Library of Scotland, these historical sources are far more accessible than the manuscript. Among scholars, they are well-known, and often referenced and consulted.

Those records bearing Marie Maitland's name have long been there in plain sight. Yet I am the first to have gone looking for them, to have specifically sought them out in order to tell her story.

And if Marie's story – that of the socially elite sister of Secretary Lethington and Chancellor Maitland – can have gone untold all this time, who knows how many more records of women's lives, and sapphic women's lives, are out there, just waiting to be discovered and shared?

In her own context, Marie Maitland is a powerful demonstration that strong, independent-minded women, and women who love women, have always existed, even – perhaps especially – in difficult and dangerous times. In the four centuries and more since her death, however, the treatment of Marie's story is emblematic of how such histories, even where we have the records of them, are all too often undermined.

We can lament and write into the gaps in recorded history, which absolutely exist, but we also still have work to do to squeeze all that we can from what is actually there: like the story of Marie Maitland.

*

Much of history is inaccessible to the layperson. The further back you go, the more difficult engagement with the primary records becomes, and the more specialist training is required. To read Marie's manuscript, and the historical documents relating to her, for example, you need both the palaeographical skills to read (the now obsolete) secretary hand script, and the language skills to read historical Scots, along with sufficient knowledge of the period to allow you to assess the deciphered contents. You also, of course, need to know where, and how, to go looking for the records in the first place.

Historians wield great power in gatekeeping access to the recorded past, in deciding which histories deserve to be told, and how. And the decision to tell, or not tell, certain histories is not just an academic concern but has real social consequence. A direct line connects the persecution of 'sodomites' in Marie's time, and Section 28 and its prohibition of the 'promotion of homosexuality' in my own.

In 1570, when Marie was in her early twenties, John Swan and John Litster were found guilty of the 'crime' of sodomy and sentenced to be strangled and burned at the stake at Edinburgh's Castle Hill.

In 1625, not long after Marie's death, two women named Elspeth Faulds and Margaret Armour, of the parish of Eaglesham, were found guilty by the Glasgow Presbytery (the kirk being responsible for enforcing moral discipline) of the scandalous behaviour of 'sodomy'. Publicly shamed, they were also prohibited from one another's company under pain of excommunication; that is, complete social ostracisation, which was a serious penalty at the time, when the kirk was the centre of life and society.*

Just five years later, in 1630, Michael Erksine was accused of engaging in both sodomy and sorcery. Found guilty of both charges, he was burned at the stake.†

Fast forward a few centuries and, in 1921, a Glasgow MP proposed an amendment to the law to formally criminalise female 'homosexuality' by making 'any act of gross indecency between female persons . . . a misdemeanor and punishable in the same manner as any such act committed by male persons'. For context, just the year before, in 1920, the Craigie edition of Marie's manuscript was published, in which poem 49 was dismissed as an 'Address of Friendship'.

During the debate on the amendment, one MP argued that there were only three ways to deal with women such as me, my wife or Marie:

---

* Between the love poetry preserved in Marie's manuscript, completed in 1586, and the surviving conviction for 'female sodomy' in 1625, it is in the early modern period – so hostile to women, let alone women who loved women – that we find our first explicit documentary evidence for women who love women in Scotland: one defiant, in the voice of the women themselves, one condemnatory, in the voice of the kirk.

† Witchcraft was a statutory crime in Scotland from 1563, when the Witchcraft Act was enacted, to 1736.

> The first is the death sentence. That has been tried in old times, and, though drastic, it does do what is required – that is, stamp them out. The second is to look upon them frankly as lunatics, and lock them up for the rest of their lives. That is a very satisfactory way also. It gets rid of them. The third way is to leave them entirely alone, not notice them, not advertise them.[7]

Ultimately, the amendment was not agreed to, and they went with the latter approach: of simply not advertising our existence.* And, eventually, that third option was expressly written into law.

An anti-gay censorship clause was still in force while I was at primary school. The very idea of some people being gay was still something to 'protect' children from. The long shadow cast by Section 28 also defined my high-school years in the 2000s. LGBT+ people, past or present, did not meaningfully appear in any lesson. It was as if people like me (not that I knew myself as such at the time) didn't exist and never had – and, by implication, shouldn't exist at all.

I later studied Scottish History at the University of St Andrews, Scotland's oldest university (pleasingly, the same university attended by Marie's father and brothers, if not her). We studied the reign of Mary, Queen of Scots inside out, including her famed Secretary Lethington – but there was no mention of William Maitland's remarkable sister, Marie. The 1603 Union of Crowns and the

* The amendment was also passed to the House of Lords, where the debate was opened by the Earl of Malmesbury as follows: 'My Lords, I am extremely sorry to raise a discussion upon what must be, to all of us, a most disgusting and polluting subject.' See: https://api.parliament.uk/historic-hansard/lords/1921/aug/15/commons-amendment-2

1707 Union of Parliaments also loomed large on the curriculum. We studied each in great political, religious and economic detail. But there was no hint that both of the monarchs associated with those momentous events, King James VI & I and Queen Anne respectively, were also significant figures of LGBT+ history, or of any other such aspect of Scottish history. Just like at school, it was as if no such thing existed.

When inclusive education was officially launched in Scotland in 2021, I said: 'These resources will be transformational for Scotland's LGBT+ bairns. They definitely would have been for me.'

I really meant that, and I still do.

These days, I have learned to love myself, as a gay woman. But it took me such a long and painful time to get here. Learning about someone like Marie Maitland during those tender, vulnerable years at school would have made that process so much easier.

It's too late for me now, but it makes me so proud and happy that children in Scottish state schools today are growing up with an education that is changing lives for the better, even saving them – and that their learning about the story of Marie Maitland is part of that.

We all need and deserve to see ourselves reflected back in the world around us, in what we are taught at school, and in the histories that we are told: to feel valid, included and worthy. We need mirrors, or we cannot see ourselves. And we need windows into other people's lives, lives that are different to ours, so that we can better understand and empathise with each other.

*

It should never have taken a part-time historian with a day job, who also happens to be a gay woman, stumbling upon Marie's poetry for its significance to be excitedly shouted about from the rooftops. It should not fall to us ourselves to seek out and meaningfully tell our own stories, because others have failed or refused to do so. Nonetheless, it is an honour, and hugely exciting, to be the person reconstructing and sharing Marie Maitland's amazing story.

After centuries of neglect, Marie is now taught about in Scottish state schools. She has been spoken about in the chamber of the modern Scottish Parliament and in the Great Hall of Holyrood Palace, and her imagined portrait hangs in the Scottish National Portrait Gallery.*

This book will, I hope, spark yet more celebration. I look forward to Marie having a statue – like Sappho in Lesbos and Anne Lister in Halifax – as well as a square in Edinburgh's Makars Court, proclaiming her name along with a line from her verse.†

Marie's home of Lethington Castle still stands, but it is no longer owned by the Maitland family and has long since been renamed 'Lennoxlove'. I look forward to the groups of guided tours, which visit during the summer months, learning about Marie while walking through the same halls that she once did.

Pepys Library, meanwhile, is home to a manuscript containing among the earliest known lesbian love poetry since Sappho, but

---

* While her brother William features on the processional frieze of Scottish history that runs around the sides of the Scottish National Portrait Gallery's stunning great hall. Identified as 'Lethington', he stands out in his red costume against the textured gold backdrop, turned, like Bothwell and Rizzio, towards Mary, Queen of Scots. Only 155 figures were chosen to embody Scotland's entire past and Marie's eldest brother was one of the men (they are overwhelmingly men) who made the cut.

† Makars Court is an evolving national literary monument in the centre of Edinburgh, where the words of Scottish writers are inscribed in the flagstones on the ground.

you would, at present, have no idea. I am glad that the university has agreed to work with the National Library of Scotland to digitise Marie's manuscript, so that anyone can enjoy its wonders on screen, freely and easily, even while it remains 'entombed' in Cambridge. I have also not given up entirely on seeing it returned to Scotland, at the very least on temporary loan, for an exhibition in the nation where Marie was born and lived, where she created it – and where it really belongs.

I also look forward to continuing to collaborate with Time for Inclusive Education, and with the many others who have supported me in sharing Marie's story over the past years – as well as with others who I have yet to meet.

I hope that this is just the beginning.

*

If I am eager for people to discover the story of Marie's life shared in this book, I am also excited about what further new information might come to light in the future: both about Marie and about other figures of recorded LGBT+ history, whose names we don't yet know.

Just as I was finalising this book for submission in late 2025, I received an email informing me that I had been granted access to a privately held manuscript that I had requested to see some time prior: Marie's father's history of the house of Douglas. Never printed, it exists only in manuscript form. I duly paid the fee and made my way down the Royal Mile – past St Giles, where Marie did her legal business, past her old townhouse opposite the Tron – and down North Bridge to National Records of Scotland. There ensconsed in the historical search room, I discovered on one of the manuscript's pages an inscription in italic, in the hand of someone who seems to have been just learning to write the script. More investigation needs to be done, but this could well be the handiwork of a young Marie, in what could be the earliest known writing in her own hand.

I am also aware of the existence of other tantalising sources, which may well contain material relating to Marie, and which it would be thrilling to get my hands on. These materials are held privately, and I have thus far been denied research access to them, but I hope that that might one day change.

Our understanding of history is always evolving, not static. This is just the start, as we reassess the records to see what has always been there, but unearthed, and unsung.

*

Like Sappho, Marie wanted to be remembered.

She left records, in her own hand, in the hope of making her immortal name.

Finally, after more than four centuries in the dark, she has.

Poem 49

As phoebus in his spheris hicht
precellis the kaip Crepusculein
And phoebe all the starris licht
Your splendour so madame I wein
Dois onlie pas all feminine
In sapience superlative
Indewit with vertewis sa devine
As leirned pallas redivive

And as by hid vertew unknawin
The adamant drawis yron thairtill
Your courtes nature so has drawin
My hairt youris to continew still
Sa greit Joy dois my spreit fulfill
contempling your perfectioun
Ye weild me holie at your will
and raviss my affectioun

Your perles Vertew dois provoike
and loving kyndnes so dois move
My Mynd to freindschip reciprocot
That treuth sall try sa far above
The auntient heroicis love
as salbe thocht prodigious
and plaine experience sall prove
Mair holie and religious

Poem 49

In amitie perithous
To theseus was not so traist
Nor Till Achilles patroclus
nor pilades to trew orest
Not Yit achates luif so lest
to gud Enee nor sic freindschip
David to Ionathan profest
nor Titus trew to kynd Iosip

Nor Yit Penelope I wiss
so luiffed ulisses in hir dayis
Nor Ruth the kynd moabitiss
Nohemie as the scripture sayis
nor portia whais worthie prayiss
In romaine historeis we reid
Wha did devoir the fyrie brayiss
To follow brutus to the deid

Wald michtie Jove grant me the hap
With you to have your brutus pairt
and metamorphosing our schap
My sex intill his vaill convert
No brutus then sould caus us smart
as we doe now unhappie wemen
Then sould we bayth with Joyfull hairt
honour and bliss the band of hymen

Yea certainlie we sould efface
Pollux and castoris memorie
and gif that thay desservit place
amang the starris for loyaltie

Then our mair perfyte amitie
mair worthie recompence sould merit
In hevin eternall deitie
amang the goddis till Inherit

And as we ar thocht till our wo
nature and fortoun doe coniure
and hymen also be our fo
Yit luif of vertew dois procuire
freindschip and amitie sa suire
with sa greit fervencie and force
Sa constantlie whilk sall Induire
That not bot deid sall us divorce

And thocht adversitie us vex
Yit be our freindschip salbe sein
Thair is mair constancie in our sex
Then ever amang men has bein
no troubill, torment, greif, or tein
nor erthlie thing sall us dissever
Sic constancie sall us mantein
In perfyte amitie for ever

Poem 72

Gif faithfulnes ye find,
And that your mynd content
Ane band heirby I bind
Of firme fayth and fervent
And to be permanent,
For ocht that may befall,
My hairt heir I present
In pledge perpetuall

Quhilk simplie I resing
As hostage in your hand
And willinglie it bring
To bind it in sic band
As plesis yow command
To lest till I may leif,
Quhilk is the gadge and pand
Maist suir that I can geif

Resave it then, and treit it
As treuth sall try my part
Gif I be fals, forleit it
And let me suffer smert
Deil efter my desert
Than dreid I no disdaine
Bot houpis to have ane hairt
In recompence againe

Poem 72

Gif loyaltie may love
Ane recompence procuire
Or honest mening move
Your favour to induire
Gif lawtie you alluire,
Or constance mak yow kynd,
Firme faith sall me assuire
And treuth content your mynd

Poem 89

As absence is the greatest fo
That Cupids clientis dois suspect
Lang out of sicht engendris so
To presence the contrair effect
And as oblivion dois deject
The building of remembrance
So lak of memorie neglect
The deidis deserving recompance

Of absence langour dois proceid
And langour breidis melancolie
Melancolie procuiris the deid
By sindrie kyndis of meladie
Thus may I gatther easalie
That absence is ane homeceid
To martyre men maist cruellie
Except thair be found out remeid

Now thocht the causer of thir thre
Langour melancolie, and deid,
This present tyme dois threattin me
To pour thir plages on my heid
Laking that grace my cause to pleid
At Bewteis bar to seek refuge
Yit in your justice I confeid
Absence my richt sall not prejudge

Poem 89

Thocht other loveries doe alledge
For to defend thair libertie
Sum other caussis to repledge
Thame selfis from absence tyrannie
Yit into that securitie
With thame I put na confidence
Suppose in love my constancie
Deservis als great recompance

To find ane trew Penelope
Quhair other sum hes wrocht in vaine
Yit I belief to find you sa
And constanter for to remaine
In easing thus your loveris paine
As scho was to be registrat;
And sua thocht absence me disdaine
I shall induire the last combat

Thocht absence be
The meladie
Tormenting me
With daylie greif
Your constancie
May remedie
Gif not: I die
Without relief

A note on language, dates and documents

Most of the sources relating to Marie's life – both poetic and documentary – were first written down in what is now historical (specifically, 'early modern') Scots, which was then still the language of the Scottish kingdom.

In terms of script, many were written in 'Scottish secretary hand', a now obsolete script that was used predominantly by male record keepers during the early modern period. Nowadays, palaeographical training is required to be able to read and transcribe it.

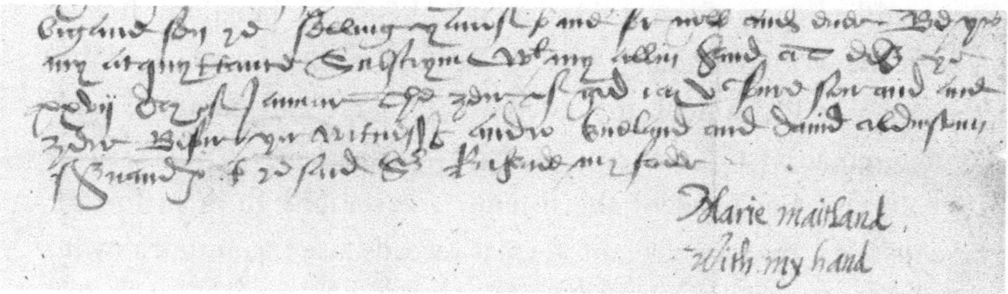

Adv Ms 80.2.3. Extract from an acquittance of January 1582, showing lines of writing in secretary hand script, followed by Marie's signature in italic script. With thanks to the National Library of Scotland for permission to use this image.

Scots is a West Germanic language, closely related to English. Each began as a dialect of Anglo-Saxon, brought to British shores by Germanic invaders in the early centuries AD. In Scotland, a northern dialect of Anglo-Saxon developed into the Scots language, in line with the formation of the medieval Scottish kingdom; in England, meanwhile, a southern dialect developed into English.

By the Middle Ages, Scots had established itself as the language of the Scottish kingdom, displacing Gaelic as the main spoken language and Latin as the main written language. It held sway in this position for centuries. Then, from the latter part of the sixteenth century onwards, a series of factors led to Scots being displaced by English as the language of state, and in formal and written settings more generally. Paramount among these factors were the dominance of English-language Bibles during the Reformation and the removal of the Royal Court to London following the Union of Crowns in 1603, under James VI/I, followed by the Union of Parliaments just over a century later, in 1707.

During Marie's lifetime, however, Scots was still the unquestioned language of the still independent Scottish kingdom. It was both the written language of state and the spoken language of the street – of Parliament and poetry, commerce and contracts and monarch and pauper alike.

In this book, all of the (literal) translations from historical Scots texts, both poetry and formal records, are the author's own. For the ease of the reader, when quoting from historical Scots texts, modernisation of spelling has often been silently introduced, while maintaining a strong sense of the original Scots. For example, in words such as 'hes', the 'e' is presented as an 'a' to give 'has', for clarity. Historical Scots 'quh' is often made 'wh' and the historical Scots ȝ (yogh) is represented as 'y'. Where u/v/w and i/j were used interchangeably in the past, the modern equivalent has been used here. Contractions are also expanded, to aid easy comprehension: for example, 'kny[ch]t' is presented simply as 'knycht'. Past tense verbal endings in '-it' (which remain a feature of Modern Scots) are generally left untouched, as are historical Scots plurals and possessives in '-is', to convey the flavour of the historical language, without compromising understanding.

Quotes from texts are clearly marked. Sometimes a full translation into English is provided; sometimes just the more challenging historical Scots words are translated in square brackets. On some occasions, the word has been deemed challenging because it is historical and now obsolete, such that even a Modern Scots speaker would not be familiar with it. On other occasions, it has been deemed challenging on the basis that someone unfamiliar with Modern Scots would not immediately know what it means, even if most Modern Scots speakers would.

*

The civil Statutory Registers of Births, Deaths and Marriages in Scotland – and the compulsory and systematic registering of those events – were not introduced until the year 1855. During the early modern period covered by this book, a person's year of birth is, therefore, often only a best guess, based on other known facts, and taking into account generalities, such as that the average age of marriage for an elite woman was eighteen, or that boys tended to matriculate at university around the age of fourteen, or a bit younger. Fortunately, from the historian's perspective, the elite status of Marie's family, together with the fact that they were a family highly adept at using the law to protect and further their interests, means that a whole range of contemporary records pertaining to them were created at the time, and have survived. They help us to reconstruct Marie's life.

*

Until the year 1600 in Scotland, the new year began on 25 March, not 1 January. For the ease of the reader, to ensure chronological clarity and avoid confusion, modern dating has been adopted, where relevant.

For example, the primary records relating to Marie's dowry investment are dated in the contemporary records as February 1578; however, in modern terms, the year 1579 had commenced. These 'dual dates' are sometimes written as 'February 1578/79'. Similarly, Marie's father died on what was, in their time, 20 March 1585; from our modern perspective, though, the year 1586 had already begun.

*

During Marie's time, Scotland had its own currency in the form of the pound or £ Scots. The Scots merk was worth two-thirds of a Scots pound. The merk was mostly a unit of account, hence its appearance in many of the contracts considered in this book, but it was also occasionally minted.

Due to inflation and other factors, accurate modern equivalents are tricky to provide. However, the following contemporary references may help ground the reader in relation to Marie's world and the figures quoted in this book.

When Jonet Cunynghame, the widow of a burgess of Edinburgh, William Bothwell, died in 1591, her debts included 40 merks (26 pounds, 13 shillings and 4 pence) owed for one year's rent of a house on the Canongate (to maltman burgess, Thomas Ramsay).

When Isobel Maitland died in 1621, she was due her gentlewoman, Margaret, £24, or 32 merks, for her half-year's fee. She was also due two other female servants, Bessie and Jonet,

10 merks each for their half-year's fee. A male steward, David, was due £60 for his half-year's fee. Isobel's 'cuik [cook] boy', Robert, by comparison, was due 5 merks for his half-year's fee. Isobel also had, by way of example, a library valued at £10 and a cow valued at 20 merks.

When Alexander Lauder younger died in 1623, he had a grey mare valued at £30 and a cow valued at 20 merks. He was due 50 merks to the late Archibald Geddes, merchant burgess of Edinburgh (that is, to his heirs and executors) for the Whitsunday term's (half-year) rent of his chambers. He was also due two female servants, Katharine and Jeane, 40 merks each for their year's fee.

When Alexander Lauder elder died in 1627, he was due 100 merks for the rent of his dwelling house in Edinburgh from Lady Curriehill elder. He himself was due to the town of Edinburgh for tack duty of the teinds [tithes] of the lands of Beirhill, 10 merks; similarly, to George Hereot for the tack duty of the half teinds of Alderstoune, 19 merks; and to the laird of Corstorphine for tack duty of the teinds of half Platt, 10 merks.

Acknowledgements

To my wife, Eilidh. You are the reason I get up in the morning, let alone the reason I have been able to write a book. This book is dedicated to you, as am I. You have been my co-creator and my champion at every stage of telling Marie's story: from the first discovery of her manuscript and the conception of her imagined portrait, to being in the front row of every talk I have ever given and, now, through your hand in editing the pages of this book.

Readers can thank Eilidh for, among other things: the existence of chapter 6; the very title of the book; and every reference to a term still being in use in the Scots legal system today (she is a lawyer).

Eilidh, I thank you for all of this, too, and so much more. I love you.

*

To my wonderful and precious friends, my chosen family. Thank you for your grounding love and support, your good humour and encouragement throughout the writing of this book, and much else besides. Not only could I not do any of it without you, there would be no joy in such. Thank you so much, for everything.

I also express my deepest gratitude to Doreen M, who has nurtured and empowered me unquantifiably, and to Debra C, for her constantly steadying and inspiring energy.

I am immensely grateful, too, to the brilliant in-laws I have been fortunate enough to gain — with special mention to my father-in-law, Jimmie, the best self-taught historian I ken.

*

To the early readers who believed in this book long before it had an agent or a publisher, and who gave me invaluable feedback on tentative first drafts, thank you so much: in particular, Tammas Clark, Liz Thomson, Auksė Beatričė Katarskytė, Rea Cris, Ross Crawford and Carolyn Montgomery. Special thanks are also due to author and poet extraordinaire Michael Pedersen, whose generosity of spirit knows no bounds. Michael, I will always be immensely touched by the time and energy you devoted to me, a fledgling author, and my very rough draft, at such an early stage. Please know how much your encouragement and enthusiasm meant at a pivotal moment; thank you so much.

To my fabulous and ferocious literary agent, Caro Clarke, of Portobello Literary: thank you for keeping me right, and for protecting my rights, every step of the way (and for your delicious homemade jam and cocktail recipes!). Massive thanks, too, to Margaux Vialleron for all her support and efforts on translation rights.

To the entire team at my fantastic publisher, Headline Press: thank you so much for believing in me and in this book, and for applying all your expertise and energies to making it the best it possibly could be — especially my wonderful editor, Holly Purdham. Thank you so much, Holly, for your profound empathy and shared passion for uncovering this untold story, and for your wisdom, enthusiasm and frequently hilarious comments on drafts. I couldn't have dreamed of a better editor — you literally have a Sappho tattoo! — and it's been an absolute joy working with you. Special mentions, too, to Alara Delfosse for her amazing work on publicity; Alice Clarke for the gorgeous and seductive cover design; Phoebe Kalid for the stunning digital assets; Aruna Vasudevan for the diligent and thoughtful copy edit; Wilf Dickie, for the beautiful typesetting; and Emma Horton for the careful proofread.

Writing a book is one thing, but standing on a stage speaking about it to audiences is quite another. I am therefore also hugely grateful to presenter, journalist and public-speaking coach Zara Janjua for the enriching and empowering training day we undertook together, and all the support she has given me since.

*

So much of this book is based on the study of primary records, possible only because they are diligently cared for by institutions and archives. I am exceptionally grateful to the National Library of Scotland, where I undertook huge swathes of the research and writing of this book, always ably assisted and enthusiastically supported by the fabulous team there. Special mentions to Peter Findlay, Ulrike Hogg, Kenny Redpath, Martha Burns Findlay, Ciara Colthart, Caspian Alexander-Reid and Alison Stevenson. When I wasn't at the National Library, I was generally at National Records of Scotland, and I similarly express my gratitude to the brilliant team there who responded to many research queries and enabled my access to countless precious records over the years; special mentions to Jessica Evershed and Jo Dixon. My thanks, too, to Jennifer Findlay, Head of Library and Archive Services at the Scottish Courts and Tribunals Service, for her generous assistance on the location of historical courts and graveyards; to Catherine Sutherland, Special Collections Librarian at Magdalene College, University of Cambridge, who most helpfully assisted with queries and facilitated my multiple research visits to consult the manuscripts held at Pepys Library; and to the teams at Glasgow City Archives and the University of Edinburgh's special collections department.

I sincerely thank Roger Mason, Professor Emeritus, for all that he has done over his long and distinguished career to promote

Scottish history as a discipline, and especially for his founding of the Institute of Scottish Historical Research at the University of St Andrews, where I had the great privilege and pleasure of undertaking an MLitt in Scottish Historical Studies under his tutelage. I have always been able to rely on both his scholarly wisdom and, latterly, our firm friendship.

I am immensely indebted, too, to professional palaeographer Robert Urquhart, who drew on his decades of experience and expertise, which include twenty years at the National Archives of Scotland, to assist me in the task of the painstaking transcription and analysis of many of the newly unearthed primary records discussed in this book. Over cake and coffee in numerous Edinburgh cafés, and across countless email threads, at often highly unsociable times, Robert, ever patient, devoted many hours of his life to discussing with me the finer details of the life of Marie Maitland, as the raw documentary evidence developed, bit by bit, into this narrative of her life. I could not have written this book without him.

Many scholars shared rich and nuanced takes on their areas of expertise and assisted me with specific and tricky questions. I am particularly indebted to Dr Amy Blakeway for both her unparalleled insights into the 1540s and her general robust feedback on draft chapters; and to Associate Professor Kelsey Jackson Williams for the vast amounts of time and energy devoted to discussing the finer semantic nuances of early modern Scots words, for his own exemplary academic approach to writing about Marie Maitland and for first suggesting the possibility that the manuscript's poems might contain anagrams. I am also grateful to Nelli Pekurinen, a BA (Hons) student of Associate Professor Williams, for sharing with me a copy of her dissertation, in which she undertook the first full codicological survey of the *Maitland Quarto*, and for our rich discussions about all things paper, ink and authorship.

The insights of Dr Rebecca Mason, who wrote her PhD on women's legal status and property rights in early modern Scotland, have been invaluable in understanding Marie in her historical context. Dr Mason is an inspiration when it comes to doing socially-conscious history with a purpose, and I am grateful to her for critically reading key sections of this book and for sharing advance sight of material from her own forthcoming book — as well as for always promptly replying to very involved text messages about annualrents, whatever the day or hour!

This book is also all the stronger for the input of Dr Suzanna Millar, who generously shared her expertise in both biblical Hebrew and queer hermeneutics and closely reviewed draft sections of the book. Dr Millar also did me the honour of inviting me to lecture on the scriptural aspects of Marie's poetry at the School of Divinity at the University of Edinburgh. I am grateful to everyone who attended and thoughtfully engaged with that lecture, and especially to the students and scholars who delivered academic responses on the day.

One of the Privy Seal records cited in this book shifts from Scots into Latin midway through, and Latin experts Dr Francis Young and Pauline Jarvis came to the rescue in assisting me with its reading, for which I sincerely thank them. I am also most grateful to Steven Veerapen — author of *The Wisest Fool: The Lavish Life of James VI and I* — for his insight into the King's role (or lack of) in relation to the marriage referred to in chapter 8, based on his expert knowledge of the sources for James' Scottish reign. I am indebted, too, to John Corbett for his invaluable expert insight on matters of historical Scots pronunciation.

Special thanks are also due to scholars Dr Alan MacDonald, Dr Jade Scott, Dr Bess Rhodes, Dr Sajed Chowdhury, Dr Jamie Reid-Baxter, Dr Anna Kłosowska, Dr Jessica DeVos and Christian Clarkson for their enriching contributions to various aspects of my research and for fruitful pointers shared. I am also indebted to Annie McGuire for her assistance with all my questions about Catholicism, and Leah Hazard for all my questions about wombs.

I acknowledge my debt to the work of all previous scholars who have written to any extent about Marie Maitland, the wider Maitland family or the Maitland manuscripts, both in centuries past and more recently, whose contributions I build on and, in good academic tradition, sometimes challenge.

*

Many other people and organisations have supported me in sharing Marie's story, in many different ways, over the past half decade, and I could not be more grateful to each and every one of them. If that is you, in any way, I thank you, sincerely and deeply. Your encouragement and enthusiasm inspired me to keep researching and writing about Marie, and convinced me of the appetite and need for this book. The below list is far from exhaustive, but a few names merit special mention.

Jordan Daly and Liam Stevenson: you have changed the world through your campaigning and my life through your friendship. It feels special, and right, that Marie has been part of inclusive education in Scotland from day one. Thank you both so much, for everything.

Josie Duncan: you light up every room you enter, and I am over the moon that my work on Marie brought us together. I can still hardly believe that you have been moved to write such beautiful and powerful songs inspired by Marie's love poetry. What joy it is to hear you sing them, breathing new sapphic life into centuries-old words.

Rona Munro: I was in awe of you and your transformational approach to telling Scotland's history through your magnificent James Plays series for many years before I had the honour of working alongside you, let alone of becoming your friend. The experience of being involved as a historical consultant in your magnificent play *Katherine: James V* was utterly thrilling, and an incredibly powerful demonstration for me of the real-world merit of what I was doing in researching and sharing Marie's story. My sincere thanks, too, to Raw Material and the entire brilliant cast and team behind *Katherine* for all your infectiously motivational energy and support. I absolutely loved meeting and working with you all.

Amina Shah: Scotland is so fortunate to have you as its National Librarian, and I am personally so fortunate to have had you in my corner, championing me and my work at every opportunity over the past few years. Thank you so much for all that you are and all that you do, and for all your support with this book. It means the world.

Sara Sheridan: thank you for being the inimitable and inspirational woman that you are (I can hear you telling me to pick just one adjective; on this occasion, though, I am keeping both!) and for your mentorship and friendship, both of which have been indispensable companions throughout my writing journey. Not only do you devote yourself to celebrating women from the past, you also always go out of your way to support women today, using every platform you have at your disposal. You even got Marie projected onto the side of Edinburgh Castle! (To my delight, Sara also features Marie in her enthralling latest novel, *The Jewel Keepers*, which I urge you to seek out — not least as Sara was able to give her a much happier ending in fiction than she seems to have had in reality.)

Special mentions are also due to the fabulous teams at Historic Environment Scotland, HistFest, the Chartered Institute of Library and Information Professionals, *Somewhere: For Us* magazine, Porty Pride, and the Scottish National Portrait Gallery (in particular Kate Anderson and Gráinne Rice); to curator Lewis Hetherington, particularly for inviting me to contribute to the anthology *who will be remembered here*; to Ione Gildroy, who attended one of my early speaking events and then conducted a beautiful interview with me for Edinburgh University's student newspaper; and to Logan McKinnon, who, in his role as warden, ensured that Marie Maitland's poetry and story featured as part of the first ever Pride event to be held at the Royal Palace of Holyrood House in 2025. Thank you all, so much.

*

Growing up, my school and my library were always places of refuge; reading and education an escape.

I owe an unquantifiable debt to all of the educators who encouraged and nurtured me, many of whom went well above and beyond in their interventions and kindness. Thank you for your positive presence and support at times in my life when it meant so much, and which helped to ensure that I found myself on a far more positive trajectory than could otherwise have been the case (with special thanks to Mr Gilmour, Mr Wyse and Mrs Dunlop).

The year that I attended summer school at the University of St Andrews, through the Sutton Trust charity, was a transformational moment in my young life for which I will always be immensely grateful (with special thanks to Mike Johnson).

I must also thank Bill Anderson, owner of the very special Bouquiniste bookshop in St Andrews, for the many happy hours spent in his company there discussing literature, history and life during my student years.

The work of teachers, librarians and booksellers changed my life, offering up paths that I would not otherwise have known existed.

Both of the books that I have now published — an illustrated children's book in the Scots language, a fairytale in which the princess falls in love not with a prince, but another girl; and this book, the untold story of a real woman from Scottish history, who fell in love with and wished to marry another woman — are my gift to them. I sincerely hope that, in writing these books, I have given back something in return to be guided into the hands of those who might need them most, when they need them most.

Sources

Original Records

MS 1408 (Pepys Library, Magdalene College, Cambridge)
MS 2553 (Pepys Library, Magdalene College, Cambridge)

Adv MS 31.2.2 (National Library of Scotland)
Adv MS 80.2.3 (National Library of Scotland)
Adv MS 19.2.6 (National Library of Scotland)

CC8/2/30 (National Records of Scotland)
CC8/7/40 (National Records of Scotland)
CC8/8/23 (National Records of Scotland)
CC8/8/31 (National Records of Scotland)
CC8/8/33 (National Records of Scotland)
CC8/8/35 (National Records of Scotland)
CC8/8/37 (National Records of Scotland)
CC8/8/50 (National Records of Scotland)
CC8/8/51 (National Records of Scotland)
CC8/8/52 (National Records of Scotland)
CC8/8/54 (National Records of Scotland)
GD89/1/446 (National Records of Scotland)
RD1/1 (National Records of Scotland)
RD1/3/3 (National Records of Scotland)
RD1/4 (National Records of Scotland)
RD1/6/1 (National Records of Scotland)
RD1/9 (National Records of Scotland)
RD1/17/1 (National Records of Scotland)

RD1/18 (National Records of Scotland)
RD1/24/2 (National Records of Scotland)
RD1/28 (National Records of Scotland)

NRAS2177/1 (Douglas-Hamilton family, Dukes of Hamilton and Brandon)

De.3.71 (University of Edinburgh Archive and Manuscript Collections)

CH2/171/36/fol. 320 (Glasgow City Archives, Glasgow Presbytery Records)

SP52/26/2 (The National Archives)

Reference

A Dictionary of the Older Scottish Tongue (up to 1700): https://dsl.ac.uk/
Records of the Parliaments of Scotland to 1707, ed. K. M. Brown et al, University of St Andrews, 2007–25 < https://www.rps.ac.uk/>
The Register of the Privy Council of Scotland (various volumes)
The Register of the Privy Seal of Scotland (various volumes)
The Register of the Great Seal of Scotland (various volumes)

Books and Articles

Andreadis, Harriette, *Sappho in Early Modern England: Female Same-Sex Literary Erotics 1550–1714*. University of Chicago Press, 2001.
Bain, Joseph (ed.) *Poems of Sir Richard Maitland.* Maitland Club, 1830.

Bawcutt, Priscilla, '"My bright buke": Women and Their books in Medieval and Renaissance Scotland', in *Medieval Women: Texts and Contexts in Late Medieval Britain: Essays for Felicity Riddy*, ed. J. Wogan-Browne et al. Turnhout, 2000, pp. 17–34 (23).

Bawcutt, Priscilla, 'Manuscript Miscellanies in Scotland from the Fifteenth to the Seventeenth Centuries', in *Older Scots Literature*, ed. Sally Mapstone. John Donald, 2005, pp. 189–210.

Bergeron, David, *King James & Letters of Homoerotic Desire*. Univeristy of Iowa Press, 1999.

Blakeway, A., *Regency in Sixteenth-Century Scotland*. St Andrews Studies in Scottish History. Boydell Press, 2015.

Borris, Kenneth (ed.), *Same-Sex Desire in the English Renaissance, A Sourcebook of Texts, 1470–1650*. Routledge, 2004.

Boswell, John, *Christianity, Social Tolerance, and Homosexuality: Gay People in Western Europe from the Beginning of the Christian Era to the Fourteenth Century*. University of Chicago Press, 1980.

Boswell, John, *The Marriage of Likeness: Same-Sex Unions in Pre-Modern Europe*. Villard Books, 1994.

Brown, James, *The Epitaphs and Monumental Inscriptions in Greyfriars Churchyard, Edinburgh*. J. Moodie Miller, 1867.

Brown, Keith, *Noble Society in Scotland: Wealth, Family and Culture, from Reformation to Revolution*. Edinburgh University Press, 2000.

Buchanan, George, *The Works of Mr. George Buchanan, in the Scottish language: containing The Chamaeleon, a satire against the Laird of Lidingtone. And an Admonition to the true Lords, maintainers of justice, and obedience to the King's grace*, ed. D. Webster. Webster, 1823.

Buchanan, George, *Vernacular Writings of George Buchanan*, ed. P. Hume Brown. William Blackwood and Sons, 1892.

Bulloch, J. (trans.), *The Confession of the Faith and Doctrine Believed and Professed by the Protestants Of Scotland.* The Saint Andrew Press, 1984.

Chowdhury, Sajed Ali, *Dissident Metaphysics in Renaissance Women's Poetry*, DPhil thesis, University of Sussex, 2012.

Chowdhury, Sajed Ali, '"Thair is mair constancie in o[u]r sex / Then euer ama[n]g men hes bein": The Metaphysics of Authorship in the *Maitland Quarto* Manuscript (ca. 1586)', *Textual Cultures*, 7: no. 1, (2012), pp. 50–76.

Coutts, Winifred, *The Business of the College of Justice in 1600: How It Reflects the Economic and Social Life of Scots Men and Women.* Stair Society, 2003.

Craigie, W. A. (ed.), *The Maitland Folio Manuscript I.* Scottish Text Society, 1919.

Craigie, W. A. (ed.), *The Maitland Quarto Manuscript.* Scottish Text Society, 1920.

Craigie, W. A. (ed.), *The Maitland Folio Manuscript II.* Scottish Text Society, 1927.

Crawfurd, George, *The lives and characters, of the officers of the crown and state in Scotland, from the beginning of the reign of King David I. to the union ... Collected from original charters, chartularies.* Printed by Robert Fleming and Company, 1736.

Dawson, Jane, '"Richt honorabill" ladies: Noble Power and Aristocratic Women in Sixteenth-Century Scotland', *The Scottish Historical Review*, 103:3 (2024), 361–91.

Donoghue, Emma, *Inseparable: Desire Between Women in Literature.* Picador, 2013.

Dunnigan, Sarah, 'Scottish Women Writers, c.1560–1650', in *A History of Scottish Women's Writing*, ed. Douglas Gifford and Dorothy McMillan. Edinburgh University Press, 1997, pp. 15–43.

Dunnigan, Sarah, 'Undoing the Double Tress: Scotland, Early Modern Women's Writing, and the Location of Critical Desires', *Feminist Studies*, 29:2 (2003), 298–319.

Dunnigan, Sarah, 'Feminising the Early-Modern Erotic: Female Voiced Lyrics and Mary Queen of Scots', in *Older Scots Literature*, ed. Sally Mapstone. John Donald, 2005, pp. 441–66.

Dunnigan, Sarah, 'Women's Writing to 1700', in *A Companion to Scottish Literature*, ed. Gerry Carruthers. Wiley, 2023, 406–418.

Durkan, John, *Scottish Schools and Schoolmasters, 1560–1633*, ed. and rev. Jamie Reid-Baxter. Scottish History Society, Fifth Series, vol. 19. Boydell & Brewer, 2013.

Ewan, E. and Meikle, M. (eds), *Women in Scotland, c.1100–c.1750*. Tuckwell Press, 1999.

Faderman, Lillian, *Surpassing the Love of Men: Romantic Friendship and Love between Women from the Renaissance to the Present*. The Women's Press, 1985.

Farnsworth, Jane, 'Voicing Female Desire in "Poem XLIX"', *Studies in English Literature 1500–1700*, 36:1 (1996), 37–72.

Goodare, Julian and Lynch, Michael (eds), *The Reign of James VI*. Tuckwell Press, 2000.

Goodare, Julian, Martin, Lauren and Miller, Joyce (eds), *Witchcraft and Belief in Early Modern Scotland*. Palgrave Macmillan, 2007.

Gouldesbrough, Peter (ed.), *Formulary of Old Scots Legal Documents*. Stair Society, 1985.

Grant, Francis J. (ed.), *Index to Genealogies, Birthbriefs and Funeral Escutcheons, Recorded in the Lyon Office*. Scottish Record Society, 1908.

Grant, Francis J. (ed.), *The Commissariot Record of Edinburgh, Register of Testaments, Part I*, Volumes 1 to 35, 1514–1600. British Record Society, 1897.

Guy, John, *My Heart Is My Own: The Life of Mary Queen of Scots*. Fourth Estate, 2004.

Harvey, C. and McLeod, J. (eds), *Calendar of writs preserved at Yester House, 1166–1625*. Scottish Record Society, 1930.

Hazlett, William Ian P. (ed.), *A Companion to the Reformation in Scotland, ca. 1525–1638: Frameworks of Change and Development*. Brill, 2023.

Heale, Elizabeth, *Fathers and Daughters: Four Women and Their Family Albums of Verse*. Cambridge University Press, 2023.

Hilton, Lisa, *Elizabeth: Renaissance Prince*. Weidenfeld & Nicolson, 2014.

Hobby, Elaine, *Virtue of Necessity: English Women's Writing, 1646–88*. Virago, 1988.

Hutson, Lorna, *England's Insular Imagining: The Elizabethan Erasure of Scotland*. Cambridge University Press, 2023.

Juhala, Amy L., *The Household and Court of King James VI of Scotland, 1567–1603*, PhD thesis, University of Edinburgh, 2000.

King, Pamela M., 'Lethington, Marie Maitland, and the "Maitland Quarto": Memorialisation and Performance in Times of "Troubill" for Scotland', in *Writing Scottishness: Writing and the Shaping of National Identities*. Eds Ian Brown and Clarissa Godard Desmarest. Association for Scottish Literary Studies, 2023, 20–43.

Knox, John, *The history of the Reformation of religion within the realm of Scotland*, ed. Guthrie, C. J. Adam and Charles Black, 1899.

Lawrence-Mathers, Anne and Hardman, Phillipa (eds), *Women and Writing, c.1340–c.1650: The Domestication of Print Culture*. Boydell & Brewer, 2010.

Lee, Maurice, *John Maitland of Thirlestane and the Foundation of the Stewart Despotism in Scotland*. Princeton University Press, 1959.

Leslie of Balquhain, C. (ed.), *Historical Records of the Family of Leslie from 1067 to 1868–9, Collected from Public Records and Authentic*

Private Sources, by Colonel Charles Leslie of Balquhain, vol 1. Edmonston and Douglas, 1869.

Loughlin, Marie (ed.), *Same-Sex Desire in Early Modern England, 1550–1735: An Anthology of Literary Texts and Contexts*. Manchester University Press, 2014.

Loughlin, Mark, *The Career of Maitland of Lethington c.1526–1573*, PhD thesis, University of Edinburgh, 1991.

Love, Harold, *Scribal Publication in Seventeenth-Century England*. Clarendon Press, 1993.

MacCulloch, Diarmid, 'Reformation time and sexual revolution (Counter-Reformation and Judeo-Christian tradition in Europe)', *New England Review-Middlebury Series*, 24:4 (2003), 6–31.

MacDonald, Alasdair, *George Lauder (1603–1670): Life and Writings*, Studies in Renaissance Literature series, no. 35. D. S. Brewer, 2018).

Mackenzie, John (ed.), *Chronicle of the Kings of Scotland, from Fergus the First, to James the Sixth*. Maitland Club, 1830.

Maitland, James, *A narrative of the principal acts of the regency, during the minority of Mary, Queen of Scotland*, ed. W. S. Fitch. Ipswich, 1833.

Maitland, Sir Richard, *The History of the House of Seytoun to the Year M.D.LIX*, ed. J. Fullarton. Maitland Club, 1833.

Mapstone, Sally (ed.), *Older Scots Literature*. John Donald, 2005.

Marshall, Rosalind K., *Virgins and Viragos: A History of Women in Scotland from 1080 to 1980*. Collins, 1983.

Martin, Joanna, 'The *Maitland Quarto* Manuscript and the Literary Culture of the Reign of James VI', in *James VI and I, Literature and Scotland: Tides of Change, 1567–1625*, ed. D. Parkinson. Peeters, 2013, pp. 65–81.

Martin, Joanna, 'Women as readers, writers, and book owners in late sixteenth-century Scotland: the *Maitland Quarto* manuscript', *The Bottle Imp*, 14 (2013).

Martin, Joanna (ed.), *The Maitland Quarto: A New Edition of Cambridge, Magdalen College, Pepys Library MS 1408*. Scottish Text Society, 2015.

Martin, J. and McLune, K., 'The *Maitland Folio* and *Quarto* Manuscripts in Context', *English Manuscript Studies, 1100–1700: Tudor Manuscripts 1485–1603*, 15 (2009), 237–623.

Mason, Rebecca, 'Married Women, Property and Paraphernalia in Early Modern Scotland', *Gender, Law and Economic Wellbeing in Early Modern and Modern Europe*, ed. Anna Bellavitis and Beatrice Zucca Micheletto. Routledge, 2018, pp. 200–214.

Mason, Rebecca, *'With Hir Gudis and Geir': Married Women Negotiating the Law of Property in the Courts of Seventeenth-Century Scotland*, unpublished PhD thesis, University of Glasgow, 2019.

Mason, Rebecca, 'Property over Patriarchy? Remarried Widows as Litigants in the Records of Glasgow's Commissary Court, 1615–94', in *Litigating Women: Gender and Justice in Europe, c.1300–c.1800*, ed. Teresa Phipps and Deborah Youngs. Routledge, 2022, pp. 133–51.

Mason, Rebecca, 'Coercion or Consent? Women, Property and Legal Authority in Early Modern Scotland', *Scottish Historical Review*, 102:2 (2023), 232–53.

Mason, Rebecca, '"Scottish Portias" Revisited: Women in the Courts in Early Modern Scottish Towns', in *Gender in Scotland, 1400–1800: Place, Faith and Politics*, ed. Mairi Cowan, Janay Nugent and Cathryn Spence. Edinburgh University Press, 2024, pp. 31–47.

Mason, Rebecca, *Women, Property and the Law in Early Modern Scotland*. Forthcoming.

Mason, Roger, *Kingship and the Commonweal: Political Thought in Renaissance and Reformation Scotland*. Tuckwell Press, 1998.

Mason, Roger, 'The idea of the commonweal in sixteenth-century Scotland', *Journal of the Northern Renaissance*, 15 (2025).

McDiarmid, Matthew P., 'Notes on the Poems of John Stewart of Baldynneis', *The Review of English Studies*, 24:93 (1948), 12–18.

McDiarmid, Matthew P., 'John Stewart of Baldynneis', *The Scottish Historical Review*, 29:107 (1950), 52–63.

McKechnie, Hector, 'Practicks, 1469–1700', in *An Introductory Survey of the Sources and Literature of Scots Laws*. Stair Society, 1936.

McKechnie, William, 'Thomas Maitland', *The Scottish Historical Review*, 4:15 (1907).

Melville, Sir James of Halhill, *Memoirs of his own life*, ed. T. Thomson. Bannatyne Club, 1827.

Miller, R., *The Municipal Buildings of Edinburgh 1145–1895: A Sketch of Their History for Seven Hundred Years Written Mainly from the Original Records*. Edinburgh Town Council, 1895.

Mitchell, Claire and Venditozzi, Zoe, *How to Kill a Witch: A Guide for the Patriarchy*. Monoray, 2025.

Morrison, Mary, 'Henri Estienne and Sappho', *Bibliothèque d'Humanisme et Renaissance*, 24:2 (1962), 388–91.

Munro, Rona, *Mary*. Nick Hern Books, 2022.

Munro, Rona, *James V: Katherine*. Nick Hern Books, 2024.

Newlyn, Evelyn S., 'A Methodology for Reading Against the Culture: Anonymous Women Poets, and the *Maitland Quarto* Manuscript (c. 1586)', in *Women and the Feminine in Medieval and Early Modern Scottish Writing*, ed. Sarah M. Dunnigan, C. Marie Harker and Evelyn S. Newlyn. Palgrave Macmillan, 2004, pp. 89–103.

Parker, Heather, *'In all gudly haste': The Formation of Marriage in Scotland, c.1350–1600*, PhD thesis, University of Guelph, 2012.

Paterson, Raymond, *King Lauderdale: The Corruption of Power*. John Donald, 2003.

Pekurinen, Nelli, *A Codicological Study of the* Maitland Quarto *Manuscript*, BA Honours dissertation, University of Stirling, 2024.

Pender, P. and Smith, R. (eds.), *The Palgrave Encyclopedia of Early Modern Women's Writing*. Palgrave Macmillan, living reference work (2020). https://link.springer.com/referencework/10.1007/978-3-030-01537-4.

Pinkerton, John (ed.), *Ancient Scottish Poems Never Before in Print*, 2 vols. Printed for Charles Dilly; and for William Creech at Edinburgh, 1786.

Ray, Meredith, *Twenty-Five Women Who Shaped the Italian Renaissance*. Routledge, 2024.

Redmond Chang, Leah, *Young Queens: Three Renaissance Women and the Price of Power*. Bloomsbury Circus, 2023.

Reid, S., 'Mary's Courier, Buchanan's Disciple: introducing Thomas Maitland (c. 1545–1572)', *Bridging the Continental Divide*, a project led by the University of Glasgow and funded by the Arts and Humanities Research Council, 2012–15. https://www.dps.gla.ac.uk/research-articles/display/?fid=maitland1.

Reid, S., *The Early Life of James VI: A Long Apprenticeship, 1566–1585*. John Donald, 2023.

Robertson, Jospeh (ed.), *Lives of Scottish Poets*, Society of Ancient Scots, 1821.

Sanderson, Margaret, *A Kindly Place? Living in Sixteenth-Century Scotland*. Tuckwell Press, 2002.

Sappho, *If Not, Winter: The Complete Fragments of Sappho*, ed. and trans. Anne Carson. Little Brown Book Group, 2003.

Sappho, *Songs and Poems, Translated from the Greek*, ed. and trans. Chris Preddle. Irish Pages Press, 2022.

Schwartz, Louis, '17th-century childbirth: "exquisite torment and infinite grace"', *The Lancet*, 377:9776 (2011), 1486–1487.

Scott, Jade, *Captive Queen: The Decrypted History of Mary, Queen of Scots*. Michael O'Mara Books Ltd, 2024.

Sexton, Kristi Rene, *A Crisis of Friendship: Calculation and Betrayal in Shakespeare's* The Merchant of Venice *and* Othello, the Moor of Venice, Masters thesis, University of Tennessee, 2016.

Simpson, Grant G., *Scottish Handwriting, 1150–1650: An Introduction to the Reading of Documents*. Bratton Publishing Ltd, 1973.

Simpson, W. D., 'Hatton House, Midlothian', *Proceedings of the Society of Antiquaries of Scotland*, 79 (1946), 15–26.

Skelton, John, *Maitland of Lethington, and the Scotland of Mary Stuart; A History*, volumes 1 and 2. William Blackwood and Sons, 1887–8.

Smith, Jane Stewart, *The grange of St. Giles, the Bass: and the other baronial homes of the Dick-Lauder family*. T. and A. Constable, Edinburgh, 1898.

Spence, Cathryn, *'Given up by herself': Women's Wills in Late Sixteenth-Century Edinburgh*, MA thesis, University of Guelph, 2006.

Stedall, Robert, *Mary Queen of Scots' Secretary: William Maitland – Politician, Reformer and Conspirator*. Pen & Sword Books, 2021.

Stevenson, J., 'Reading, Writing and Gender in Early Modern Scotland', *The Seventeenth Century*, 27:3 (2012), 335–74. doi: 10.7227/TSC.27.3.5.

Stevenson, J. and Davidson, P. et al. (eds), *Early Modern Women Poets (1520–1700): An Anthology*. Oxford University Press, 2001.

Summers, Claude (ed.), *Homosexuality in Renaissance and Enlightenment England: Literary Representations in Historical Context*. Routledge, 1992.

Sutherland, Robert (ed.), *The practiques of Sir Richard Maitland of Lethington : from December 1550–October 1577: a transcription of John Orr's MS, Glasgow University Library MS Gen 1333*. Scottish Record Society, 2007.

Thomson, T. (ed.), *The historie and life of King James the Sext: being an account of the affairs of Scotland, from the year 1566, to the year 1596; with a short contribution to the year 1617*. Bannatyne Club, 1825.

Thomson, T. (ed.), *A diurnal of remarkable occurrents that have passed within the country of Scotland since the deathof King James the Fourth till the year MDLXXV. From a manuscript of the sixteenth century, in the possession of Sir John Maxwell of Pollock, baronet.* Bannatyne Club, 1833.

Todd, Margo, *The Culture of Protestantism in Early Modern Scotland.* Yale University Press, 2002.

Tytler, Patrick Fraser, *An account of the life and writings of Sir Thomas Craig of Riccarton: including biographical sketches of the most eminent legal characters, since the institution of the Court of Session by James V. till the period of the union of the crowns.* Printed for W. & C. Tait, 1823.

Veerapen, Steven, *The Wisest Fool: The Lavish Life of James VI and I.* Birlinn, 2024.

Verweij, Sebastiaan, *The Literary Culture of Early Modern Scotland: Manuscript Production and Transmission, 1560–1625.* Oxford University Press, 2016.

Williams, Ethel Carleton, *Anne of Denmark: Wife of James VI of Scotland, James I of England.* Longmans, 1970.

Williams, Kelsey Jackson, 'A "Scoto-British-European" Rediscovered: the Life and Writings of George Lauder', *Studies in Scottish Literature*, 45:1 (2019), 107–12.

Williams, Kelsey Jackson, 'Poets in the Age of James VI', in *A Companion to Scottish Literature*, ed. Gerry Carruthers. Wiley, 2023, 393–405.

Wormald, Jenny, *Court, Kirk, and Community: Scotland 1470–1625.* Toronto University Press, 1981.

Wynne, Frank (ed.), *Queer: LGBTQ Writing from Ancient Times to Yesterday.* Head of Zeus, 2021.

Yandell, C., '"*L'Amour au féminin?*" Ronsard and Pontus de Tyard Speaking as Women', in *Ronsard, Figure de la variété*, ed. Colette H. Winn. Droz, 2002, 65–77.

Young, Margaret (ed.), *The Parliaments of Scotland – Burgh & Shire Commissioners*, vol. 2. Scottish Committee on the History of Parliament, 1993.

Notes

Preface

1 'Anne Lister and Shibden Hall', Historic England: https://historicengland.org.uk/research/inclusive-heritage/lgbtq-heritage-project/love-and-intimacy/anne-lister-and-shibden-hall/

Chapter One

1 Poem 68, *Maitland Quarto* manuscript, Marie Maitland.
2 Poem 11, *Maitland Quarto* manuscript, Sir Richard Maitland of Lethington.
3 Knox, as quoted in Mark Loughlin, '*The Career of Maitland of Lethington c.1526–1573*' (PhD thesis, University of Edinburgh, 1991), p. 26.
4 Poem 8, *Maitland Quarto* manuscript, Sir Richard Maitland of Lethington.
5 James Maitland, *A narrative of the principal acts of the regency, during the minority of Mary, Queen of Scotland*, ed. W. S. Fitch (Ipswich, 1833), p. 14.
6 Poem 6, *Maitland Quarto* manuscript, Sir Richard Maitland of Lethington.
7 Sir Richard Maitland, *The History of the House of Seytoun to the Year M.D.LIX*, ed. J. Fullarton (Maitland Club, 1833), p. 30.

Chapter Two

1 Poem 9, *Maitland Quarto* manuscript, Sir Richard Maitland of Lethington.
2 'The whilk [which] day in presence of the Lords of Counsell compeired [appeared] Sir Richard Maitland of Lethingtoune and conform to ane wreating [document] given by the Quein's grace desireing the Lords to admitt him to be ane of their ordinary number (for he was ane extraordinary Lord all that tym).' As quoted in *Poems of Sir Richard Maitland*, ed. Joseph Bain (Maitland Club, 1830), p. xxxiv.
3 *Ibid.*
4 'Ane letter maid to Schir Richart Maitland of Lethingtoun Knycht, makand him Keipar of owre Soverane Ladeis Privie Seill and gevis to him thairof for all the dayis of his liffe.' *Ibid.*
5 *Ibid.*

6 John Skelton, *Maitland of Lethington, and the Scotland of Mary Stuart; A History* (William Blackwood & Sons, 1887–8) vol. 1, p. 19.
7 Patrick Fraser Tytler, *An account of the life and writings of Sir Thomas Craig of Riccarton: including biographical sketches of the most eminent legal characters, since the institution of the Court of Session by James V. till the period of the union of the crowns* (printed for W. & C. Tait, 1823).
8 Hector McKechnie, 'Practicks, 1469–1700', in *An Introductory Survey of the Sources and Literature of Scots Laws* (Stair Society, 1936), p. 30.
9 Skelton, *Maitland of Lethington, and the Scotland of Mary Stuart*, vol. II, pp. 6–7.
10 Sir James Melville Halhill, *Memoirs of His Own Life*, ed. by T. Thomson. From the original manuscript (Edinburgh, Bannatyne Club, 1827), p.120.
11 *Ibid.*, p. 177.
12 *Ibid.*, p. 180.

Chapter Three

1 Poem 14, *Maitland Quarto* manuscript, Sir Richard of Lethington.
2 Poem 34, *Maitland Quarto* manuscript, Sir Richard of Lethington.
3 Poem 46, *Maitland Quarto* manuscript, Marie Maitland.
4 Poem 24, *Maitland Quarto* manuscript, Sir Richard Maitland of Lethington.
5 *Poems of Sir Richard Maitland*, ed. Joseph Bain, p. xlix.
6 Poem 20, *Maitland Quarto* manuscript, Sir Richard Maitland.
7 Poem 68, *Maitland Quarto* manuscript, Marie Maitland.

Chapter Four

1 *The Dictionary of the Older Scottish Tongue* lists many other contemporary examples attesting to the dominance of this meaning of the verb. "Revis, *v.*". Dictionaries of the Scots Language. Online (accessed 16 Nov 2025): http://www.dsl.ac.uk/entry/dost/revis
2 Translation of Homer by Richmond Lattimore, as quoted in Frank Wynne (ed.), *Queer: LGBTQ Writing from Ancient Times to Yesterday* (Head of Zeus, 2021), p. 3.
3 Book of Ruth 1:15–17.
4 Poem 77, *Maitland Quarto* manuscript.

5 Poem 85, *Maitland Quarto* manuscript, anonymous.
6 As quoted in: Kristi Rene Sexton, *A Crisis of Friendship: Calculation and Betrayal in Shakespeare's* The Merchant of Venice *and* Othello, the Moor of Venice (Master's thesis, University of Tennessee, 2016), p. 13.

Chapter Five

1 "Wedset, *v.*", Dictionaries of the Scots Language. Online (accessed 16 Nov 2025): http://www.dsl.ac.uk/entry/dost/wedsett_v
2 The letter is preserved among the special collections of the University of Aberdeen.

Chapter Six

1 See Leah Redmond Chang, *Young Queens: Three Renaissance Women and the Price of Power* (Bloomsbury Circus, 2023), p. 409.
2 "Pand, *n.*[2]", Dictionaries of the Scots Language. Online (accessed 16 Nov 2025): http://www.dsl.ac.uk/entry/dost/pand_n_2
3 For example, 'We beand copuled and juned in lauchfull mariage/I treatet, obeyed and served the said Williame' (1560). "Tret, *v.*", Dictionaries of the Scots Language. Online (accessed 16 Nov 2025): http://www.dsl.ac.uk/entry/dost/trete_v
4 Meredith Ray, *Twenty-Five Women Who Shaped the Italian Renaissance* (Routledge, 2024), p. 110.
5 These editions included the 'Ode to Aphrodite' and 'Fragment 31'. See Mary Morrison, 'Henri Estienne and Sappho', *Bibliothèque d'Humanisme et Renaissance*, 24:2 (1962) 388–391.
6 *Songs and Poems*, trans. Chris Preddle (Irish Pages Press, 2022), p. 15.
7 Again, in Preddle's beautiful modern translation, p. 35.
8 This time the translation is Anne Carson's sensual rendering of her ancient verse, in *If Not, Winter: The Complete Fragments of Sappho* (Little, Brown Book Group, 2003) 184–187.

Chapter Seven

1 "Replege, *v.*", Dictionaries of the Scots Language. Online (accessed 17 Nov 2025): http://www.dsl.ac.uk/entry/dost/replege_v
2 *Excercitatio Alphabetica* was published on the Continent in 1569.

Chapter Eight

1 Keith Brown, *Noble Society in Scotland: Wealth, Family and Culture, from Reformation to Revolution* (Edinburgh University Press, 2000), p. 117.
2 *Ibid.*, p. 123.
3 John Mackenzie (ed.), *Chronicle of the Kings of Scotland from Fergus the First, to James the Sixth* (Maitland Club, 1830), p. 157.
4 Masson, David (ed.) *The register of the Privy Council of Scotland. Volume 3, A.D. 1578–1585*, Edinburgh: H. M. General Register House, 1880, p. 597.
5 Tytler, *An account of the life and writings of Sir Thomas Craig of Riccarton*, p. 203.
6 T. Thomson (ed.), *The historie and life of King James the Sext: being an account of the affairs of Scotland, from the year 1566, to the year 1596; with a short continuation to the year 1617, 1825* (Bannatyne Club, 1825) p. 179.
7 Heather Parker, *'In all gudly haste': The Formation of Marriage in Scotland, c. 1350–1600* (PhD thesis, University of Guelph, 2012).

Chapter Nine

1 Amy L. Juhala, *The Household and Court of King James VI of Scotland, 1567–1603* (PhD thesis, University of Edinburgh, 2000), p. 205.
2 Ethel Carleton Williams, *Anne of Denmark: Wife of James VI of Scotland, James I of England* (Longmans, 1970), pp. 30–31.
3 Alisdair MacDonald, *George Lauder (1603–1670): Life and Writings*, Studies in Renaissance Literature series, no. 35 (D. S. Brewer, 2018).
4 Cathryn Spence, *'Given up by herself': Women's Wills in Late Sixteenth-Century Edinburgh* (MA thesis, University of Guelph, 2006), pp. 53–4.

Afterword

1 'Information for Researchers' from the Pepys Library website: https://www.magd.cam.ac.uk/visitors-and-conferencing/pepys-library/pepys-library-information-researchers (last accessed 10 May 2026).
2 S. Dunnigan, 'Maitland, Mary (*d.* 1596)' *Oxford Dictionary of National Biography* (2004): https://www.oxforddnb.com/view/10.1093/ref:odnb/9780198614128.001.0001/odnb-9780198614128-e-68146 (last accessed 17 November 2025).

3 Martin, Joanna (ed.), *The Maitland Quarto: A New Edition of Cambridge, Magdalen College, Pepys Library MS 1408*. Scottish Text Society, 2015, p. 371.

4 *Ibid.*, p. 375.

5 See 2015 edition commentary, p. 416; Joanna Martin, 'Women as readers, writers, and book owners in late sixteenth-century Scotland: the *Maitland Quarto* manuscript', *The Bottle Imp*, 14 (2013).

6 'The Maitland Quarto and Poem 49', Ashley Douglas, National Library of Scotland (2021): https://wee-windaes.nls.uk/the-maitland-quarto-and-poem-49/ See also 'Marie Maitland: Scotland's Sixteenth-Century Sappho', Ashley Douglas, National Galleries of Scotland (2023): https://www.nationalgalleries.org/art-and-artists/features/marie-maitland-scotlands-16th-century-sappho

7 See '"Sapphic Sedition": Lesbians and Law in the 1921 Criminal Law Amendment Act': https://blogs.bodleian.ox.ac.uk/lawbod/2025/06/20/sapphic-sedition-lesbians-and-law-in-the-1921-criminal-law-amendment-act/

ASHLEY DOUGLAS is a Scottish historian and translator. She has two master's degrees, including an MLitt in Scottish History from the University of St Andrews. Since graduating in 2016, Ashley has developed a national profile and successful career as a translator, historian, and consultant, specialising in LGBT history and the Scots language. She has worked with a range of national heritage, literary and educational organisations, including the National Library of Scotland, Historic Environment Scotland, Time for Inclusive Education, and Scottish National Galleries. She has also been engaged as historical consultant for two of the plays in Rona Munro's acclaimed *The James Plays* series.

RAISING READERS
Books Build Bright Futures

Dear Reader,

We'd love your attention for one more page to tell you about the crisis in children's reading, and what we can all do.

Studies have shown that reading for fun is the **single biggest predictor of a child's future success** – more than family circumstance, parents' educational background or income. It improves academic results, mental health, wealth, communication skills and ambition.

The number of children reading for fun is in rapid decline. Young people have a lot of competition for their time, and a worryingly high number do not have a single book at home.

Our business works extensively with schools, libraries and literacy charities, but here are some ways we can all raise more readers:

- Reading to children for just 10 minutes a day makes a difference
- Don't give up if your children aren't regular readers – there will be books for them!
- Visit bookshops and libraries to get recommendations
- Encourage them to listen to audiobooks
- Support school libraries
- Give books as gifts

Thank you for reading.
www.JoinRaisingReaders.com